COMMERCIAL DRIVER'S LICENSE
(CDL)

Professional Driver's Study Manual

William C. Atkinson/Ron Raslowsky

pound square inch = PSI

This publication is designed to provide accurate and authoritative information regarding the subject matter covered. It is sold with the understanding that the publisher is not engaged in rendering legal, accounting, or other professional services. If legal advice or other expert assistance is required, the services of a competent professional should be sought. *(From the declaration of Principles jointly adopted by a committee of American Bar Association and a Committee of Publishers and Associates).*

This Study Manual has been developed to assist all commercial driver applicants to prepare for and pass the National Commercial Driver's License as administered by the 50 States.

For information regarding other CDL study material available from National Safety Compliance Services, Inc., dba CTTS call: 1-800-869-3926.

COMMERCIAL DRIVER'S LICENSE (CDL)

Professional Driver's Study Manual

William C. Atkinson/Ron Raslowsky

KENDALL/HUNT PUBLISHING COMPANY
4050 Westmark Drive   Dubuque, Iowa 52002

CREDITS AND ACKNOWLEDGEMENTS

To all the private companies, manufacturers, state trucking associations and individuals who have supplied the many illustrations, photographs and forms used throughout this manual, my deepest gratitude and appreciation.

There have been so many that have been so helpful that it is impossible to remember and list them all. I have done the best that I could and they are given the proper credit and acknowledgement below. For those that I fail to list, rest assured that I am in your debt and thank you profusely.

To the hundreds of truckers, motor coach operators and bus operators who have, over my 20+ (we won't say exactly how many) years in the transportation industry . . . it is for you that this manual has been written. Without your help, compassion, understanding and knowledge which you so freely gave, this manual would never have been written. My hope is that it will help our brothers and sisters to easily and safely join our ranks as professional drivers.

Sincerely,

William C. Atkinson,
Author

CONTRIBUTORS

Blue Bird Corporation

Freightliner Corporation

Navistar International Transportation
    Corporation

Caterpillar Engine Division

Ford Motor Company—Truck Operations

Kenworth Trucks

Peterbuilt Trucks

Eaton Truck Components

Sealco Air Controls

CONTENTS

Congratulations!

You have just purchased the best CDL training manual available. This manual, when used in conjunction with the supplemental videos, is the best CDL training system available anywhere. It will provide you with everything necessary to assist you in preparing for and passing the Commercial Drivers License tests the *FIRST TIME.*

This material was written by "Bill" Atkinson and the experts of CTTS™/Safety Products, Ltd., with the support and help of many trucking, motor coach and transit company professionals.

The complete CDL Training System consists of this manual and ten supplemental video cassette tapes. CTTS has produced a video for EACH CDL test, plus a Skills Test Video and a Pre-Trip Inspection for Tractor-Trailer and one for Straight trucks.

The ideal method of study is to read a chapter in the manual and then when you see, **"WATCH VIDEO ON CHAPTER ___ NOW,"** you will stop reading and watch the video for that particular chapter.

There is a video for each of the CDL written tests. The Pre-Trip Inspection Videos and the Skills Test Video will help you to pass the hands on skills portion of the CDL test the FIRST time.

If you would like information about any of the videos, call 1 (800) 869-3926.

If you decided to purchase only this manual, that's OK, you still have what you need to prepare for the CDL tests. The written material covers everything you will need to know.

Whether you are an experienced "old hand" at driving, or just beginning your professional driving career, we know you'll find this information helpful. It has been written for everyone, young or old, experienced or inexperienced. Some of you old timers may think it's too simple, or you may think you already know it all. Just keep this in mind, many things have changed in the past 10 to 30 years since you started driving. Rules and regulations have changed, engines and transmission systems have changed, and there have been major changes in the industry due to deregulation.

Even though you are an experienced driver with many years of safe driving, you are still be required to know about these changes—(and know them the way the Department of Transportation wants you to know them) in order to pass the CDL tests.

This book is not just a CDL Study Manual. It is also a great driver safety manual. It does contain the latest CDL tests questions and answers, but just as important, it is full of safe driving tips which will help to make you a safer and better driver.

Today, in our industry a driver shortage exists, or perhaps I should say, there exists a shortage of **QUALITY** professional drivers. As a **QUALITY** professional driver, you can now earn an excellent wage, befitting your true professional status. You are now more respected than ever, and the image of the **"KNIGHTS OF THE HIGHWAYS"** is returning to our industry. I am excited, as I am sure you are, to be part of this movement.

This book is dedicated to all of you, the men and women of the transportation industry who play such an important role in the economy of our great nation.

So, study hard and **GOOD LUCK!**

Study Tips

The CDL tests are tough! *In order to pass these tests, you must read this entire manual.* As you read this manual, you will notice that certain words or phrases are printed in **<u>BOLD CAPITAL LETTERS AND ARE UNDERLINED.</u>**

Anything printed in **<u>BOLD CAPITAL LETTERS AND UNDERLINED</u>** is almost surely going to be on your CDL tests. You will need to know these items completely and thoroughly. While it is important that you read and understand the entire manual—pay careful attention to those items written in **<u>BOLD CAPITAL LETTERS AND UNDERLINED.</u>** At the end of each chapter you will find a test. Read and

re-read the chapters until you can answer the questions on these tests with 100% accuracy. After you've read the entire manual and have taken the tests at the end of each chapter, then you are ready to take the final examinations located at the back of the manual.

Study Tip #1

Set aside a place and time to study. For some of us the best time to study is in the morning. For others, the best time to study is late at night. It can be while you are waiting to get loaded or unloaded, or maybe you can find time to study while eating dinner at a truck stop. Whatever works for you. The important thing is to *plan* your study periods. Set aside a certain time *each day* and then stick to that schedule!

Study Tip #2

Study in "short bursts." If you plan to study one hour a day, try to do it in two 30-minute sessions. It seems that most folks, when studying, tend to learn and remember best the material at the beginning of the study period and then again just at the end of the study period. If you study for one hour straight, you'll have one beginning and one ending. If you study in two 30-minute sessions, you'll have two beginnings and two endings. Better yet, try studying in four 15-minute sessions, that way you'll have four beginnings and four endings. Experiment with it and see what works best for you.

Study Tip #3

Take notes. You *MUST* take notes. Get yourself a notebook and keep it with this manual at all times. There is a relationship between the eye, the brain, and the hands. It's an accepted fact that if you write down what your eyes have seen and your brain has interpreted, you tend to learn and remember it more quickly. So, *TAKE NOTES*. Whenever you see something you believe to be important, write it down.- Whenever you see something in this manual printed in **BOLD CAPITAL LETTERS AND UNDERLINED**, you must write it down, it probably is going to be on your examinations. Keep your notebook with this manual at all times. After you have finished reading this manual, and provided you've taken good notes, and written down everything that was in **BOLD CAPITAL LETTERS AND UNDERLINED**, you will then have your own condensed study guide to use.

Study Tip #4

Study with a friend or spouse. Studying with someone will make learning fun. Challenge and test each other to see who is learning it quicker and more thoroughly. We realize that if you are an over-the-road driver or a line haul driver, and don't get home every night, it makes it difficult to study with someone. What you can do, however, is challenge a friend or spouse to read certain chapters of the manual and then test each other when you return. If you really want to make it fun, the loser buys coffee, lunch or maybe even dinner. Having a challenge like this can help make studying fun. Studying doesn't have to be dull. With a little imagination, and remembering that we don't have a choice, we have to know this material, we can make this trip go a little faster and much more enjoyable. Since we are required to pass the CDL, we might as well have a good time doing it.

Study Tip #5

Set a goal for yourself. Before beginning to read this study guide, set a goal for the number of pages you want to read during each study session. Don't set your goal too high or too low. *Quality not quantity is what counts.* If you read the entire manual in a week, and don't understand it, what have you accomplished?

Make your goals realistic and attainable. Your goal will be your plan, and once you set it, stick to it.

Study Tip #6

Testing for success. At the end of each chapter is a test. The test is for you to see what you have learned. Tell yourself right now that your ultimate goal is to know the correct answers for all of the test questions. When you've accomplished that, you are ready for the CDL Tests.

Word Key

Throughout this manual we will be using abbreviations in many instances. The Commercial Driver's License (CDL) examination will use abbreviations and initials frequently. Listed below are the ones that you will see most often.

BAC	Blood Alcohol Concentration
CDL	Commercial Driver's License
CDLIS	Commercial Driver's License Information System
CMVSA/86	The Commercial Motor Vehicle Safety Act of 1986
CMV	Commercial Motor Vehicle
DMV	Department of Motor Vehicles
DOT	Department of Transportation
ERG	Emergency Response Guide
ERT	Emergency Response Team
FHWA	Federal Highway Administration
FMCSR	Federal Motor Carrier Safety Regulations
GCWR	Gross Combination Weight Rating
GVW	Gross Vehicle Weight
GVWR	Gross Vehicle Weight Rating
HAZMAT	Hazardous Material
HM	Hazardous Material
ID	Identification Number
MDM	Model Driver's Manual (issued by each state)
NA	North American (Hazardous Material ID Number)
ORM	Other Regulated Material
PSI	Pounds per Square Inch
PTI	Pre-Trip Inspection
RQ	Regulated Quantity
UN	United Nations (Hazardous Material ID Number)
PGIA	Pounds per square inch absolute

The Commercial Motor Vehicle Safety Act of 1986 CMVSA/86

It is the CMVSA/86 that established the National Driver's Licensing Program, which is more commonly known as the Commercial Driver's License (CDL).

On October 18, 1986, the United States Congress, in response to a great deal of pressure from the public for increased highway safety, enacted the CMVSA/86. The Act requires, among other things, that all 50 states conduct uniform testing and licensing of all commercial drivers within each state (uniform means that the tests must be similar in all states).

Since the original CDL test questions were released in 1986, many changes have occurred. This Manual reflects the latest questions to the CDL tests as issued by the American Association of Motor Vehicle Administrators and provided to each State.

It takes special skills and knowledge to safely handle a tractor-trailer, doubles or a large transit bus. The United States Congress, by enacting the CMVSA/86, is ensuring that all 50 states implement standard testing and licensing procedures. It requires that all driver applicants take a series of written tests, depending on the type of equipment they will be operating, and that all applicants take a skills (driving) test in the type of vehicle they will actually be driving on the job. The ultimate goal of the CMVSA/86 is to make sure that all individuals driving a commercial vehicle today, and in the future, have the skills, knowledge and training necessary to drive them safely and in accordance with all the rules and regulations established by the United States Department of Transportation.

Commercial Motor Vehicle Safety Act of 1986

Major Provisions of the Act

- SINGLE LICENSE

  NO COMMERCIAL VEHICLE OPERATOR MAY POSSESS MORE THAN ONE LICENSE. LICENSE MUST BE ISSUED FROM DRIVER'S STATE OF LEGAL RESIDENCE

  Penalties for possessing more than one license range up to $5,000.00 and possible jail term.

- TESTING AND LICENSING STANDARDS

  Establishes testing and licensing requirements for all commercial drivers. The Act establishes commercial motor vehicle groups and required endorsements.

- REPORTING

  THE ACT **REQUIRES ALL COMMERCIAL DRIVERS TO REPORT ALL MOVING VIOLATIONS TO THEIR HOME STATE OF RESIDENCE AND TO THEIR EMPLOYER WITHIN 30 DAYS OF CONVICTION.** Also, *it requires drivers to report any suspensions or revocations, cancellation or disqualifications to their employers before the end of the business day following notification.*

- DISQUALIFICATIONS

  A commercial driver may face disqualification for a specific period of time for the following:

  —60 DAY DISQUALIFICATION—Any commercial driver who, in a three year period, is convicted of two *serious traffic violations in a commercial motor vehicle.*

---

*Serious Traffic Violation . . . Reckless operation, excessive speed (15 mph over posted speed limit), any traffic control violation involving a fatal accident, following too closely, erratic or unsafe lane change. Please note, states may add to this list; check with your Department of Motor Vehicles.

—120 DAY DISQUALIFICATION—Any commercial driver who, in a three-year period, is convicted of *three *serious traffic violations,* will be disqualified for *not less than* 120 days.

—ONE YEAR DISQUALIFICATION—First offense, and is convicted of:
- Driving a commercial vehicle while under the influence of alcohol or a controlled substance (illegal drugs)
- Leaving the scene of an accident while operating a commercial vehicle
- Operating a commercial vehicle while committing a felony

—THREE YEAR DISQUALIFICATION—If a commercial driver is found to have been convicted of any of the *previous* three violations, and was transporting hazardous material, the disqualification period will be *three years.*

—LIFETIME DISQUALIFICATION—Second violations involving any of the three listed under the one-year disqualifications while operating a CMV or—a second conviction of operating a CMV while under the influence of alcohol or a controlled substance, will result in a *lifetime disqualification.*

PLEASE NOTE: These disqualifications are the minimums required by the CMVSA/86. It is possible that individual states may add to this list and make the penalties more severe.

It's pretty obvious that the United States Congress has decided to play hard ball. The Congress, the public and the professional drivers have had it with the "druggies," the "boozers" and the "cowboy-type" drivers in the industry. For those drivers who drink and drive—or drive and pop pills, or smoke dope, or fool around with nose candy, their driving career is coming to an end. The penalties are severe, the fines are stiff and the honest, hard-working professional drivers like yourself, "ain't gonna take it any more."

DOT Is Writing Federal Alcohol Testing Rules

Congress Considers Drug, Alcohol Testing Mandates

Lawmakers pushing for mandatory drug testing of truck drivers have strong hopes that Congress will act on legislation this year that would make government-ordered random testing a reality.

At the same time, mandatory testing for alcohol abuse is growing more likely.

ATA Drug Test Policy Toughened

American Trucking Associations further strengthened its policy against illegal drug use last ⁓k by supporting mandatory ⁓sting.

⁓tion already had ⁓porting ran-
⁓tion of
⁓ri-

Approximate Blood Alcohol Percentage							
Drinks	**Body Weight in Pounds**						
	100	120	140	160	180	200	220	240
1	.04	.03	.03	.03	.02	.02	.02	.02
2	.08	.06	.05	.05	.04	.04	.03	.03
3	.11	.09	.08	.07	.06	.06	.05	.05
4	.15	.12	.11	.09	.08	.08	.07	.06
5	.19	.16	.13	.12	.11	.09	.09	.08
6	.23	.19	.16	.14	.13	.11	.10	.09
7	.26	.22	.19	.16	.15	.13	.12	.11

In this chart you will notice that it only takes two drinks to place a person of 180 pounds in the .04 level. So, if you weigh 180 pounds and you stop for lunch and have two beers, you will be legally drunk. Is it worth losing your license for one year? Or, if you were hauling hazardous material, is it worth losing your license for three years? Wonder if your family would think it was worth it? . . .

The best method of control is not to consume any alcohol during those times that you are working, or subject to be called to work. Also, keep this in mind. The alcohol content in one bottle of beer, one glass of wine and one shot of whiskey is all the same. So if you say to yourself, "I'm just having a couple of beers," the only person you will be fooling will be *yourself!*

Legal Blood Alcohol Level

A quick word about drinking and the new legal blood alcohol level, also known as BAC (blood alcohol concentration). The BAC level for commercial drivers has changed. The previous level was .10, the new level is now .04, less than half of the previous level. This law was put into effect on October 27, 1988. If you are stopped at a roadside inspection and have a BAC of .04 or higher, and are driving a commercial vehicle, you will be arrested for DUI, driving under the influence. If at the time of the check your BAC is found to be at .02, but less than

.04, you will be put out of service for 24 hours. *Try to explain that to your dispatcher.*

If you test at .04 or higher, your employer is required to refer you to a Substance Abuse Professional (SAP). The SAP will evaluate you for possible alcohol misuse and/or substance abuse. If the SAP recommends treatment, you must complete the treatment. If you do not complete the treatment you will NEVER be allowed to drive a commercial motor vehicle again. After completing the treatment and before returning to work you must take a "return-to-duty" test with a result below .02. You will then be subject to a minimum of at least six random tests during the next 12 months.

The previous chart provides a guideline about the effect of alcohol. Again, this is a general guideline and each individual may respond differently to certain situations.

Alcohol testing for commercial drivers is now required by the Department of Transportation.

Effective January 1, 1995, companies with 50 or more drivers will be required to begin alcohol testing of its commercial drivers. Companies with less than 50 drivers will not have to comply until the following January. *ALL* commercial drivers are affected by the regulations regardless of whether they drive interstate or intrastate.

Drivers are subject to five types of testing: reasonable suspicion, post-accident, random testing, follow-up and return to duty.

The original requirements for random testing required that a company test at least 25% of its drivers annually. That has been adjusted and companies now are required to test only 10% of its drivers on a random basis.

It should be noted that several organizations are opposing these new alcohol testing rules and are attempting to have them modified. Therefore, it is possible that certain portions of the rules may change prior to actual implementation.

In regards to substance abuse testing, the DOT has in the past only required that interstate drivers be tested. Since January 1, 1995, *ALL* drivers who hold a commercial driver's license fall under the substance abuse testing and training regulations.

Classifications

Which CDL Classification Will You Need?

It's not really all that complicated, the CDL classifications are divided into three categories:

1. CLASS A—COMBINATION

   All tractor-trailer drivers must have a "Class A" CDL *provided* the trailer GVWR* is *MORE THAN* 10,000 lbs, *AND* . . . when you *ADD* the weight of the tractor, the *TOTAL* GCVWR** of both is more than 26,000 lbs. Also, anyone pulling any type of doubles or triples must have a "Class A" CDL. Tractor semi-trailer type buses fall into this category. In certain states, tow-truck operators who tow vehicles that exceed 10,000 lbs GVWR, or if the combination of the tow truck and towed vehicle exceed 26,000 GCVWR, may be required to have a "Class A" CDL. Check with your state DMV.

2. CLASS B—HEAVY STRAIGHT TRUCK OR BUS

   If you operate a large straight truck or bus with a GVWR of *MORE THAN* 26,000 lbs, you will need a "Class B" CDL. You may pull a trailer provided the GVWR of the trailer is not more than 10,000 lbs. Articulated buses would fall into this category.

3. CLASS C—SMALL VEHICLES

   To determine if the driver of a small vehicle such as a van, mini-bus or

*GVWR—Gross Vehicle Weight Rating. The amount of weight for which the vehicle was designed.
**GCVWR—Gross Combination Vehicle Weight Rating

car, needs a CDL, the type of cargo, not the weight, is the determining factor.

A. If you transport hazardous materials which require hazardous material placards,* you will need a "Class C" CDL, regardless of the weight.

B. If you operate a small passenger vehicle designed to carry *MORE THAN* 15 persons, including the driver, you will need a "Class C" CDL.**

If you want to get a license to drive this type of vehicle or a similar tank vehicle*	Study these sections of the driver's manual
	Chapter 1 CMVSA Chapter 2 Classifications Chapter 3 General Knowledge Part 1 Chapter 3 General Knowledge Part 2 Chapter 5 Air Brakes Chapter 6 Combination Vehicles Chapter 7 Haz Mat (if needed)
	Chapter 1 CMVSA Chapter 2 Classifications Chapter 3 General Knowledge Part 1 Chapter 3 General Knowledge Part 2 Chapter 5 Air Brakes Chapter 6 Combination Vehicles (expect double/triple info) Chapter 7 Haz Mat (if needed)
	Chapter 1 CMVSA Chapter 2 Classifications Chapter 3 General Knowledge Part 1 Chapter 3 General Knowledge Part 2 Chapter 4 Transporting Passengers Chapter 5 Air Brakes (if needed)
	Chapter 1 CMVSA Chapter 2 Classifications Chapter 3 General Knowledge Part 1 Chapter 3 General Knowledge Part 2 Chapter 5 Air Brakes Chapter 7 Haz Mat (if needed)
(CDL required only if these vehicles are used to haul hazardous materials) 	Chapter 1 CMVSA Chapter 3 General Knowledge Part 1 Chapter 3 General Knowledge Part 2 Chapter 7 Haz Mat (if needed)

* Hazardous Materials Placards - Diamond shaped warning signs which are affixed to all 4-sides of a vehicle, indicating the nature of the hazardous material being transported.

** Some states are considering lowering the passenger requirements to less than the Federal standard of 15. check with your state DMV.

Endorsements and What They Are

We have already discussed the three major classifications of the CDL; they are:

1. Class A
2. Class B
3. Class C

The CDL regulations require that you take additional tests (called endorsements) depending on the cargo you transport (haul), and the type of vehicle you drive. The endorsements are divided into the following categories:

"P"   for PASSENGER VEHICLE
"H"   for HAZARDOUS MATERIAL
"T"   for DOUBLE and TRIPLE TRAILERS
"N"   for TANK VEHICLES
"X"   for COMBINATION HAZARDOUS MATERIAL and TANK VEHICLE

Now, let's discuss each one of these individually so you can determine which of the endorsements you will need.

"P" for Passenger Vehicle

The CDL regulations require that a person take the passenger vehicle test if he/she operates a vehicle *designed* to transport *more than* 15 persons including the driver. The key word here is *DESIGNED*. It doesn't make any difference that you may never transport more than 5 or 6 passengers at a time. If your vehicle is *designed* to transport *more than* 15 passengers, including the driver, you *MUST* take the passenger vehicle endorsement. Upon passing the test, your CDL license will have the letter "P" stamped on it, indicating you are qualified to transport passengers.

IMPORTANT NOTE : Each state has the right to make the requirements more strict. For example, the states may change the regulation to fewer than 16 persons. Check with your state DMV to make sure.

"H" for Hazardous Material

Drivers who haul hazardous materials in such an amount that hazardous material placards must be displayed on the vehicle, *MUST* take the hazardous material endorsement test. It makes no difference what type of vehicle you drive—a bus, truck, van, or car; if you transport enough hazardous material to require a placard, you will need this endorsement.

"T" for Doubles and Triples

If you pull doubles or triples, you will need to take the "T" endorsement test. This test is designed to test your knowledge of pulling doubles and triples as they require specialized skills. Only "Class A" drivers are eligible to take this endorsement.

"N" for Tank Vehicles

Since hauling liquids and gases requires specialized knowledge, the CDL regulations require that any person driving liquid tank vehicles must take a special endorsement to demonstrate his/her knowledge of tanker operations. This endorsement is required for all liquid tanker drivers *NOT* hauling hazardous material. If you operate a tanker, *and* transport hazardous material in enough quantity to require hazardous material placards, you will be required to have the following endorsement.

"X" for Combination Hazardous Material and Tank Vehicles

If you drive a tanker and haul hazardous material, you will be required to take *BOTH* the Hazardous Material endorsement test, and the Tank Vehicle endorsement test. When you pass both of these, you will then receive the "X" endorsement on your CDL license, instead of the "N" or "H" endorsements.

Air Brake Test

If you operate a vehicle, with air brakes, you must take a test designed to measure your knowledge about air brake systems. This is primarily a concern for "Class A" and "Class B" vehicles, since the majority of them are equipped with air brakes. If you do not take the air brake test, your license will be marked with the words "AIR BRAKE RESTRICTION," which means that you *CANNOT* operate any vehicle with an air brake system. When you take the skills (driving test) portion of the CDL, and you are going to be taking the air brake test, you *MUST* take the skills test in a vehicle equipped with air brakes.

An Explanation of the CDL Written Tests

The CDL tests are divided into the following seven categories:

1. **THE GENERAL KNOWLEDGE TEST** All CDL applicants are required to take this test regardless of whether they are Class A, B, or C. When

you go in to take your test, this is the first one you will take. In most states, you must pass this test before you will be permitted to take any of the others.

The six remaining tests are the Specialized Knowledge tests. You will take *ONLY* the ones you need, depending on the vehicle you drive or the product or number of people you transport.

2. **PASSENGER VEHICLE TEST** You will take this test if you drive a vehicle designed to carry more than 15 persons, including the driver.

3. **HAZARDOUS MATERIAL TEST** If you haul hazardous material in a quantity large enough to require placards, you will take this test.

4. **DOUBLES and TRIPLES TEST** Only those "Class A" drivers pulling doubles or triples will be required to take this test.

5. **TANK VEHICLES TEST** You will take this test if you drive a tanker hauling liquids or gases.

6. **COMBINATION VEHICLES TEST** All "Class A" drivers are required to take this test. It is designed to measure the knowledge needed to operate combination vehicles such as tractor-trailers and tractor semi-trailer type buses. Articulated buses do not need this endorsement.

7. **AIR BRAKE TEST** Any driver operating a vehicle equipped with air brakes must take the air brake test, which will remove the air brake restriction, allowing him/her to operate vehicles equipped with air brakes.

As you can see, some drivers will be required to take just two of the tests, where others may be required to take all the tests. For example, a school bus operator, operating a bus without air brakes, would only be required to have the general knowledge test and the passenger vehicle test. But, a driver for a large freight company, like Roadway or Yellow, might need the general knowledge, the air brake, the hazardous material, the combination, and the triples and doubles test.

You can now determine which of the tests you are required to take and then study those sections of the manual which cover those endorsements.

About the Test

Each state is giving virtually the same tests. Each state has a "pool" of about 450 test questions to choose from. They will choose questions from this "pool" to create the individual tests. For example, if you went in to take the General Knowledge Test on Monday and failed, when you return again on Tuesday to retake it, the questions will *not* be the same. This will be true of all the tests.

In most states, the CDL tests will be given as a written test; however, some states will be using "computers," or what are also known as automated testing devices. These are really quite simple to use. You will sit down in front of a piece of equipment that looks like a television. You will read the questions on a screen. All questions will be multiple choice. After reading the question, you will push button "A," "B," "C," or "D." The "TV" screen will then display the next question where you will repeat the process. In those states where they will be using automated testing devices, you will have a choice of using it, or taking a written test.

All states are required to give oral tests. These are for the drivers who may have some reading problems. The examiner will read the question out loud, and you can answer out loud. In all states the questions are multiple choice, however many states are changing the oral tests to true and false, but there will be more questions on the true and false tests. Some states are also giving the tests in a foreign language. The only test not allowed to be given orally or in another language is the hazardous material test.

In most states the CDL written tests are multiple choice, however, some states have chosen to use true or false questions on the written test. Whether you take a true or false or a multiple choice test you still must get 80% correct on *each one* in order to pass.

How Many Questions on Each Test?

We wish we could tell you exactly how many questions will be on each test, but the number of questions on each varies from state to state. In the course of writing this manual, we have talked to more than half of the states and have asked them how many questions will be on each of them. The following is what the states tell us you can expect.

Name	Number of Questions	Correct Answers in Order to Pass
General Knowledge	50	40
Air Brake	25	20
Combination	20	16
Doubles and Triples	20	16
Hazardous Material	30	24
Passenger Vehicle	20	16
Tank Vehicle	20	16

Taking the Test

Each of the questions on the tests will have four possible answers: "A," "B," "C," or "D." *Only one is correct!* You might think that two of the answers seem awfully close, but there will only be one correct answer. Read the question as many times as necessary. Then, through the process of elimination (narrowing down the choices), you will eventually arrive at the correct answer. If after you have narrowed down the choices, you still have two answers that seem to be correct, select the answer you think is most correct. If you've narrowed it down to two choices, you have a 50/50 chance of getting it correct. The *ABSOLUTE WORST* thing to do is leave it blank. *IT WILL BE COUNTED AS AN INCORRECT ANSWER*, so *ALWAYS* answer each question!

Take all the time you need. There is *NO TIME LIMIT*. Just relax, take your time, read the questions carefully and you'll do just fine.

If you have trouble reading, or get so darn nervous when taking tests that you usually "bomb" them, ask to take an oral test. If you have reading difficulties, most states will allow you to take the tests orally. In other words, the state will have an examiner read the questions to you and you will answer them out loud.

Check with your local Department of Motor Vehicles to get information about taking tests orally.

Let's Take a Test

At the end of each chapter, you will see the words *"LET'S TAKE A TEST."* This will be your opportunity to test your knowledge on the material we have covered up to that point. It will also give you a chance to begin getting used to answering test questions. The format for these tests will be similar to the tests for the CDL.

☞ Now LET'S TAKE A TEST

CMVSA/86—CDL Requirements Test

Study each question carefully and then indicate your choice by drawing a circle around the letter you have chosen.

1. The "P" endorsement (PASSENGER VEHICLE) is required if:

   A. the driver transports 15 or more passengers, including the driver
   B. the driver operates a vehicle designed to transport more than 15 persons, including the driver
   C. operates a passenger bus for hire
   D. the driver transports passengers more than six months of the year

2. The new BAC (Blood Alcohol Concentration) level is:

   A. .10
   B. .07
   C. .04
   D. .05

3. If you operate a tractor-trailer tanker, which is air-brake equipped, you will be required to take:

   A. Tank Vehicle and Hazardous Material endorsements
   B. Tank Vehicle, Air Brake, and Combination endorsements
   C. Tank Vehicle, Air Brake, Combination, and Hazardous Material endorsements
   D. Tank Vehicle, Air Brake, Combination endorsements, and the General Knowledge Test

4. The penalty for operating a commercial vehicle without a CDL can be as high as:

   A. $2,500
   B. $5,000
   C. $10,000
   D. $500

5. The Commercial Motor Vehicle Safety Act of 1986 requires that if you are convicted of a traffic violation (except parking) you must notify your employer within how many days after the conviction?

   A. 10
   B. 15
   C. 30
   D. 45

6. You must have the Hazardous Materials endorsement if:

   A. you transport hazardous material on a regular basis
   B. you haul hazardous material only in a tractor-trailer
   C. you haul hazardous material in such a quantity that "Hazardous Material" placards are required
   D. you haul hazardous material only on a full-time basis

7. You have never received the Hazardous Material endorsement. When can you haul hazardous material legally?

   A. when the load does not require a placard
   B. never
   C. only as long as you drive intrastate
   D. only during daylight hours

8. You will lose your CDL for one year upon the first conviction of which of the following:

   A. you drive a commercial motor vehicle under the influence of alcohol or a controlled substance (drugs)
   B. you leave the scene of an accident involving a commercial motor vehicle you were driving
   C. you used a commercial motor vehicle to commit a felony
   D. all of the above

9. If you are convicted a second time for driving under the influence of drugs, you will lose your license for:

   A. one year
   B. three years
   C. five years
   D. lifetime

10. If you are stopped by the authorities and your BAC is less than .04, but you have any detectable amount, you will:

    A. be suspended for 30 days
    B. be placed out-of-service for 24 hours
    C. lose your license for 60 days
    D. lose your license for 3 years

Answers

1. B   6. C
2. C   7. A
3. D   8. D
4. B   9. D
5. C   10. B

If you were able to answer all of the questions correctly—*GOOD JOB!* If you missed any, reread the material again until you know it with 100% accuracy.

General Knowledge

Part 1: Driving Safely

Who must study this section?

ALL APPLICANTS FOR THE CDL MUST READ THIS CHAPTER AND TAKE THE GENERAL KNOWLEDGE TEST.

The Commercial Motor Vehicle Safety Act of 1986, and the CDL requirements, came about because of an increased demand for highway safety. This section will deal with all the aspects of safety that you will be required to know in order to pass the General Knowledge Test. As you read, remember to look for those words or phrases written in **BOLD CAPITAL LETTERS AND UNDERLINED.** Whenever you see them, you can just about bet that the next time you see them they will be on the CDL examinations. *TAKE NOTES*, write your notes down in a separate notebook so that you'll have the key words and phrases to study. Now let's get started . . .

Commercial motor vehicle safety begins with the inspection of the vehicle. **THERE ARE THREE TYPES ON INSPECTIONS:**
1. **PRE-TRIP INSPECTION**
2. **EN ROUTE INSPECTION**
3. **AFTER TRIP OR POST-TRIP INSPECTION**

Pre-Trip Inspection

Federal Motor Carrier Safety Regulations (FMCSR) require that commercial motor vehicles, **OPERATING IN INTER-STATE TRANSPORTATION,** be inspected prior to beginning of each trip.

The FMCSR, Part 392.7, states:

"No motor vehicle shall be driven unless the driver thereof shall have satisfied himself that the following parts and accessories are in good working order, nor shall any driver fail to use or make use of such parts and accessories when and as needed:

- Service brakes, including trailer brake connections
- Parking (hand) brake
- Steering mechanism
- Lighting devices and reflectors
- Tires
- Horn
- Windshield wiper or wipers
- Rear-vision mirror or mirrors
- Coupling devices

So, as you can see, if you operate in inter-state transportation, you must complete a pre-trip inspection.

What about drivers operating in intra-state transportation? Many states have adopted the federal pre-trip regulations for intra-state carriers. In other words, some states require that all carriers, both inter- and intra-state, require their drivers to conduct a pre-trip inspection prior to driving the truck. Check with your state to see if they require a pre-trip inspection for intra-state operations. Even if they do not, common sense tells you that you should never drive a vehicle until you have made sure it is safe. After all, it's your career and life that may be lost if you have an accident.

Purpose of a Pre-Trip Inspection (PTI)

You do a PTI before each trip to find problems which may affect the safe operation of the vehicle or which may cause a crash or breakdown.

What we will cover in this chapter are the critical items which you must know and memorize. Again, take good notes, look for the words or phrases written in **BOLD CAPITAL LETTERS AND UNDERLINED.** Be sure to write these down in your personal notebook and study them frequently.

Proper Pre-Trip Inspection Procedures

The key to performing a proper pre-trip inspection is **CONSISTENCY.** In other words, establish a routine for your PTI, and then **DO IT THE SAME WAY EVERY TIME.** It doesn't make that much difference in what order you do the PTI. The important thing is that you check all the required items exactly the same way each time.

In the next few pages, we will give you a suggested 7-step procedure for a proper pre-trip. Located at the back of this manual is a detachable "Pre-Trip Inspection Checklist." Use this as a study guide. You may also use this checklist when performing the pre-trip inspection portion of the skills (driving) test. Chapter 10 covers in detail who must take the skills test and how it will be conducted.

7-Step Pre-Trip Inspection

The 7-step procedure should be conducted in the following order:
1. Vehicle overview
2. Check engine compartment
3. Start engine and inspect inside the cab
4. Turn off engine and check lights
5. Do walkaround inspection
6. Check signal lights
7. Start the engine and check brake system

Step 1—Vehicle Overview

Approach the unit looking for any major defects. Look for leaks, flat tires, or vehicle leaning to one side (indicating broken suspension). Visually check the area around the vehicle for anything which might present a hazard to the vehicle: people, broken glass, low wires, etc.

Driver's Vehicle Inspection Report

Check the previous vehicle inspection report. Determine if any defects were noted (written-up) by the previous driver. If so, were the items repaired?

Step 2—Check Engine Compartment

- **<u>CHECK THAT PARKING BRAKE IS APPLIED, AND/OR WHEELS CHOCKED</u>**
- Tilt cab or raise hood and check the following:
- Fluid levels
  - —Check condition of all hoses, belts, air connection and lines, electrical wiring
  - —When checking belts, look for tightness, fraying, cracks, etc.
  - —When checking electrical wiring, look for fraying, cracks, and worn or burned spots

- Check steering mechanism
  - —Look for missing nuts, bolts, cotter keys or other parts
  - —Look for bent, loose or broken parts; such as steering column, steering gear box or tie rods
  - —If power steering equipped—look at hoses, pumps, and fluid level; check for leaks
  - —**<u>STEERING WHEEL PLAY OF MORE THAN 10 DEGREES (ABOUT 2 INCHES MOVEMENT OF THE RIM OF A 20-INCH STEERING WHEEL) MAY MAKE IT HEARD TO STEER</u>**

Steering System Components

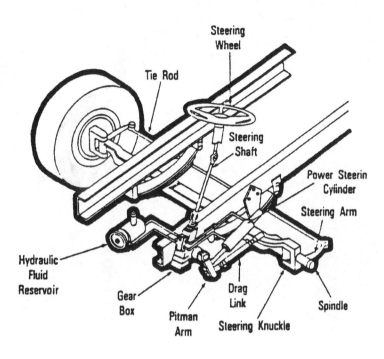

IMPORTANT—KEY PARTS OF THE STEERING SYSTEM MAY BE FOUND ON THE CDL GENERAL KNOWLEDGE TEST. LEARN AND MEMORIZE ALL OF THE KEY PARTS.

Check Brakes in Engine Compartment

- Look for cracked drums
- Look for shoes or pads with oil, grease or brake fluid on them
- **LOOK FOR BRAKE SHOES THAT ARE WORN DANGEROUSLY THIN, MISSING OR BROKEN**

Secure engine compartment door, hood or cab.

Step 3—Start Engine and Inspect Inside the Cab

- Check brakes
- Place transmission in neutral (automatics—place in "park")
- Depress clutch (if equipped)
- Start engine
- Listen for unusual noises and check gauges and instruments
    —oil gauge
    —ammeter/voltmeter
    —water temperature
    —oil temperature
    —warning lights and buzzers

All gauges should be within normal operating ranges.

Check vehicle controls

- steering wheel
- clutch
- accelerator
- brake controls

—brake pedal

—trailer brake (if equipped)

—parking brake

—engine retarder (Jake Brake—Williams Blue Ox, etc., if equipped)

- transmission controls
- inter-axle differential lock (if equipped)
- windshield wipers/washers
- light controls

  —headlights

  —dimmer switch

  —turn signals

  —4-way flashers

  —clearance and marker light switch(s)

Check mirrors and windshields

- cracks
- dirty
- legal stickers and windshield decals
- mirrors adjusted properly

Check emergency equipment

- **<u>SAFETY EQUIPMENT</u>**

—SPARE ELECTRICAL FUSES (UNLESS EQUIPPED WITH CIR-CUIT BREAKERS)
—THREE RED REFLECTIVE TRIANGLES
—PROPERLY CHARGED AND RATED FIRE EXTINGUISHERS

Step 4—Turn Off Engine and Check Lights

Make sure the parking brake is set, turn off the engine, **AND TAKE THE KEY WITH YOU.** Turn on headlights (low beams) and four-way flashers, and get out.

- Go to front of vehicle and check that low beams are on and both of the four-way flashers are working
- Push dimmer switch and check that high beams work
- Turn off headlights and four-way hazard warning flashers
- Turn on parking, clearance, side-marker and identification lights
- Turn on right-turn signal, and start walkaround inspection

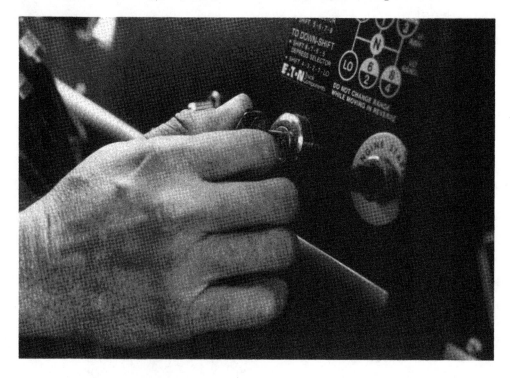

Step 5—Walkaround Inspection

General

- Walkaround and inspect
- Clean all lights, reflectors and glass as you walkaround the unit

Left Front Side

- Driver's door glass should be clean
- Door latches or lock work properly
- Left front wheel
  —Condition of wheel and rim—missing, bent, broken studs, clamps, lugs; any signs of misalignment
  —**LOOK FOR RUST AROUND LUG NUTS—THIS WILL INDICATE THEY MAY BE LOOSE**
  —Condition of tires—properly inflated, valve stem and cap OK, no serious cuts, bulges, tread wear. **STEERING TIRES MUST HAVE AT LEAST 4/32" OF TREAD DEPTH IN THE DEEPEST GROOVE**
  —Use wrench to test rust-streaked lug nuts, indicating looseness
  —Hub oil level OK, no leaks
- Left front suspension
  —**IF ONE-FOURTH OF THE LEAVES IN A LEAF SPRING IS MISSING OR BROKEN THE VEHICLE WILL BE PLACED "OUT-OF-SERVICE."**
  —Condition of spring, spring hangers, shackles, u-bolts
  —shock absorber condition
- Left front brake
  —Condition of brake drum
  —Condition of hoses

Front

- Condition of front axle
- Condition of steering system
  - No loose, worn, bent, damaged or missing parts
- Condition of windshield
  - Check for damage and clean if dirty
  - Check windshield wiper arms for proper spring tension
  - Check wiper blades for damage, "stiff" rubber, and for proper attachment
- Lights and reflectors
  - Parking, clearance and identification lights clean, operating and proper color (amber at front)
  - Reflectors clean and proper color (amber at front)
- Right front turn signal light clean, operating, and proper color (amber or white on signals facing forward)

Right Side

- Right front: check all items as done on left front
- Primary and safety cab locks engaged (if cab-over-engine design)
- Right fuel tank(s)
  - Securely mounted, not damaged or leaking
  - Fuel crossover line secure
  - Tank(s) contain enough fuel
  - Cap(s) on and secure
  - Fuel caps must have rubber gasket
- Condition of visible parts
  - Rear of engine—not leaking
  - Transmission—not leaking
  - Exhaust system—secure, not leaking, not touching wires, fuel or air lines
  - Frame and cross members—no bends, cracks
  - Air lines and electrical wiring—secured against snagging, rubbing, wearing
  - Spare tire carrier or rack not damaged (if so equipped)
  - Spare tire and/or wheel securely mounted in rack
  - Spare tire and wheel adequate (proper size, properly inflated)
- Cargo securement (trucks)
  - Cargo properly blocked, braced, tied, chained, etc.

—Headerboard (headache rack) secured (if required)

—Side boards, stakes strong enough, free of damage, properly set in place (if so equipped)

—Canvas or tarp (if required) properly secured to prevent tearing, flapping or blocking of mirrors

—If oversize, all required signs must be safely and properly mounted and all required permits in driver's possession

—Curbside cargo compartment doors securely closed, latched/locked; required security seals in place

Right Rear

- Condition of wheels and rims—no missing, bent, broken spacers, studs, clamps, lugs
- Condition of tires—properly inflated, valve stems and caps OK, no serious cuts, bulges, tread wear, tires not rubbing against each other and nothing stuck between them. **<u>ALL TIRES EXCEPT STEERING TIRES MUST HAVE AT LEAST 2/32 INCH OF TREAD DEPTH IN THE DEEPEST GROOVE.</u>**
- Tires same type, e.g., not mixed radial and bias types. (radials and bias ply may not be mixed on the same axle)
- Tires evenly matched (same sizes)
- Wheel bearing/seals not leaking
- Suspension
  —Condition of spring(s), spring hangers, shackles and u-bolts
  —Axle secure
  —Powered axle(s) not leaking lube (gear) oil
  —Condition of shock absorber(s)
  —If retractable axle equipped, check condition of lift mechanism; if air powered, check for leaks
- Brakes
  —Condition of brake drum(s)
  —Condition of hoses—look for any wear due to rubbing
- Lights and reflectors
  —Side-marker lights clean, operating and proper color (red at rear, others amber)
  —Side-marker reflectors clean and proper color (red at rear, others amber)

Rear

- Lights and reflectors
  - —Rear clearance and identification lights clean, operating and proper color (red at rear)
  - —Reflectors clean and proper color (red at rear)
  - —Tail lights clean, operating and proper color (red at rear)
  - —Right rear turn signal operating, and proper color (red, yellow, or amber at rear)
- License plate(s) present, clean and secured
- Splash guards present, not damaged, properly fastened, not dragging on ground or rubbing tires
- Cargo secure (trucks)
  - —Cargo properly blocked, braced, tied, chained, etc.
  - —Tailboards up and properly secured
  - —End gates free of damage, properly secured in stake sockets
  - —Canvas or tarp (if required) properly secured to prevent tearing or billowing to block either the rear-view mirrors or to cover rear lights.
  - —If over-length, or over-width, make sure all signs and/or additional lights/flags are safely and properly mounted and all required permits are in driver's possession
  - —Rear doors securely closed, latched/locked

Left Side

- Check all items as done on right side, plus:
  - —Battery (if not mounted in engine compartment)
  - —Battery box securely mounted to vehicle
  - —Box has secure cover
  - —Battery(s) secured against movement
  - —Battery(s) not broken or leaking
  - —Fluid in battery(s) at proper level (except maintenance-free type)
  - —Cell caps present and securely tightened (except maintenance-free type)
  - —Vents in cell caps free of foreign material (except maintenance-free type)

Step 6—Check Signal Lights

Get In and Turn Off Lights

- Turn off all lights
- Turn on stop lights (apply trailer hand brake, or have a helper push on the brake pedal)
- Turn on left-turn signal

Get Out and Check Lights

- Left front turn signal light clean, operating and proper color (amber or white on signals facing the front)
- Left rear turn signal light and both stop lights clean, operating and proper color (red, yellow, or amber)

Step 7—Start the Engine and Check Brake System

Get In Vehicle

- Turn off lights not needed for driving
- Check for all required papers, trip manifests, permits, etc.
- Secure all loose articles in cab (they might interfere with operation of the controls, or hit you in a crash)
- Start the engine

Test For Hydraulic Leaks. **IF THE VEHICLE HAS HYDRAULIC BRAKES, PUMP THE BRAKE PEDAL THREE TIMES. THEN APPLY FIRM PRESSURE TO THE PEDAL AND HOLD FOR FIVE SECONDS. THE PEDAL SHOULD NOT MOVE.** If it does, there may be a leak or other problem. Get it fixed before driving.

If the vehicle has air brakes, do the checks described in Chapter 5, *AIR BRAKES*.

Test Parking Brake

- **WITH THE VEHICLE FULLY STOPPED, APPLY PARKING BRAKES AND GENTLY ATTEMPT TO MOVE THE VEHICLE. PARKING BRAKES MUST HOLD THE VEHICLE.**

Test Service Brake Stopping Action

- **GO 3 TO 5 MILES PER HOUR**
- **PUSH BRAKE PEDAL FIRMLY**

- **<u>VEHICLE SHOULD STOP IMMEDIATELY</u>**
- **<u>"PULLING" TO ONE SIDE OR THE OTHER CAN MEAN BRAKE TROUBLE</u>**
- **<u>ANY UNUSUAL BRAKE PEDAL "FEEL" OR DELAYED STOPPING ACTION CAN MEAN TROUBLE</u>**

This completes the pre-trip inspection. If you find anything wrong during the pre-trip inspection which may affect the safe operation of the vehicle, Federal and State regulations require that these items be repaired before beginning your trip.

Enroute Inspections

During your trip you must, at all times, be aware of the condition of your vehicle. Constantly monitor your gauges, controls and mirrors.

<u>DRIVERS OF TRUCKS AND TRUCK-TRACTORS ARE REQUIRED TO STOP AND INSPECT THE VEHICLE WITHIN THE FIRST 25 MILES OF A TRIP AND EVERY 150 MILES OR EVERY 3 HOURS AFTERWARD.</u>

- Check these things:
  - —cargo doors
  - —cargo securement
  - —tires
  - —coupling devices

—brakes (are they getting hot?)

—lights (at night)

After-Trip Inspection

Federal law requires that inter-state drivers complete an after-trip inspection. The driver must list any defects discovered during the trip. A copy of this report must remain in the truck. In some states, intra-state drivers must also fill out this report. Check with your state to make sure.

KEEP IN MIND THAT A FEDERAL INSPECTOR DOES HAVE THE RIGHT TO INSPECT YOUR TRUCK OR BUS AND ALSO HAS THE AUTHORITY TO PLACE IT "OUT-OF-SERVICE."

☞ LET'S TAKE A TEST

General Knowledge Vehicle Inspections

Study each question carefully and then indicate your choice by drawing a circle around the letter you have chosen, or filling in the correct answers, or indicating if it is true or false.

1. The pre-trip vehicle inspection described in this section consists of how many steps?

   A. 4
   B. 6
   C. 7
   D. 9

2. Name five key components of the steering system.

   1.
   2.
   3.
   4.
   5.

3. Name the three types of inspections.

   1.
   2.
   3.

4. The driver's vehicle inspection report must be filled out:

   A. at the beginning of the trip
   B. half way through the trip
   C. the following morning
   D. at the end of the trip

5. Brake shoes must not be less than, or:

   A. worn dangerously thin, missing or broken
   B. 2/32-inch thick
   C. 3/52-inch thick
   D. 4/52-inch thick

6.   Where must the ignition (starter) key be during the pre-trip inspection walkaround?

   A. in the ignition
   B. in your pocket
   C. on the dashboard
   D. on the driver's seat

7.   How many red reflective triangles are you required to carry?

   A. 6
   B. 2
   C. 4
   D. 3

8.   Drivers of truck and truck-tractors are required to inspect their vehicles within how many miles after starting the trip?

   A. 150
   B. 75
   C. 25 / 50
   D. 100

9. When checking your wheels and rims during the pre-trip inspection, look for:

   A. broken studs
   B. missing lug nuts
   C. cracked rims
   D. all of the above

10. Steering tires must have at least:

   A. 4/32-inch of tread depth
   B. 2/32-inch of tread depth
   C. 3/32-inch of tread depth
   D. 5/32-inch of tread depth

11. Can federal inspectors inspect your truck or bus?

   A. yes, and they have the authority to place you "out-of-service"
   B. yes, but they have no authority to place you out of service
   C. yes, but only at a point of entry
   D. no

12. How many missing or broken leaves in leaf spring will cause your vehicle to be placed "out-of-service"?

   A. one-fourth of the total number

   B. one-half of the total number

   C. one-third of the total number

   D. any

Answers

1. C

2. Steering wheel
   Tie Rod
   Spindle
   Pittman arm
   Drag link
   Gear box
   Steering arm
   Steering shaft

3. Pre-trip
   En route
   After-trip

4. D

5. A

6. B

7. D

8. C

9. D

10. A

11. A

12. A

If you were able to answer all of the questions correctly—*GOOD JOB!* If you missed any, read the material again until you know it with 100% accuracy.

Basic Control

IN ORDER TO SAFELY DRIVE A COMMERCIAL VEHICLE, YOU NEED TO BE AN EXPERT IN CONTROLLING ITS SPEED AND DIRECTION. To be able to achieve this, you must have a basic understanding of the four elements of vehicle control:

1. Accelerating
2. Steering
3. Shifting gears
4. Braking

During this section we will discuss these four elements in detail. Many of you experienced drivers will already be familiar with much of this information. However, we will be using some terminology, or words, which you may not be familiar with, so it's important that you read this section and become familiar with these new words. Many of them will probably be on your test.

Before beginning this section on Basic Control, let's first talk about seatbelts and their use. FMCSR, Part 392.16 states "A motor vehicle which has a seatbelt assembly installed at the driver's seat shall not be driven unless the driver has properly restrained himself with the seatbelt assembly."

It is a Federal regulation that all inter-state drivers must wear seat belts. In many states, the law requires that seat belts be worn. There are two reasons that the Federal regulation requires the use of seat belts:

1. To help you maintain control of your vehicle. Any driver who has ever run off the road, had a front tire blow-out when heavily loaded or hit a curb at a high rate of speed, can tell you how violent it is. Many drivers are thrown from the seat and lose control of the vehicle and their life, when in many cases, the seat belt would have kept them in the seat and allowed them to control the vehicle.

2. Statistics prove, time and time again, *SEATBELTS SAVE LIVES.* So buckle up—and let's get started!

Accelerating

The key to proper acceleration is to do it smoothly with the proper coordination between the clutch and the accelerator pedal.

Rough acceleration is caused by either taking the foot off the clutch too fast, or by pressing the accelerator too hard, or both. When this happens you may experience what is called an **ACCELERATION SPIN OR SLIDE.** An acceleration slide happens when too much power, too quickly, has been applied to the drive wheels, causing them to lose traction. In a truck-tractor this could cause the tractor to spin around and cause a tractor jackknife. When going up a hill or mountain on wet, snowy or icy roads, an acceleration slide can happen which will cause you to "break traction." **IF AN ACCELERATION SPIN OCCURS, ALL YOU NEED TO DO IS SIMPLY LET UP ON THE ACCELERATOR.** This will reduce the power to the drive wheels and stop the slide, enabling your drive wheels to regain traction.

When beginning to move on snowy or icy roads, too much acceleration will cause a loss of traction. Take your foot off the accelerator, stopping the spin. Start out again using less power. In some cases, you may need to choose a higher gear when starting out. This will reduce the amount of power going to the drive wheels.

Another problem encountered when starting out, especially among novice drivers, is the **ROLLBACK.** This occurs when the driver either fails to press on the accelerator enough, or doesn't let his foot off the clutch in the same movement as he/she steps on the accelerator. This happens most often when stopped on an upgrade. To prevent this from happening, partly engage the clutch before removing the foot from the brake, then release the clutch smoothly as the accelerator is depressed. **WHATEVER YOU DO, DON'T ROLL BACK!** You may hit someone behind you. **IF NECESSARY, APPLY THE PARKING BRAKE** until the clutch release and the proper pressure to the accelerator has been obtained.

Rough and jerky acceleration can result in severe drive-train damage. Always start out smoothly and slowly.

Steering

ALWAYS PLACE YOUR HANDS ON THE OPPOSITE SIDE OF THE STEERING WHEEL. This allows you to maintain control of the vehicle in the event of a front tire blow-out or hitting a curb or pothole. The correct position to hold the steering wheel is with your hands at the 3 o'clock and 9 o'clock positions.

Backing Safely

- **BACK ONLY WHEN YOU HAVE TO.**
- **BACK ONLY ON THE DRIVER'S SIDE WHENEVER POSSIBLE.** You can see better with less chance of having an accident.
- Back slowly.
- **USE A HELPER WHENEVER POSSIBLE BECAUSE OF THE BLIND SPOTS, BUT ESTABLISH WITH THE HELPER THE HAND SIGNALS TO USE AND MAKE SURE YOU ARE THE SAME ON THE SIGNAL TO "STOP."**
- Before backing, always get out and check out the area.
- **WHENEVER YOU BACK A TRAILER—TRY TO POSITION YOUR VEHICLE SO YOU CAN BACK IN A STRAIGHT LINE.**
- Never back if you can avoid it. Most minor accidents occur when backing; avoid it if you can.
- When pulling into a parking place, truck stop, etc., try to position your vehicle so you won't have to back out.
- Take as many **"PULL UPS"** as necessary. If the truck or trailer begins to get out of alignment, **PULL UP AND STRAIGHTEN IT OUT** and then start backing again.

Shifting Gears

Most trucks and truck-tractors are designed to be double-clutched. You clutch when coming out of gear and then again when going back into gear. **YOU SHOULD DOUBLE-CLUTCH AT EVERY SHIFT.**

Steps in shifting manual transmissions:

- Upshifting
    —Release accelerator, push in clutch, move shifter to neutral position
    —Release clutch
    —Depress clutch and move shifter lever to higher gear
    —Release clutch and smoothly press accelerator at the same time
- Downshifting
    —Release accelerator, push in clutch, move shifter to neutral
    —Release clutch and press accelerator to increase engine rpm's (usually an increase of 200 to 500 rpm's depending on make of engine).
    —Depress clutch and shift to lower gear.
    —Release clutch and press accelerator smoothly.

Knowing when to upshift . . .

Every vehicle has an engine operating rpm range. On older truck-tractors with diesel engines, the range was usually 1700-2100 rpm's. In newer diesel engines this range is usually 1300-1800 rpm's. Check your vehicle's manual to find the rpm operating range for your equipment.

After you've driven for awhile, **YOU'LL BE ABLE TO TELL WHEN TO SHIFT FROM THE ENGINE SOUNDS.** Until then—use the tachometer—as you reach the top of the range—you upshift to the next higher gear.

Progressive shifting is a new method of shifting. Its purpose is to save fuel by allowing the driver to shift at lower rpm's in the lower gears. In the higher gears the shifting takes place at "progressively" higher rpm's on each shift.

Knowing when to downshift . . .

Again, read the vehicle manual to determine the proper rpm operating range. When the engine speed (rpm) reaches the lower level, you clutch—shift—clutch again and shift to the next lower gear.

With practice (all you "old-timers" are already doing it), you'll be shifting by the:

ENGINE SOUND

SPEEDOMETER

TACHOMETER

After you've driven awhile, you'll know what gear will correspond to which speeds, so the engine sounds and speedometer will more often tell you when to shift than the tachometer.

When should you downshift?

1. Before starting down a hill—**DOWNSHIFT BEFORE STARTING DOWN A HILL.** Get into a gear, (usually lower than the one you use to climb up the hill) and allow the brakes and the engine to control your speed going down.

2. **DOWNSHIFT BEFORE ENTERING A CURVE, NEVER WHILE YOU'RE IN IT. THIS ALLOWS YOU TO USE SOME POWER THROUGH THE CURVE.**

Engine Retarders

What's an engine retarder? Most drivers know them as a "Jake Brake" or a Williams "Blue OX" brake. While these are two of the more popular retarders on the market, there are many types of retarders being manufactured by many different companies.

AN ENGINE RETARDER SIMPLY ALLOWS THE VEHICLE'S ENGINE TO BE USED TO HELP SLOW IT DOWN. This is particularly useful on long downgrades when excessive braking can cause the brakes to heat up and fade. **BRAKE FADE IS WHEN THE BRAKES BEGIN TO LOSE THEIR STOPPING POWER.**

All retarders are controlled by the driver with a switch on or near the instrument panel.

Caution: If driving on snowy or icy roads, your wheels naturally have less traction than when on dry roads. Using an engine retarder in these conditions could cause your drive wheels to skid. **IT IS BEST NOT TO USE AN ENGINE RETARDER WHEN DRIVING ON WET, ICY OR SNOW-COVERED ROADS. ENGINE RETARDERS CAN CAUSE THE TRUCK TO GO INTO A SKID ON WET, ICY OR SNOW-COVERED ROADS.**

Professional Driving Techniques

Driving a commercial vehicle is a tough job. It takes longer to get the truck moving, longer to slow it down, longer to stop and longer to turn. Because of this **YOU WILL NEED LARGER GAPS IN TRAFFIC WHEN MERGING.** Professional drivers must be more aware of their driving environment than do their nonprofessional counterparts driving their "4-wheelers." More is expected from you, the professional driver. After all, it's what you do for a living. You ought to be good at it.

In order to safely and professionally operate a commercial vehicle, you must have sharply developed driving skills and techniques. The skills and techniques we are going to discuss in this section are:

- Reading the road
- Communicating
- Speed management
- Space management
- Night driving
- Adverse driving conditions
- Driving hazards

Reading the Road

You can't be a safe driver if you don't know what's going on around you. "Reading the Road" means watching everything that is going on in front of you, next to you and behind you.

When driving, you must maintain a **"12-15 SECOND EYE LEAD TIME."** This means that you look down the road to a point that will take your vehicle 12-15 seconds to reach. In the city, this will be 2-3 city blocks; **AT HIGHWAY**

SPEEDS, THIS WILL BE APPROXIMATELY 1/4 MILE. By looking that far ahead you will be able to see things happening that may affect you—in plenty of time to react calmly and professionally. Next time you are driving, practice this. Pick out an object ahead of you and start counting; one-thousand-one, one-thousand-two, one-thousand-three, etc., etc. See how long it takes you to reach it. With practice, you'll find yourself automatically looking ahead 12-15 seconds.

What do you look for? When looking ahead 12 to 15 seconds, you are looking for anything which may affect you or your vehicle. You will be looking for two major items:

1. **LOOK FOR TRAFFIC**
2. **LOOK FOR ROAD CONDITIONS**
   WHILE DRIVING DOWN THE ROAD YOU SHOULD BE LOOKING BACK AND FORTH AND NEAR AND FAR AT ALL TIMES.

When looking at or for traffic, you'll be scanning intersections, watching driveways, looking for brake lights or turn signals, or anything which may affect your path of travel.

Road conditions such as curves, hills, merging lanes, construction, and new traffic lights or signals are just some of the conditions that you must be looking for.

Professional drivers look in their mirrors **OFTEN,** every 5 to 8 seconds. Because all commercial vehicles have **BLIND SPOTS,** the driver constantly scans his mirrors to see vehicles entering and exiting those blind spots. It is critical that the driver know where other traffic is at all times. If a rapid lane change or an emergency evasive maneuver has to be done quickly, the driver might not have time to look in his mirrors, but if he's constantly checking them every 5 to 8 seconds, he/she will always know the location of the other traffic in relationship to his/her own vehicle. Looking in the mirrors will also allow the driver to check his trailer frequently, looking for flat tires, open doors, loose tarp straps, etc. **WHEN USING "SPOT" OR CONVEX MIRRORS, EVERYTHING WILL APPEAR SMALLER AND FARTHER AWAY THAN THEY REALLY ARE. ALWAYS CHECK AND ADJUST MIRRORS PRIOR TO THE BEGINNING OF EACH TRIP.**

Never stare or focus for too long a time at the mirrors or at any object. When traveling at 55 mph, your vehicle will travel approximately 80 feet per second. If you stare at something for just a few seconds, you and your vehicle will travel a considerable distance "blind." Another reason for not staring is that when you focus on an object such as your mirror or someone standing on the corner, you will temporarily lose your peripheral vision (your side vision). When that happens, you won't be able to see anything out of the "corner of your eye," which could be disastrous if something was coming at you from the side. Don't stare at traffic signals when sitting at a light. If you do, you'll lose that peripheral vision—that's why so many accidents happen at intersections.

Communicating

Communicating with other motorists means to tell them what you are doing. **YOU MUST COMMUNICATE YOUR INTENTIONS TO OTHERS. YOU "COMMUNICATE" WITH TURN SIGNALS, BRAKE LIGHTS, HEADLIGHTS, 4-WAYS AND THE HORN.** These are also the way other motorists "communicate" their intentions to you. There are other methods that communication can take. For example, you are in the center lane of a 3-lane interstate. Just ahead of you in the right lane is a lady driving a 4-wheeler. You see her turn her head to the left and look over her left shoulder. What do you think she's communicating to you? That's right, she's telling you that she's thinking about moving left into your lane. Because you were observant, you saw that communication in enough time to react to it properly.

Turn signals are a major form of communication. They tell oncoming traffic and traffic behind you what you are going to do. Not only are turn signals a good safe driving habit, for commercial drivers, *they are the law*.

Here are three rules for using turn signals:

1. Signal early—**<u>SIGNAL 100 FEET BEFORE THE LANE CHANGE. CHECK YOUR MIRRORS BEFORE AND AFTER YOU SIGNAL TO MAKE SURE NO ONE HAS MOVED OUT OF YOUR BLIND SPOT.</u>**

2. Signal continuously throughout the turn. You'll need both hands on the wheel for turning. **<u>CHECK YOUR MIRRORS AGAIN.</u>**

3. **<u>CANCEL THE TURN SIGNAL ONLY AFTER THE TURN HAS BEEN COMPLETED AND CHECK YOUR MIRRORS AFTER TURN IS COMPLETED.</u>**
   PLEASE NOTE: It used to be, "back in the old days," when trucks went much slower than cars, we would signal the drivers following us that it was OK to pass. Today, not only is that not necessary, **<u>IT IS UNSAFE AND AGAINST THE LAW. NEVER DO IT!</u>**

4. Lane changes—whenever changing lanes, put on your signal at least 100 feet before making the change, and then cancel it as soon as you are in the lane.

5. When merging onto a freeway or exiting, signal your intentions well in advance—let everybody know what you want to do.

<u>WHEN SLOWING DOWN OR IN TIGHT TURNS WHERE YOU'LL ALMOST HAVE TO STOP—FLASH YOUR BRAKE LIGHTS A FEW TIMES SO THAT THE MOTORISTS BEHIND YOU WILL KNOW THAT YOU ARE SLOWING DOWN.</u> Also, whenever you begin to slow down, always look in your mirror to see how closely traffic is following. Most rear-end collisions could have been prevented if the lead driver had looked in his mirror. It may mean you miss your turn or exit, but that's better than having an accident that might have been prevented.

<u>WHEN PASSING,</u> don't assume the drivers of the car you are about to pass, or that a pedestrian, or a child on a bicycle, can see you. **<u>TAP YOUR HORN LIGHTLY</u>** (where legal), or at night **<u>FLASH YOUR HIGH BEAMS</u>** and let them know you are coming around.

In cloudy, overcast, rainy, or in any driving conditions that make it hard to see, **<u>TURN ON YOUR HEADLIGHTS AND CLEARANCE MARKER LIGHTS.</u>**

If it's hard for you to see them, it's hard for them to see you. Even though your rig may be 55 feet long, they still might not see you. How many times at an accident scene, where a truck and car collided, have you heard the driver of the car say *"but officer, I just didn't see him"*? Another good rule of thumb, whenever you have to use your windshield wipers, turn on your lights as well.

If, because of mechanical problems or some other reason, it is necessary for you to pull over to the side of the road, **TURN ON YOUR 4-WAY FLASHERS IMMEDIATELY.** This is especially true at night. There have been many drivers killed who ran into the back of a truck parked along the highway without their 4-ways flashing.

If you do stop alongside the road, and are going to be there any length of time, **YOU MUST SET OUT THE REFLECTIVE TRIANGLES WITHIN 10 MINUTES.**

The warning devices should be placed in the following manner:

Emergency Warning Devices

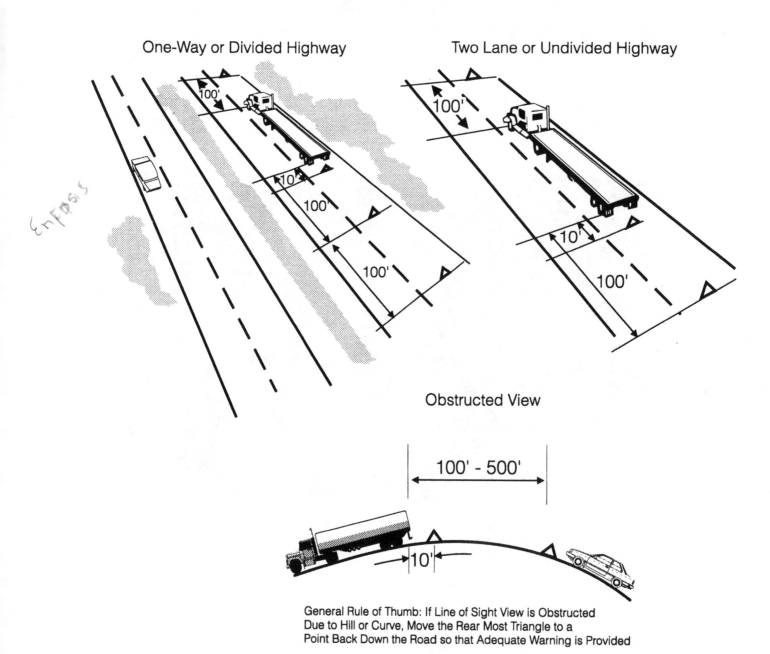

One-Way or Divided Highway

Two Lane or Undivided Highway

Obstructed View

General Rule of Thumb: If Line of Sight View is Obstructed
Due to Hill or Curve, Move the Rear Most Triangle to a
Point Back Down the Road so that Adequate Warning is Provided

Note: **YOU MUST KNOW THE PROPER PLACEMENT OF THE REFLECTIVE TRIANGLES FOR EACH SITUATION.**

The horn is an excellent way to communicate your presence and intentions; however, only use it when necessary. A couple of friendly taps on the horn will let others know what you are going to do. The horn should never be used in anger. A loud blast of the horn, especially an air horn, can be dangerous, and will communicate that a non-professional is driving that rig. The best advice is to never allow your emotions to control your actions while driving.

Speed Management

Controlling, or managing, your speed, is essential when driving a commercial vehicle. In the majority of all fatal accidents involving commercial vehicles, speed was a major factor.

It is necessary that the speed of your vehicle be adjusted to the driving conditions. Heavy traffic, weather, construction, school zones, etc., all dictate that your speed must adjust accordingly. Failure to adjust your speed may put you in a situation where you will not have the time to react the way you should if an emergency happens.

Let's talk about stopping distance. Three factors determine how long it takes to stop:

1. **PERCEPTION DISTANCE**
2. **REACTION DISTANCE**
3. **BRAKING DISTANCE**

Let's talk about a formula you can use to figure out how many feet your vehicle is traveling per second. If you take the number, 1.47, and multiply it times your speed, it will tell you how many feet you are traveling each second. Here are some examples:

25mph	45mph	55mph	65mph
x1.47	x1.47	x1.47	x1.47
36.75 feet per second	66.15 feet per second	80.85 feet per second	95.55 feet per second

As you can see, at 55 mph, your vehicle will travel almost 81 fps (feet per second) and at 65 mph, it will travel 96 fps. Let's say you are traveling down the road at 65 mph (legal in many states), and you look in your mirror for three seconds. During that three seconds, your vehicle will travel almost the length of a football field! Most of us don't realize we're moving that fast. That's why it is so critical that we always maintain a good following distance, and why it is so important to **MAINTAIN AN EYE LEAD TIME OF 12-15 SECONDS.**

To determine how long it takes a vehicle to stop, we must understand the three factors involved. Perception distance, reaction distance and braking distance add up to the total stopping distance of any vehicle.

PERCEPTION DISTANCE is the distance your vehicle will travel from the time your eyes see a hazard and your brain tells you that it is a hazard and you must do something about it. With the average driver, this takes about 3/4 of a second. At 55 mph, your vehicle will travel about 60 feet during that 3/4 of a second.

REACTION DISTANCE is the time it takes for your foot to come off the accelerator and hit the brake pedal. Again, it will take the average driver about 3/4 of a second to do this, and again, at 55 mph, your vehicle will travel approximately another 60 feet during this time.

BRAKING DISTANCE, also called brake lag, is the distance the vehicle will travel from the time the brakes are applied until it stops. This distance will vary with the weight of the vehicle, the adjustment of the brakes and the road conditions; wet, dry, icy, etc. Taking a speed of 55 mph, on dry roads, properly adjusted brakes, and an average load of 35,000 lbs, it will take approximately 182 feet to stop.

Now, let's look at the total stopping distance at 55 mph:

Perception distance	60 feet
Reaction distance	60 feet
Braking distance	182 feet
Total stopping distance	302 feet

AT 55 MPH, IT WILL TAKE YOU THE LENGTH OF A FOOTBALL FIELD TO STOP, assuming brakes are all properly adjusted and you are driving on dry roads.

Now that you know how to calculate total stopping distance, let's look at the effects of speed and road conditions on total stopping distance.

Whenever you **DOUBLE YOUR SPEED**—it will take **FOUR TIMES LONGER** to stop your vehicle! If a crash occurs, it will have four times the destructive power!

What about the effect of vehicle weight on stopping distance? This is sometimes a little confusing to drivers because we think that the heavier the load, the longer it takes to stop. The fact is, **EMPTY TRUCKS TAKE LONGER TO STOP, HEAVIER TRUCKS WILL STOP IN A SHORTER DISTANCE.** The reason for this is **FRICTION**. The more friction between the tires and the road surface, the sooner the truck will stop. **HEAVIER TRUCKS HAVE MORE FRICTION; EMPTY TRUCKS HAVE LESS. BOBTAILS (TRACTOR WITHOUT A TRAILER) HAVE THE LEAST AMOUNT OF FRICTION AND, AS MOST EXPERIENCED DRIVERS WILL TELL YOU, THEY TAKE THE LONGEST AMOUNT OF TIME TO STOP, ESPECIALLY ON WET ROADS.**

Let's look at some road and traffic conditions that will affect stopping distances and steering:

- Slippery surfaces—It will take you longer to stop on wet, snowy or icy roadways. **WET ROADS CAN DOUBLE YOUR STOPPING DISTANCE. REDUCE YOUR SPEED BY AT LEAST 1/3. IF TRAVELING 55—SLOW DOWN TO 35.**
  —SNOW-COVERED ROADS WILL MAKE STOPPING DISTANCES EVEN LONGER. REDUCE SPEED BY AT LEAST 1/2.
  —ICY ROADS MEAN YOU SHOULD SLOW TO A CRAWL AND STOP AS SOON AS YOU CAN SAFELY DO SO.
- Shaded areas—when the temperature is just above freezing, watch out for shaded areas. The rest of the roadway may have thawed out, but shaded areas may remain icy.
- When the temperature is just at the freezing mark of 32 degrees, watch out! Ice and snow will be wet at this temperature. **WET SNOW OR ICE IS SLIPPERIER THAN DRY SNOW OR ICE.**
- Black ice—**THIS IS A LAYER OF ICE SO THIN THAT THE ROAD SURFACE IS SEEN THROUGH IT.** The road will look wet. One way to tell if the roadway is beginning to freeze is to watch the spray being created by the wheels of the vehicle ahead of you. If the spray stops, the roadway has gone from wet to frozen. Another way to tell is if ice begins to form on windshields, mirrors or antennas.

- Bridges will remain frozen longer than the rest of the roadway and will be the first to freeze. This is caused by the cooling effect of the air passing below and over the bridge.
- Rain—The roadway is at its most slippery right after rain begins to fall. The rain forces the oil, asphalt and grime out of the cracks and crevices in the road surface. The rain then mixes with this material and lays on the surface making the roadway extremely slick. If the rain continues, it will wash away this mixture and the road will become less slippery. **WHEN VISIBILITY IS REDUCED BY SNOW OR RAIN, TURN ON YOUR HEADLIGHTS.**

Hydroplaning

HYDROPLANING IS WHEN THE TIRES ACTUALLY RIDE ON A THIN FILM OF WATER BETWEEN THE ROADWAY AND THE TIRES. The best way to describe this is to say that your tires are actually water skiing. **WHEN HYDROPLANING OCCURS—YOU MAY LOSE ALL TRACTION—BRAKING AND STEERING.** Your only course of action is to simply take your foot off the accelerator, and depress the clutch. When speed decreases, your wheels will stop hydroplaning and will regain traction. **HYDROPLANING OCCURS BECAUSE OF SPEED AND/OR LACK OF TREAD ON THE TIRES AND LOW TIRE PRESSURE.** A smooth tire will hydroplane much more quickly than one with tread. It is the grooves in the tread that channel away the water. **HYDROPLANING CAN OCCUR AT SPEEDS AS LOW AS 30 MPH.**

Speed on Curves and Ramps

You must always remember that on curves and ramps, the posted speed limits are for cars, not necessarily for commercial vehicles with high centers of gravity. It is best to always travel 5 to 10 mph less on curves and ramps than the posted speed limit. **WHEN**

APPROACHING A CURVE, DOWNSHIFT AND SLOW DOWN BEFORE ENTERING IT AND THEN ACCELERATE AS YOU GO THROUGH IT. THIS WILL HELP YOU TO MAINTAIN CONTROL. Going into a curve too fast can cause the vehicle to lose traction and continue straight ahead. When this happens, the driver may attempt to stop or steer radically, which may result in a rollover. Always slow down before entering a curve.

We've talked about safe following distance and maintaining a 12-to-15-second eye lead time, but in certain conditions this can be difficult to do. In fog, heavy rain or blinding snow, you must adjust your driving and your vehicle's speed. **IF CONDITIONS ARE BAD—USE YOUR HEADLIGHTS** and maybe even your 4-way flashers to communicate your presence. If it is necessary to stop—pull off the roadway as far as possible, make sure your 4-ways are on—and set out your reflective triangles *as quickly as possible*. When setting out your triangles, be careful. Remember, oncoming traffic will have a difficult time seeing you walking down the road. **ALWAYS OPEN ONE OF THE TRIANGLES AND CARRY IT ABOUT CHEST HIGH WITH THE REFLECTIVE SIDE FACING ONCOMING TRAFFIC.**

Traffic Flow—When traveling in heavy traffic, **THE SAFEST SPEED TO TRAVEL IS THE SPEED OF THE OTHER VEHICLES, NOT SLOWER, NOT FASTER.** Always maintain a safe following distance.

Night Driving—Don't overdrive your headlights. When driving with your low beams, 40 mph is the top speed at which you'll be able to stop if something is in the roadway at the furthest reach of your headlights. **ALWAYS USE YOUR HIGH BEAMS WHENEVER SAFE AND LEGAL TO DO SO.** Never use them when closely following another vehicle or when traffic is approaching. When driving at night, keep your eyes moving. This will help prevent "highway hypnosis" or "white line hypnosis," and allow you to scan the side of the roadway for hazards.

Downgrades—The best rule of thumb is to use a lower gear going down the hill than the one you used to climb up. **SHIFT DOWN TO A LOWER GEAR BEFORE STARTING DOWN THE GRADE, AND THEN "SNUB" OR STAB THE BRAKES WHEN THE VEHICLE SPEED REACHES THE "SAFE SPEED." MAINTAIN BRAKING PRESSURE UNTIL YOUR VEHICLE SPEED IS AT LEAST 5 MPH UNDER THE "SAFE SPEED." "SAFE**

SPEED" MEANS THE POSTED TRUCK OR BUS SPEED LIMIT FOR THE HILL. Before starting down the grade, make sure that all brakes are properly adjusted.

Space Management

Managing space means to always have a place to go if you need it—or to leave yourself an out. In order to have a place to go, you must manage space. You do this by always maintaining a safe following distance and by always watching your mirror to see where other traffic is, in relationship to your vehicle.

How much space, or following distance, do you need to maintain? Here's the formula:

FOR EVERY 10 FEET OF YOUR VEHICLE LENGTH, YOU NEED ONE SECOND FOR SPEEDS UP TO 40 MPH:
40-ft vehicle + 30 mph = 4 seconds

FOR SPEEDS OVER 40 MPH, YOU ADD ONE SECOND:
40-ft vehicle + 50 mph = 5 seconds

IF YOUR VEHICLE IS 45 FEET LONG, YOU ROUND IT UP TO THE NEXT HIGHER NUMBER:
45-ft vehicle + 50 mph = 6 seconds

Tailgaters—How do you handle tailgaters? First rule is always to stay to the right whenever possible. Never pass another commercial vehicle when going up hill if it is going to take a long time to do it. Motorists behind you are going to get angry and will certainly be following you too closely and may attempt to pass when it isn't safe.

When being tailgated, the best course of action for you is to **INCREASE YOUR FOLLOWING DISTANCE**. This will give you a chance to slow down gradually if road and traffic conditions make it necessary. Tap your brake lights several times before you begin to slow down; this will give the motorists behind you advance warning that you are getting ready to stop.

WHEN BEING TAILGATED NEVER FLASH YOUR BRAKE LIGHTS AT THE VEHICLE BEHIND YOU JUST TO GET THEM TO BACK OFF . . . it will only upset the driver of that vehicle and may lead to road rage.

Managing the space to your sides is simply a matter of watching your mirrors frequently, every 5 to 8 seconds. **STAY CENTERED IN YOUR LANE, AVOID TRAVELING RIGHT NEXT TO ANOTHER VEHICLE AND NEVER DRIVE IN ANOTHER VEHICLE'S BLIND SPOT.** Always try to leave yourself an out.

You always want to keep a space to your left, your right, immediately behind and ahead of you.

When operating a commercial vehicle, several factors come into play which normally will not affect other vehicles; these are:

Strong winds

Overhead hazards

Turns

STRONG WINDS—may make operating a commercial vehicle more hazardous. Gusts of winds have been known to blow tractor-trailers over. **<u>BE ESPECIALLY CAUTIOUS ON HIGH BRIDGES AND WHEN EXITING TUNNELS. AVOID DRIVING ALONGSIDE OTHER VEHICLES WHEN IN THESE CONDITIONS.</u>**

Overhead hazards—are a very real threat to trucks and buses. Never assume that the signs indicating the height of an overpass are correct. Newly paved roads or snow packed roads can change the height clearance. **<u>RUNNING EMPTY AS OPPOSED TO RUNNING LOADED WILL AFFECT THE HEIGHT OF YOUR VEHICLE.</u>** Running through a tunnel or under a bridge at a speed which can cause your trailer or truck to bounce can cause you to hit the top. A sign for a low overpass may be missing. All of these factors must be considered when driving a commercial vehicle.

Whenever you approach a low overpass, approach with caution. If you have any doubt about it at all, slow down, put on your 4-way flashers and stop if necessary. Move toward the center of the road and proceed through slowly, keeping an eye on the clearance.

Backing—Whenever backing, always check out the area before beginning to back. Get out of the truck and walk the path your vehicle will take. Look for any overhead hazards, overhangs of buildings, signs, or low electrical wires. Also look for any hazards on the ground which may affect your path of travel.

Another hazard unique to commercial vehicles is the space below the vehicle. This is especially true for auto carriers, low boys and platform trailers with drop frames. When crossing railroad tracks, when traveling over crossovers with a high bank, the trailers can get hung up, and may require a tow truck to get unstuck. The best rule of thumb here is, if in doubt, Don't!

Turning—**<u>WHEN MAKING A RIGHT TURN, KEEP YOUR TRAILER AS CLOSE TO THE CURB AS POSSIBLE.</u>** This will prevent another vehicle or a bicyclist from "squeezing" between you and the curb. Stay as close to the right side of the curb as possible throughout the turn, only swing left to turn right if absolutely necessary and only at the last minute, keeping the trailer right next to the curb (see diagrams below).

When making left turns, follow these procedures:

- Reach the center of the intersection before starting the turn.
- **<u>IF THERE ARE TWO LEFT-TURN LANES, STAY IN THE ONE TO THE RIGHT.</u>**
- Check left mirror for others turning left.
- Make the turn, watching traffic and left mirror for trailer swing.
- If entering two lanes after making turn, stay in right lane (see diagram below). Make sure you have the space and time necessary to complete the turn without interfering with oncoming traffic.

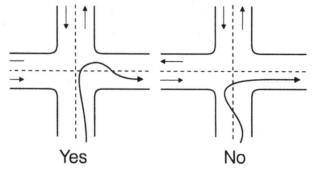

Yes   No

PLEASE NOTE: ➡️

If you are taking the road test the examiner may instruct you to begin your turn from the left-turn lane instead of from the right lane—if so—just remember you should end up in the left lane of the street you are turning onto—check your right mirror, turn on your right-turn signal and then move to the right lane as soon as you can do so safely.

If there are two left turn lanes, use the right hand lane.

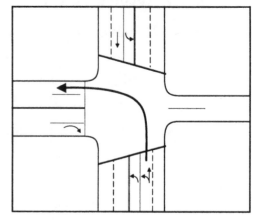

Night Driving

Driving at night is more dangerous. Drivers can't see as well at night and therefore have less time to respond to hazards. When driving at night, you must be more alert.

Vision—Obviously, people can't see as well at night—our eyes need more time to adjust. This is especially true of persons over the age of 40. Experts tell us that our night vision (the ability to see at night) begins to diminish after the age of 40.

Glare—Glare created by headlights is a major problem encountered when driving at night. This is especially true on two-lane roads. When blinded by the headlights of an oncoming vehicle, it takes several seconds to regain our vision. When traveling at highway speeds, this means we may travel several hundred feet blind! To minimize the glare, look to the **RIGHT SIDE OF THE ROADWAY**—watch the shoulder line; this will help to reduce the effects of oncoming headlights. **NEVER USE YOUR HIGH BEAMS WITHIN 500 FEET** of approaching traffic or when following traffic. If an oncoming vehicle has his bright lights on, it is OK to flash yours at him quickly to remind him to dim his, but if he refuses to, the worst thing you can do is to turn yours on high beam and leave them on. If you do that, you're not only breaking the law, but you'll now have two blind drivers coming at each other. It's best just to look at the side of the road and not to get angry. Remember, never let your emotions drive the vehicle!

Fatigue—What do you do when you get so tired you can hardly stay awake? **THE ONLY SAFE THING TO DO IS GET OFF THE ROAD AND GET SOME SLEEP.** Your body's need for sleep is beyond your control. When it's time to sleep, it's time to sleep, and nothing else will help. Coffee won't do it. The caffeine in coffee only stimulates the nervous system. It may help you to stay awake, but you'll still be fatigued and less alert—and you will not be able to respond to an emergency as quickly, or as well, as when you are alert and well rested. Fatigue, and drivers falling asleep at the wheel, is a major factor in truck accidents.

Don't become a statistic.

WHEN YOU ARE TIRED, GET OFF THE ROAD AND GET SOME SLEEP. It's certainly better to be a little late, than never to get there at all.

City Lights and Glare—Driving in a city or among many signs, lights and signals can be confusing and dangerous. Glare from all these lights can mix with each other making traffic signals difficult to see. Whenever driving in these conditions, especially in an unfamiliar city—go slower—take it easy—and don't rush.

Drunk Drivers—When driving at night, be especially watchful for drunk drivers, especially on weekends. Watch for vehicles going too fast, or too slow—or weaving in and out of traffic. Watch for drivers that stop in the roadway for no apparent reason. These are all signs of a drunk driver. Give them a wide berth. If possible, try to get in touch with the police on your CB radio and report any drivers you suspect are driving while intoxicated.

Other tips for night driving:
- Keep your headlights clean
- Keep your windshield clean—inside and out
- Clean all marker lights, brake lights and turn signals and
- make sure they're working
- Clean your mirrors

- **LOW BEAMS ALLOW YOU TO SEE ABOUT 250 FEET AHEAD; HIGH BEAMS ABOUT 350-500 FEET AHEAD**

Dirty headlights and windshields can reduce your visibility by 30%!

- Never wear sunglasses at night—they can reduce your night vision by 20%
- If you wear eye glasses—keep 'em clean
- Use high beams whenever possible
- **NEVER DRIVE WHEN SLEEPY! GET OFF THE ROAD AND GET SOME SLEEP!**

Hazardous Driving Conditions

Winter Driving—Driving during the winter involves additional hazards for all drivers. The careful professional driver can reduce and eliminate many of the hazards by taking a few extra precautions. *You must first prepare your vehicle* by checking the following items:

- Cooling systems—Check and make sure your cooling system is full and protected with antifreeze.
- Fuel tanks—If equipped with heaters, make sure they are working and make sure all fuel lines are properly insulated and protected.
- Tires—Check and make sure that all tires have adequate tread remaining. Steering tires must not have less then 4/32 inch of tread, and remaining tires, not less than 2/32. It is a good idea to install snow tires on the driving axles. This should be done before the first snowfall is expected, taking into account the states in which the vehicle will travel.
- Tire chains—If equipped with tire chains, make sure they are the right size, check for broken links, hooks or cross links. Know how to install them if necessary.
- Wipers and washers—Make sure blades are in good condition and washer solvent bottle is full. Always carry an extra set of wiper blades with you.
- Defrosters and heaters—Make sure they are working properly. If your vehicle is equipped with auxiliary heaters such as mirror heat or battery heaters, make sure they are working.
- Lights and reflectors—Check all lights and reflectors and make sure they are working and clean. Replace any that are defective.

- Exhaust system—Check exhaust system for leaks. Look for loose parts and smoke residue around joints. Get these replaced. Carbon monoxide from gasoline engines can kill you. Don't take any chances.
- Radiator and winter fronts—Make sure radiator shutters are working correctly, and if equipped with winter fronts, make sure that they are installed correctly.

Driving in the Winter

The key word here is to *adjust!* In order to *"Drive to Survive,"** you must adjust your driving to the ever-changing road and traffic conditions.

When driving on slippery roads—the less power to the wheels—the better. When starting to move the vehicle, use the least amount of power necessary, and start out gently. Too much power will result in an over **ACCELERATION SPIN. TO STOP AN ACCELERATION SPIN, TAKE YOUR FOOT OFF THE ACCELERATOR AND DEPRESS THE CLUTCH.**

WHEN TURNING ON SNOW OR ICY ROADS—GO *SLOW* AND TURN AS GENTLY AS POSSIBLE. Adjust your following distance. It may be necessary to *double* your following distance on snow-covered and icy roadways. Extend

* State of Maryland Safety Slogan—Maryland Department of Highway Safety

your eye lead time—look further down the road for hazards which may cause you to have to stop or change lanes. This will give you the extra time you will need to make adjustments slowly and gently.

When applying the brakes—do so *gently*. Wheels will tend to lock up more quickly on snow and ice-covered roads. If you must apply the brakes—*softly and gently* is the rule. If your truck is equipped with an engine retarder, be careful when using it on icy or snow-covered roads; it may cause a spin or loss of traction.

Adjust your space and never drive close to other vehicles—*always leave yourself an out*.

Brakes may get wet when driving in inclement weather and may lose some of their braking ability. By applying very light pressure on the brake pedal, the friction between the drums and linings will cause them to dry out. **WHEN GOING THROUGH DEEP WATER, KEEPING THE BRAKES APPLIED VERY LIGHTLY WILL HELP TO KEEP THEM DRY.** If brakes have gotten wet, test them by applying pressure to the brake pedal to see how they are working. When using any of these methods, be careful not to apply so much pressure that excessive heat is built up—**THIS WILL ALSO CAUSE A LOSS OF BRAKING POWER CALLED BRAKE FADE.**— loose of brake power

WHEN DRIVING IN COLD WEATHER YOU SHOULD ALWAYS USE WINDSHIELD WASHER FLUID WHICH CONTAINS ANTI-FREEZE.

Railroad Crossings

Never try to out race a train. If you lose . . . you'll lose a lot!

When approaching a railroad crossing, always assume a train is coming. Many crossings do not have warning devices. And, often, many of those that do have warning devices aren't working properly.

Because of the size of a train, it is difficult to judge its speed. If you have your window rolled up and the radio on, you probably won't be able to hear a train coming. Follow these simple precautions and you should never have a problem when crossing railroad tracks:

- Approach cautiously with window rolled down
- Look both ways and be especially cautious with double tracks (one train may hide another)
- *NEVER* shift while crossing
- Treat railroad crossings in town as if they were just as dangerous as crossing in the country (they are!)
- Never stop on the tracks

moore than 15 seconds

- Never stop closer than 15 feet to the tracks and never more than 50 feet away
- Be prepared to stop if it becomes necessary

Hot Weather Driving

Driving in hot weather can be as hard, or harder, on a vehicle as driving in cold weather.

Before beginning the trip, check the following:

- Tires—Check air pressure and tread depth. When operating in extremely hot temperatures, **KEEP IN MIND THAT AS TEMPERATURE INCREASES SO DOES AIR PRESSURE IN THE TIRES, SO CHECK EVERY TWO HOURS OR 100 MILES. BE ESPECIALLY WATCHFUL OF RECAPPED OR RETREADED TIRES**.
- **ENGINE COOLANT**—Test as in winter driving. Make sure coolant level is full and has adequate amounts of antifreeze. Anti-freeze helps the cooling system to cool the engine. Pure water would simply boil out. When driving, keep a close eye on the water temperature gauge, especially when climbing a grade. If it reaches the red mark, indicating high temperatures—stop the truck as soon as you can do so safely. Before driving again, check the coolant level and try to determine what caused it to overheat.
  Note: *NEVER Remove The Radiator Cap Until The System Has Cooled.* Doing so may cause steam and boiling water to erupt from the radiator causing serious injury.
- **ENGINE OIL**—High heat puts tremendous strain on the engine oil. Check the oil level regularly. Watch the oil pressure gauge and if equipped, the oil temperature gauge. Loss of oil pressure can result in severe engine damage very quickly.
- **ENGINE BELTS**—Water pump, engine fan, air conditioning and many other engine parts are operated by V-belts. In hot weather, check them often. At any signs of fraying or cracking, get them replaced.
- Hoses—Check your hoses often, and especially during the pre-trip inspection. A ruptured hose can lead to engine damage and even fires. Replace them at any sign of cracks, splits or bubbles on the hose.

Mountain Driving

Long up-and-down grades must be driven cautiously by commercial vehicle operators.

Long upgrades, especially in hot weather, will create extra demands on the engine. Overheating is one of the major problems. Always make sure the coolant and oil levels are full and in good condition.

The major concern for most commercial vehicles when going down a long grade is braking. Many drivers have been killed on long downgrades because they allowed the truck to get away from them.

In this section, we will discuss a few driving techniques that all commercial drivers should do in order to safely descend long downgrades.

Proper Braking

The key to safe braking when going downhill is to get in the right gear, and then stay in it.

The driver must choose which gear he should use to descend the grade—and then get into that gear **BEFORE** starting down. How do you know what the proper gear is? It will usually be a gear **LOWER** than the one used to climb the grade. Today's modern engines have so much horsepower that very often a truck only needs to shift down once or twice in order to climb the grade. That wasn't always so. It used to be, when trucks had smaller engines, they would need to be shifted down many times in order to get up the hill. Back then the rule of thumb was to go down the hill in the same gear you went up. *Today, that just isn't true.* So, you'll probably have to choose a gear two or three gears lower than the one

you used to go up. Most long downgrades, which are a danger to trucks, will have a safe speed posted for trucks. Being familiar with your gear ratios will help you to know what gear to be in order to maintain that speed. And remember . . . before starting down, make sure all of your brakes are adjusted properly.

When brakes are applied they get hot. The hotter they get the less effective they are. Eventually they can get so hot they begin to lose their braking ability. This is called **BRAKE FADE.** How do you know when **BRAKE FADE** is occurring? *If you have to keep applying more and more pressure on the brake pedal in order to maintain the same speed,* **BRAKE FADE IS OCCURRING.** *Pull over and stop and allow them to cool before proceeding.*

The key to downhill braking is to have all of your brakes adjusted properly and to be in a low enough gear. Being in the right gear will allow you to use the braking effect of the engine to help maintain a safe speed. *LOW GEAR,* PROPERLY ADJUSTED BRAKES AND BRAKING EFFECT OF THE ENGINE are a few of the keys to safe downhill braking.

Some experts say that the proper way to brake while going downhill is to apply light, steady pressure to the brakes. Other experts say that the best way is to "snub" or "stab" the brakes on and off. Both methods can work if done properly. Light, steady pressure will work but ONLY if ALL brakes are adjusted absolutely perfectly, which is rarely the case. We think that the best way to brake downhill Is to use the *"snubbing"* or *"stabbing"* method. But again, this works only If done properly. When "snubbing" the brakes it is important that you apply enough pressure to the brake pedal to slow the vehicle to a speed at least **5 MPH UNDER THE "SAFE SPEED." "SAFE SPEED"** means the posted truck or bus speed limit. **IN ORDER FOR THE "SNUBBING" METHOD TO WORK PROPERLY, YOU MUST APPLY 20 PSI OR MORE TO THE BRAKE PEDAL. WHEN YOUR VEHICLE SPEED IS BACK UP TO THE "SAFE SPEED," YOU THEN "SNUB" THE BRAKES AGAIN.** Keep repeating this procedure until you reach the bottom of the grade.

Even though some experts recommend using light, steady pressure, we do not recommend it. Its effectiveness depends on ALL of the brakes being adjusted perfectly. If all the brakes are not adjusted properly those that are will have to work harder and can heat up, at which time, **BRAKE FADE** can occur.

If **BRAKE FADE** occurs you must stop as soon as possible. If you don't stop quickly you may not be able to stop later. If that happens you may end up using a truck escape ramp. **TRUCK ESCAPE RAMPS ARE FOR RUNAWAY TRUCKS THAT HAVE LOST THEIR BRAKES.** Escape ramps are filled with loose gravel. The loose gravel will slow the speed of the truck as it enters the escape ramp and then fill in very quickly behind the truck and trap it. If you ever end up in a truck escape ramp be prepared for a very costly towing bill, a stern lecture from your safety department, and lots of embarrassment as the other truckers wave as they go by. **ESCAPE RAMPS HAVE SAVED MANY LIVES, EQUIPMENT AND CARGO**—use them if you need to.

NEVER SHIFT GEARS WHILE GOING DOWN THE GRADE. You may get into neutral and not be able to get back into gear. If that happens, STOP IMMEDIATELY WHILE YOU STILL CAN! If you don't stop, you may become a candidate for the truck escape ramp or the hospital.

So, what are the five keys to downgrade driving?

1. **SELECT THE RIGHT GEAR**
2. **KEEP BRAKES PROPERLY ADJUSTED**
3. **USE LOW ENOUGH GEAR TO MAINTAIN "SAFE SPEED"**
4. **SNUB BRAKES TO 5 MPH UNDER "SAFE SPEED," THEN RELEASE**
5. **DON'T SHIFT**

Remember these keys, use them correctly and you'll never have a problem while going down long, dangerous grades. You'll always be the professional in control.

Certain situations are more hazardous than others—let's discuss a few of the more common ones that you will have to deal with often.

● Construction Zones—Wherever you go today, you will encounter these. **YOU MUST REDUCE SPEED AND BE ALERT FOR CONSTRUCTION WORKERS AND EQUIPMENT. YOU SHOULD ALSO TURN ON YOUR FLASHERS AND USE YOUR BRAKE LIGHTS TO WARN DRIVERS BEHIND YOU.**

   —Pavement Drop-off—These are common in construction zones but can be found anywhere. They are especially dangerous for high-center-of-gravity commercial vehicles.

   —Off-ramps/On-ramps—These are particularly dangerous as other motorists may make delayed decisions about getting on or off the freeway—and may cut in front of you to get off, or may ride the shoulder on your right trying to get onto the freeway and in front of you. Be especially cautious when coming up on-ramps—watch your mirrors often. Long on/off-ramps

with a curve may also be especially dangerous to high-center-of-gravity vehicles. Remember, the posted speed limit is standardized for cars—you need to go 5 to 10 mph slower. Hitting a curb in a curve on an on/off-ramp has caused many trucks and buses to turn over. Be careful and slow down.

Blocked Vision

Many times your vision or the vision of other motorists may be blocked by signs, trees, bushes, delivery vans, etc. This is especially true at intersections and in narrow city streets. Always be extra careful when approaching an intersection or double-parked car or delivery van.

Watch out for motorists who are driving with their vision blocked by boxes or other material in the vehicle. When you see other motorists whose windows or mirrors are covered with snow or ice or all fogged up, give them plenty of room; they probably can't see you.

Watch out for parked cars. People may be getting out—or they may pull out in front of you. Look for movement in the car—it's an indication that someone is in it, and it may become an immediate hazard to you.

Pedestrians, especially children, the elderly, and bicyclists are hazards. Give them plenty of room.

Watch for drivers who look confused or lost. Look for out-of-state tags. They are totally unpredictable and may turn in front of you or come to a dead stop right in the road.

Elderly drivers tend to drive slowly. Give them plenty of room. Remember, their eyesight and hearing may not be working as well as yours.

Look for a driver's body movement as a clue to what he/she may do. People will look in the direction they are going to go. By being alert, you can spot clues that other drivers will give you. By spotting these clues early, you will have the time you need to react safely.

Always have a plan and leave yourself an out. You must constantly be on the lookout for hazards because hazards often become emergencies very quickly. As you drive down the road looking for hazards, always leave yourself an out and always have a plan to use if necessary, and always be prepared to execute your plan if you need to. This is what defensive driving is all about.

Emergency Steering

STOPPING IS NOT ALWAYS THE SAFEST THING TO DO IN AN EMERGENCY. Many times you will not have enough room to stop, so you'll have to steer away from the hazard. **REMEMBER, YOU CAN ALMOST ALWAYS TURN TO MISS A HAZARD MORE QUICKLY THAN YOU CAN STOP.** Certain limitations will apply to top-heavy, high-center-of-gravity vehicles and combination vehicles with more than one trailer.

KEEP BOTH HANDS ON THE WHEEL—OPPOSITE EACH OTHER. In the event you must make an emergency evasive steering action, you'll need both hands on the wheel. Get in a habit of driving that way.

Here's how to turn quickly and safely in an emergency:

- With both hands on the wheel
- **DO NOT APPLY THE BRAKES WHILE TURNING.** If the wheels lock up, you'll lose your ability to steer and may skid out of control.
- Do not turn any more than necessary. Too much steering can cause skidding and rollover.
- **COUNTERSTEER**—Turn back the wheel in the **OPPOSITE** direction once you've passed the hazard. Be prepared to countersteer as soon as the hazard has been passed.

Where to Steer

IF A VEHICLE IS COMING TOWARD YOU IN YOUR LANE—STEER RIGHT, NEVER STEER LEFT.

If a hazard is blocking your lane, steering right is always the best choice; if a shoulder is present, steer onto it, if not, it is almost always better to steer right off the road. Steering left puts you into jeopardy for a head-on crash, which is almost always fatal. If you are on a freeway or roadway with several lanes going in the same direction, you will then be able to steer left or right. If you have been monitoring your mirrors every 5 to 8 seconds, and if you've left yourself an out, you'll know which way to steer.

What do you do if you have to steer off the road?

1. Firm grip on the steering wheel
2. **NO BRAKES UNTIL SPEED HAS SLOWED DOWN TO ABOUT 20 MPH**
3. **SOFT BRAKING TO A COMPLETE STOP.** (If you try to steer back onto the roadway while moving, you may roll over.) If you must return to the road without coming to a full stop, grip the wheel firmly and steer sharply back onto the roadway and then immediately countersteer to straighten the unit to prevent it from crossing the center line into oncoming traffic.

IF YOU MUST LEAVE THE ROADWAY, IT IS ALMOST ALWAYS BETTER TO COME TO A COMPLETE STOP. Always try to leave one set of wheels on the pavement; this will help you to maintain control.

Emergency Braking

Two types of emergency braking which will allow you to keep your vehicle in a straight line and to turn if necessary:

1. Controlled Braking
2. Stab Braking

CONTROLLED BRAKING (also known as squeeze braking)—is **APPLYING THE BRAKES HARD, BUT WITHOUT LOCKING THE WHEELS.** This allows you to maintain steering control, but you must keep steering movements small.

ABS — Air brake system

STAB BRAKING IS APPLYING THE BRAKES HARD UNTIL THE WHEELS LOCK UP, AND THEN RELEASING UNTIL THE WHEELS BEGIN TO ROLL, AND THEN APPLYING AGAIN, repeating this procedure until you come to a complete stop. **STAB BRAKING SHOULD NEVER BE USED WITH A VEHICLE EQUIPPED WITH ANTI-LOCK BRAKES,** as it defeats the purpose of the anti-lock brakes.

Never jam on the brakes and hold them. This will result in wheel lockup and loss of steering. **IF YOU ARE IN A DRIVE WHEEL BRAKING SKID, YOU SHOULD STOP BRAKING, TURN QUICKLY AND COUNTERSTEER.**

Brake Failure

If you keep the brakes in good condition they will rarely fail.

Hydraulic brakes—Two situations occur which will result in hydraulic brake failure.

1. Loss of hydraulic pressure
2. Brake fade on downgrades

IF YOU LOSE YOUR HYDRAULIC BRAKES DUE TO LOSS OF HYDRAULIC PRESSURE, the brakes will feel spongy and/or the pedal may go all the way to the floor. Here are some actions you can take:

1. **DOWNSHIFT**—This will help to slow the vehicle.
2. **PUMP THE BRAKE**—Sometimes pumping will generate enough pressure to stop the vehicle.
3. **USE THE PARKING BRAKE**—Since the parking brake system is separate from the regular braking system it can be used to slow or stop the vehicle. Use caution when using the parking brake so that you don't jam it on and create a spin—use it firmly but with care.

If you lose your brakes, look for an escape route or escape ramp. If you find a road traveling off in an uphill direction, try to take it if you can. Gravity will help to stop the vehicle but be careful that it doesn't start to roll back—use your parking brake or put it in gear.

Air Brake failure is discussed in Chapter 5, Air Brakes.

Tire Failure

In the event of a tire failure, here are the steps to follow:

1. Firm grip on the steering wheel
2. Stay off brakes—maintain speed until you've got the vehicle under control
3. Once the vehicle is under control, begin slowing and find a safe place to pull over.

You'll know if you have "blown" a tire because you'll feel a **VIBRATION**, hear a **LOUD BANG**, and if it is on the steering wheel, **THE STEERING WILL BECOME VERY HEAVY AND SLUGGISH**, and may become violent.

The critical steps to take in the event of a front tire blow-out are to maintain a firm grip on the steering wheel, *DO NOT TOUCH THE BRAKES*, and maintain your speed. By maintaining your speed, you keep the truck traveling in a straight line. It will want to drift toward the side where the blow-out occurred. You must maintain the forward momentum. If you slam on the brakes when the tire blows, you will *decrease* the forward momentum and *increase* the sideward momentum, which may cause you to lose control, especially if you run off the road. Don't touch your brakes until you have the vehicle firmly under control and you have slowed gradually to a safer, more controllable speed.

Skid Control and Recovery

Here are some terms with which you must become familiar:

OVERBRAKING—Braking too hard and locking the wheels. This will cause a skid
OVERSTEERING—Turning the wheels more sharply than the vehicle can handle
OVERACCELERATION—Too much power to the drive wheels
Driving too fast—Not adjusting speed to road and traffic conditions

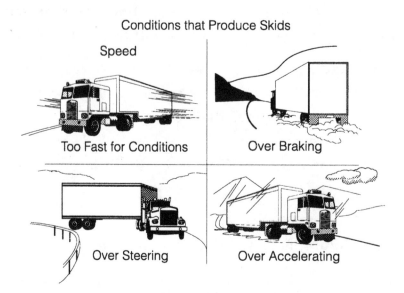

Conditions that Produce Skids

Speed

Too Fast for Conditions

Over Braking

Over Steering

Over Accelerating

The most common skid is rear wheel skid due to overacceleration or excessive braking. Overacceleration skids normally occur on snow or ice. **THEY CAN BE STOPPED BY SIMPLY TAKING YOUR FOOT OFF THE ACCELERATOR AND DEPRESSING THE CLUTCH**.

Rear wheel braking skids occur because too much pressure is applied to the brakes, causing the wheels to lock up and lose traction and then begin to skid. This will happen more frequently on wet, snow-covered or icy roadways because it takes less brake pressure to lock the brakes up. However, they also can occur on dry roads if the brakes are applied too hard.

Whenever the wheels lock up, they will attempt to take the lead. If the drive wheels lock up, they will attempt to "come around" and take the lead. This will result in the rear of the tractor sliding out to the left or right, and if it continued, would result in a tractor jackknife (see diagram).

Tractor Jackknife

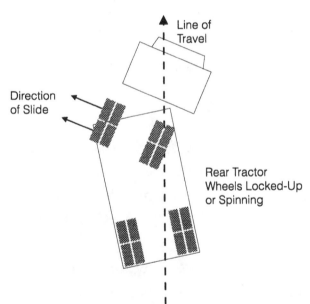

IF REAR WHEEL LOCK-UP OCCURS ON A BUS OR STRAIGHT TRUCK, THE VEHICLE WILL SKID SIDEWAYS CAUSING A "SPINOUT."

If pulling a trailer and the rear wheels of the trailer lock up, the trailer will swing out and attempt to "catch up" or pass the truck. This is called a trailer jack-knife.

How do you correct a drive wheel braking skid?

— **STOP BRAKING**—When the wheels begin to roll again they will stop sliding

—**TURN QUICKLY**—When a vehicle begins to slide sideways, quickly turn in the direction you want to go and then be prepared to

—**COUNTERSTEER**—As it turns back on course, if you don't countersteer quickly enough, you may find yourself sliding in the opposite direction

Front Wheel Skids

Most front wheel skids are caused by driving too fast for conditions. Poor tread on the steering tires and improperly loaded cargo may also contribute to steering tire skids. **WHEN IN A FRONT WHEEL SKID, THE STEERING TIRES WILL TRAVEL IN A STRAIGHT LINE, REGARDLESS OF HOW YOU TURN THE STEERING WHEEL.** The only way to stop a front wheel skid is to reduce speed until the wheels re-grip the road again. Excessive braking will just make the front wheel skid continue for as long as the brakes are locked up on the front wheels. Reduce speed by soft braking until traction has been regained.

Accident Management

As a professional, you are expected to manage the accident scene. Here are the steps to follow:

- *STOP*
- **PROTECT THE SCENE**—The **FIRST** responsibility at any accident scene is to prevent any other accidents. Set out reflective triangles and any other emergency warning equipment you may have. **IF YOUR VEHICLE IS IN-VOLVED AND IS SITTING ON THE ROADWAY, TRY TO GET ONTO THE SHOULDER IF POSSIBLE.**
- **ASSIST THE INJURED**—Unless you are trained in first aid—do not at-tempt to move an injured person unless not moving them places them in greater danger, such as a burning vehicle. You may cover them with a blan-ket, or if heavy bleeding is occurring, you may apply direct pressure to the wound, but other than that, unless properly trained, do not attempt further first aid.
- **NOTIFY THE AUTHORITIES**—Do it by way of the CB if you can—or try to get another motorist to report the accident. Be sure to give the location and if anyone is injured.

- Collect Information— Exchange information (company name, driver's license, phone numbers, etc.) with everyone involved in the accident. Attempt to get the names, addresses and phone numbers of any witnesses. Never admit fault or liability. We recommend that all drivers carry inexpensive throw-away cameras in order to take good pictures of the scene. Usually, by the time the company or insurance representatives arrive, the vehicles have been moved and much of the physical evidence has been removed. Taking a few simple pictures may prove invaluable to the driver and the company in the event of a law suit. This is called "CYA."

Here's an easy way to remember what to do at an accident:

Stop   **P**rotect   **A**ssist   **N**otify = **SPAN**

Fires

A professional needs to know the causes of truck fires and what to do if they occur.

The most common types of truck fires are:

- Spilled fuel and improper use of flares or fuses
- **TIRE FIRES—CAN BE CAUSED BY UNDERINFLATED TIRES OR DUALS THAT TOUCH**
- **ELECTRICAL SYSTEM FIRES—CAUSED BY SHORT CIRCUITS, LOOSE CONNECTIONS AND DAMAGED INSULATION**
- Fueling—Driver smoking, improper fueling, **LOOSE FUEL CONNECTIONS**
- Cargo—Flammable cargo, improperly sealed or loaded, poor ventilation
- **POOR TRAILER VENTILATION CAN CAUSE CARGO TO CATCH ON FIRE.**

Fire Prevention

During your pre-trip and en-route inspections, pay close attention to fuel systems, electrical systems, tires and cargo. Check tires often for proper inflation, that duals are not touching and that nothing has gotten wedged between the duals.

Monitor your instruments regularly for signs of anything getting hot. Monitor the mirrors frequently, looking for any smoke coming from the tires or the vehicle.

Fighting the Fire

It is essential that a professional driver know how to put out the types of fires he may encounter.

In the event of a fire, you should:

- **GET THE VEHICLE OFF THE ROAD AS QUICKLY AS POSSIBLE.**
- **PARK IN AN OPEN AREA, AWAY FROM BUILDINGS, TREES, BRUSH, OTHER VEHICLES OR ANYTHING WHICH MAY CATCH ON FIRE.**
- Use your CB or in some way notify the police or fire department of your problem and your location. If hauling hazardous materials, be sure to inform them of what materials are on board.
- Keep the fire from spreading—This is more important than trying to put the fire out. **IF THE FIRE IS IN THE ENGINE COMPARTMENT, DON'T OPEN THE HOOD.** This will allow oxygen to get to the fire which will cause it to burn more rapidly. Spray your fire extinguisher through the grill or from the underside. **IF THE FIRE IS IN THE CARGO AREA, IN A VAN, KEEP THE DOORS CLOSED**, especially if you are carrying any hazardous materials.
- Use the right fire extinguisher.
  - **B:C TYPE—DESIGNED FOR ELECTRICAL FIRES AND LIQUID FIRES**
  - **A:B:C TYPE—USED FOR ELECTRICAL, LIQUID, BURNING WOOD, PAPER AND CLOTH**
  - **NEVER USE WATER ON ELECTRICAL OR LIQUID FIRES.** You may get shocked and it will only spread the liquid fire making it worse.
  - **WATER MAY BE USED FOR TIRE FIRES**. Since a tire burns hot, it will take a lot of water to cool the tire.

If you're not sure what type of extinguisher to use—don't—wait for the fire department.

Tips on fire extinguisher use:

- Become familiar with how your extinguisher works. Do it now, don't wait until you need it.
- **STAY UPWIND OF THE FIRE.**
- **SPRAY EXTINGUISHER TOWARD THE BASE OF THE FIRE.**

- Stay as far away from the fire as possible.
- Use the powder-type extinguisher in short bursts.
- After fire is extinguished, stay with it, it may start back up again.

Staying Alert and Ready to Drive

Driving for long periods of time can be tiring. Even the best drivers become fatigued and less alert after having driven many hours. Here are a few tips to help make each trip a safe one:

Sleep—Never start a trip without your proper rest. Leaving on a trip when you are tired is dangerous and stupid. Adjust your off-duty time so you'll be rested when you leave.

Avoid Medication—Many over-the-counter drugs will make you sleepy. This is especially true of many cold medications containing an antihistamine. Read the label before taking these or any other medication.

Stay Cool—A cab that is poorly ventilated or too warm can make you sleepy. Crack a window and run the air conditioning. This will help to keep you alert.

Take Frequent Breaks—Short breaks can help keep you awake. Stop every couple of hours. Get out of the truck and stretch. Walk around the truck checking tires and lights. Doing a few jumping jacks or stretches against the truck can really "juice" you up and get the blood pumping.

When You're Sleepy—*STOP*—When you get to the point where you're tired—the only thing that will help is sleep. Pull into a rest area ("pickle-park") or off the road and get some sleep. Don't try to keep going. Fatigue and falling asleep at the wheel is a major cause of deaths among truck drivers. Don't let it happen to you. *NO LOAD IS WORTH YOUR LIFE.* If you can't pull over and get a full night's sleep, then at least take a short nap. A nap as short as a half an hour can be enough to get you going again. After taking a quick "cat-nap" and before starting to drive again, get out of the truck and stretch, maybe jog a little bit, check your tires and lights, take a quick "10-100" and you'll be ready to roll.

Drugs

DON'T TAKE DRUGS to stay awake. Uppers will kill you—you may be awake, and feel awake, but you *won't* be alert and you *won't* be able to respond quickly and professionally in an emergency. Whenever you let "bennie" drive the truck, he'll kill you.

Alcohol

Over 50% of all vehicle fatalities are alcohol related. Last year almost 24,000 people lost their lives in alcohol-related accidents.

There are many myths and facts about alcohol; let's look at a few of them:

MYTH	*FACT*
Alcohol increases your ability to drive.	Alcohol is a drug that will make you less alert and reduce your ability to drive safely.
Some people can drink a lot and not be affected by it.	Everyone who drinks is affected by alcohol.
If you eat a lot first, you won't get drunk.	Food will not keep you from getting drunk.
Coffee and a little fresh air will help a drinker sober up.	Only time will help a drinker sober up—other methods just don't work.
Stick with beer—it's not as strong as wine or whiskey.	A few beers are the same as a few shots of whiskey or a few glasses of wine.

Alcohol Content

Many people believe that it's OK to have a "couple of beers," but should stay away from the "hard stuff" when driving.

The truth is, one can of beer contains as much alcohol as one-and-one-half ounces of whiskey. And, one glass of wine has the same alcohol as one-and-one-half ounces of whiskey or one beer. So it doesn't make any difference what you drink, **<u>ONE BEER, ONE SHOT OF WHISKEY OR ONE GLASS OF WINE, THE AMOUNT OF ALCOHOL IS THE SAME</u>**.

Alcohol goes directly from you stomach to your bloodstream and then to your brain. And it does it very quickly. The drinker has no control over how long the alcohol stays in the bloodstream, and no control over how long he/she will take to sober up. Alcohol leaves the body at a specified rate, and nothing can be done to speed that up. No amount of coffee or cold showers can sober him/her up. All you'll have is a wet, cold drunk. **<u>IT TAKES THE BODY ONE HOUR TO GET RID OF THE EFFECTS OF ONE DRINK, TWO HOURS FOR TWO DRINKS, THREE HOURS FOR THREE DRINKS AND SO ON.</u>**

BAC or Blood Alcohol Concentration is determined by the amount of alcohol you drink. The more alcohol, the higher the BAC. The faster you drink, the quicker the BAC rises. Your weight also has a great deal to do with BAC. A small person will have a higher BAC than a large person drinking the same amount of alcohol. Look at the chart in the introduction to determine the BAC levels based on weight and number of drinks.

<u>ALCOHOL AFFECTS YOUR BRAIN ALMOST IMMEDIATELY. THE PART OF YOUR BRAIN AFFECTED IS THE PART THAT CONTROLS JUDGMENT AND SELF-CONTROL.</u> Because your judgment is affected, you may not know you are getting drunk. Never drive a commercial vehicle after drinking or while drinking. In order to drive a commercial vehicle safely, you must have good judgment and self-control.

After judgment and self-control are affected, muscle control and vision are the next to be affected. If you continue to drink, you will eventually pass out.

In the introduction we discussed the new BAC limits for commercial drivers, and the new penalties for drinking and driving. If you haven't read them yet, be sure to do so—and become familiar with them. *The penalties are severe! Don't take a chance!*

Illness

If you are sick or ill, you probably shouldn't drive. Colds and flu can affect your judgment and your reaction time. If possible, stay home and get well. If you're driving and become ill, you should continue driving to the nearest place where you can safely stop.

Notes

Hazardous Materials

In this section we will cover some of the hazardous materials regulations that all commercial drivers need to know. If you transport hazardous materials in a quantity that requires your vehicle to be placarded, you must read Chapter 9 and take the Hazardous Materials Endorsement Test.

What Are They?

The Federal Hazardous Materials Table names 9 different hazard classes which pose a threat to health, safety, and property during transportation. These 9 hazard classes are:

(See next page.)

Class I (Explosive)	*Explosives*
1.1	Explosive A
1.2	Explosive A or B
1.3	Explosive B
1.4	Explosive C
1.5	Blasting Agent
1.6	Explosive 1.6 (Extremely Insensitive)

Class 2 (Gases)	*Gases*
2.1	Flammable Gas
2.2	Non-Flammable Gas
2.3	Poison Gas

Class 3 (Flammable Liquids)	*Flammable Combustible Liquids*
3	Flammable Liquid
	Combustible Liquid

Class 4 (Flammable Solids)	*Flammable Solids*
4.1	Flammable Solid
4.2	Flammable Solid or Flammable Liquid (spontaneously combustible or pyroforic)
4.3	Flammable Solid—dangerous when wet

Class 5 (Oxidizing Substances)	*Oxidizing Substances*
5.1	Oxidizer
5.2	Organic Peroxide

Class 6 (Poisons)	*Poisons*
6.1	Poison B
6.2	Etiologic Agents (infectious substances)

Class 7 (Radioactive Materials)	*Radioactive Material*

Class 8 (Corrosive Material)	*Corrosive Material*

Class 9 (Miscellaneous Material)	*ORM (Other Regulated Material)*

Don't worry—You do not need to memorize these for the test.

The hazardous materials regulations exist for three major reasons:

1. **PROVIDE SAFE DRIVERS AND EQUIPMENT**
2. **COMMUNICATE THE RISK**
3. **CONTAIN THE PRODUCT**

Contain the product—Since many hazardous materials can kill or injure on contact, or by breathing it in, the rules tell the shippers how to safely package the material, and tell the drivers how to load, transport and unload the product in a way to ensure safety and avoid any leaks or spillage. These are called **CONTAINMENT RULES**.

Communicate the Risk—The rules outline the procedures which must be followed by the shipper when filling out the shipping papers and affixing labels to the packaging. Shippers must write the name of the hazard class of the product in the item description portion of the shipping paper. Similar words must be in 4-inch letters on diamond-shaped labels and attached to the packages. If labels won't fit on the package, tags must be affixed securely to the container. For example, tags would be used in some instances on gas cylinders.

Placards are diamond-shaped signs that are placed on the outside of the vehicle indicating the hazard class of the materials inside the cargo compartment. They are required to be placed on all four sides of the vehicle.

The rules tell the driver which placards must be affixed to the vehicle, thereby communicating to everyone that hazardous materials are on board. In the event of an accident, the driver may be injured or killed. The placards would then serve to tell the enforcement and emergency officials what type of hazard they are dealing with, so they will then be able to respond correctly to the situation.

The shipping papers must be tabbed or tagged and placed on top of any other shipping paper and must be within the driver's reach while he is driving. **IF THE DRIVER LEAVES THE VEHICLE, HE MUST PLACE THEM ON THE SEAT IN CLEAR VIEW, OR IN A POUCH ON THE DRIVER'S DOOR.**

Not all vehicles carrying hazardous materials are required to display placards. The rules about placards are covered more thoroughly in Chapter 9, Hazardous Materials. **YOU CAN DRIVE A VEHICLE CARRYING HAZARDOUS MATERIALS AS LONG AS IT DOES NOT REQUIRE PLACARDS. IF PLACARDS ARE REQUIRED BECAUSE OF THE NATURE OF THE PRODUCT OR**

THE QUANTITY BEING TRANSPORTED, YOU MUST HAVE THE HAZARD-OUS MATERIAL ENDORSEMENT.

Safe Drivers and Equipment—The regulations require that all drivers of placarded vehicles must know how to safely load, transport and unload hazardous products. They must have a CDL with the hazardous materials endorsement.

NEVER DRIVE A PLACARDED VEHICLE UNLESS YOU HAVE THE HAZARDOUS MATERIALS ENDORSEMENT. If you do, and are stopped by law enforcement officials, you will be cited and will not be permitted to drive the truck any further. The fines are severe.

☞ LET'S TAKE A TEST

General Knowledge: Part One

Study each question carefully and then indicate your answer by drawing a circle around the correct answer.

1. When approaching a curve you should:

   A. downshift while in the curve
   B. downshift as you come out of the curve
   C. downshift before entering a curve and accelerate slightly as you go through it
   D. downshift at any time, it doesn't make a difference

2. When driving a commercial vehicle with a height over 13 feet, you should:

   A. not worry about height clearance as long as you stay on state or federal highways
   B. assume all clearances are high enough
   C. if you aren't sure a clearance is high enough, stop and make sure
   D. all of the above

3. You should use your high beams:

   A. at all times at night
   B. OK to use during the day, but never at night
   C. may be used anytime when on a divided highway
   D. should use whenever possible and when legal

4. Controlled braking is: = squeze braking

   A. slamming on the brakes hard and making wheels lock up
   B. squeezing brakes firmly without locking them up
   C. pressing brakes until wheel lock-up occurs, releasing and then reapplying
   D. none of the above

5. Stab braking should be used:

   A. only in an emergency   than lock than release
   B. never
   C. used only on wet or snow-covered roadways
   D. whenever the driver wants to

6. While driving on a two-lane road, an approaching vehicle begins to drift into your lane, you should use which of the following techniques:

    A. brake hard, steer right
    B. steer left
    C. steer right
    D. steer straight, brake hard

7. If you experience a rear-wheel overacceleration skid, you should:

    A. apply the brakes
    B. press on the accelerator
    C. downshift
    D. release accelerator and depress clutch

8. When fighting a fire, the first thing you should do is:

    A. call the police and/or fire department
    B. open the doors on the trailer
    C. park vehicle off the road and away from buildings or anything flammable
    D. drive faster and allow the wind to put out the fire

9. Many truck fires are started by:

    A. improper fueling
    B. loose fuel connections
    C. shorts in the electrical system
    D. all of the above

10. When exiting or entering on a curved freeway ramp, you should:

    A. maintain a speed 5-10 mph under the posted speed limit
    B. maintain the posted speed limit
    C. slow down to at least 50% of the posted speed limit
    D. go faster than the posted speed limit if you are familiar with the ramp and know your vehicle can handle it

11. When do you know when it is time to shift?

    A. speedometer can tell you
    B. tachometer can tell you
    C. engine sound can tell you
    D. all of the above

12. The correct way to hold a steering wheel is:

    A. one hand on the wheel, one hand on the shifter
    B. both hands on wheel, opposite each other at the 3 o'clock and 9 o'clock positions
    C. both hands on wheel, one hand at 4 o'clock position and one at the 7 o'clock position
    D. both hands on wheel, one hand at 11 o'clock position and one hand at the 1 o'clock position

13. When driving down a long downgrade, you should:

    A. go down in the same gear you went up
    B. go down in a higher gear than the one you went up
    C. go down in a lower gear than the one you went up
    D. never use an engine retarder

14. If you have a tire blow on the steering axle, you should:

    A. stop immediately
    B. slam on the brakes
    C. speed up
    D. don't brake until the vehicle has slowed down

15. On wet roads your speed should be reduced by:

    A. 20%
    B. 1/3
    C. 1/2
    D. 60%

16. You are driving a 40-foot-long vehicle at 50 mph, the safe following distance is:

    A. 5 seconds
    B. 4 seconds
    C. 3 seconds
    D. 6 seconds

17. Which of the following vehicles will have the longest stopping distance?

    A. empty truck
    B. loaded truck
    C. bobtail tractor
    D. automobile

18. How many red reflective triangles are you required to carry?

    A. 6
    B. 2
    C. 4
    D. 3

19. You are required to inspect your truck within how many miles after beginning the trip?

    A. 100
    B. 150
    C. 25 50
    D. 200

20. You are driving your vehicle and the front wheels lock-up. Which of the following is most likely to occur?

    A. you will continue in a straight line
    B. the momentum of the truck will force it to one side
    C. the truck will stop in the shortest distance
    D. the truck will roll over

21. The pre-trip inspection described in this section consists of how many steps?

    A. 6
    B. 4
    C. 7
    D. 9

22. When driving, what is the proper eye-lead time (how far should you be looking ahead)?

   A. 2-4 seconds
   B. 3-5 seconds
   C. 8-10 seconds
   D. 12-15 seconds

23. For the average driver driving on dry pavement, with the brakes properly adjusted, how many feet will it take to stop at 55 mph?

   A. about the length of a football field = 300 feet
   B. about 100 feet
   C. about twice the length of the vehicle being driven
   D. about 200 feet

24. The new BAC (Blood Alcohol Concentration) for commercial drivers to be considered intoxicated when driving a commercial vehicle is:

   A. .04
   B. .01
   C. .05
   D. .10

25. Which of the following about emergency steering is true?

   A. quick steering movements should only be done when the wheels are locked
   B. if an oncoming driver drifts into your lane, a move to your right may be best
   C. you can almost always stop more quickly than you can turn
   D. you can steer quicker and safer with only one hand on the wheel

26. When should you test your parking brake?

   A. moving at a very slow speed
   B. while the vehicle is parked
   C. while traveling at least 10 mph
   D. when backing

27. Where should the ignition key be during the pre-trip inspection?

    A. in your pocket
    B. in the ignition
    C. on the driver's seat
    D. on the dashboard

28. If you become sleepy while driving, you should:

    A. continue driving
    B. stop as soon as possible and get some sleep
    C. drink coffee
    D. continue driving, but go slower

29. The minimum amount of tread depth allowed on steering tires is:

    A. 4/32
    B. 5/32
    C. 2/32
    D. no minimum

30. To correct a drive-wheel braking skid, you should:

    A. stop braking
    B. increase braking, turn quickly, and countersteer
    C. increase braking
    D. stop braking, turn quickly, and countersteer

31. There are two types of jackknife; they are:

    A. trailer
    B. tractor
    C. wet-road jackknife
    D. both A and B

32. What is the proper action to take if your vehicle begins to hydroplane?

    A. accelerate
    B. brake hard
    C. release accelerator
    D. release accelerator and downshift immediately

33. When traveling down a downgrade, you should:

    A. shift gears when necessary
    B. never shift gears
    C. use engine retarder only if necessary
    D. both A and C

34. When going down a long or steep downgrade you should always:

    A. use only your trailer brakes
    B. use the braking effects of the engine
    C. use controlled braking
    D. when you exceed "safe speed" by 5 mph, then brake

35. You are driving a 40-foot-long vehicle at 25 mph; the proper safe following distance is:

    A. 3 seconds
    B. 2 seconds
    C. 4 seconds
    D. 5 seconds

36. When loading a trailer, if the load is loaded all to the rear, it may result in:

    A. wheel lockup
    B. damage to steering axle
    C. poor traction on drive wheels
    D. none of the above

37. Turn signals should be used:

    A. at least 100 feet before turning or changing lanes
    B. at least 150 feet before turning or changing lanes
    C. at least 200 feet before turning or changing lanes
    D. at least 500 feet before turning or changing lanes

38. Communication means:

    A. talking with law enforcement officers
    B. to communicate your intentions to other motorists
    C. to talk on the CB radio
    D. to talk on your mobile phone

39. Which of the following about the effects of alcohol is true?

    A. coffee will sober you up
    B. only time will help a driver sober up
    C. if you eat first, you won't get drunk
    D. a shot of whiskey contains more alcohol than a glass of beer

40. Which of the following statements about mirrors is true?

    A. only one mirror is required on a truck
    B. if adjusted properly, no blind spots exist
    C. all trucks have blind spots which the mirrors cannot cover
    D. when driving down the road you need to look at your mirrors every 12-15 seconds

41. If you are looking ahead the distance you should be looking at highway speeds, you will be looking how far?

    A. 1/4 mile
    B. 1/2 mile
    C. 700 feet
    D. 1 mile

42. You are driving in heavy traffic, the speed limit is 45 mph but traffic is moving at 35 mph. The safe speed for you to be driving is:

    A. 45 mph
    B. 30 mph
    C. 40 mph
    D. 35 mph

43. If you are convicted for driving under the influence while driving a commercial vehicle, and this is your first offense, you most likely will get:

    A. a probation period of one year
    B. at least a one-year suspension of your CDL
    C. a fine of $250.00
    D. a warning

44. If you are stopped at a roadside rest and found to have a BAC
(Blood Alcohol Concentration) of .02 you will:

    A. be placed out of service for 72 hours
    B. be in deep trouble with your dispatcher
    C. be placed out of service for 24 hours
    D. both B and C

45. Which of the following statements about speed management is true?

    A. if you double your speed, stopping distance will double
    B. empty trucks and loaded trucks will have the same stopping distance
    C. if you double your speed, stopping distance will be increased by 4 times
    D. never follow closer to a vehicle than 100 feet

46. Which of the following is true about emergency driving?

    A. a truck can always be stopped quicker than it can be steered
    B. a truck can turn faster than it can stop
    C. hard braking is always the best emergency braking maneuver
    D. a truck, because of air brakes, can stop quicker than a car

47. Empty trucks:

    A. have better traction when stopping than loaded trucks
    B. stop quicker when you use only the emergency or parking brake
    C. need less following distance than loaded trucks
    D. require longer stopping distances than loaded ones

48. You are the first one on the scene of an accident. The first thing you should do is:

    A. help the injured
    B. stop other motorists for assistance
    C. protect the scene
    D. notify the authorities

49. Which is the slickest road surface?

    A. dry ice
    B. snow covered
    C. wet ice
    D. wet

50. Hydroplaning is:

    A. when your wheels lift off the roadway onto a thin film of water
    B. when excessive heat has built up in the radiator
    C. an emergency situation when a plane must use the interstate as a safe
       place to land
    D. testing the batteries for proper battery acid

51. When doing your pre-trip inspection, which of the following would you not do?

    A. check turn signals and 4-way flashers
    B. check leaf springs and shock absorbers
    C. check main bearings - dspectos
    D. check tires

52. When checking your suspension system, which of the following would you
    check?

    A. leaf springs for cracks
    B. leaking shock absorbers
    C. u-bolts and spring hangers
    D. all of the above

53. Which of the following items would you check on an en route inspection?

    A. tires
    B. cargo securement devices
    C. lights
    D. all of the above

54. A driver's vehicle inspection report form must:

    A. be filled out by the mechanic
    B. be filled out by the driver at the end of the trip
    C. be filled out by the driver for each vehicle driven
    D. both B and C

55. Brake fade is:

    A. old worn out brakes

    B. when brakes begin to lose their stopping power due to excessive heat

    C. the time it takes for brakes to apply once the brake pedal has been depressed

    D. the time it takes for brakes to regain their stopping power

56. Double clutching should be used:

    A. each time a heavy-duty truck is shifted

    B. only when loaded

    C. only by experienced drivers

    D. only when going uphill with a heavy load

57. If your engine overheats, you should:

    A. continue the trip if you have less than 25 miles to go

    B. stop immediately and try to determine the problem before proceeding

    C. proceed to the nearest truck stop

    D. stop and take off radiator cap immediately; this will allow it to cool

58. The hazardous materials regulations exist to:

    A. provide safe drivers and equipment

    B. communicate the risk

    C. contain the product

    D. all of the above

59. Placarding is an example of:

    A. containment

    B. communication

    C. controlling the risk

    D. none of the above

60. As alcohol begins to build up in the brain, what body functions are the first to be affected?

    A. liver control

    B. judgment and self-control

    C. vision

    D. muscle control

61. Water will put out which type of fire?

    A. electrical
    B. diesel fuel
    C. gasoline
    D. tire

62. When fighting a fire you should:

    A. aim at the base of the fire with the extinguisher
    B. stand downwind
    C. get as close to the fire as possible
    D. aim at the top of the fire with the extinguisher

63. Which of the following conditions will produce a skid?

    A. too fast for conditions
    B. over braking
    C. over steering
    D. all of the above

64. You are driving on a clear night with your low beam headlights on. If your headlights let you see about 250 feet ahead of you, you should adjust your speed so that you can stop within how many feet?

    A. 50 feet
    B. 100 feet
    C. 250 feet
    D. 300 feet

65. In the event of a breakdown and it is necessary to park on the shoulder of a two-lane undivided highway, you must place your reflective triangles:

    A. one triangle within 10 feet of the rear of the vehicle, and one 100 feet behind and ahead of the vehicle in the lane the vehicle is stopped in
    B. one triangle 100 feet ahead of the vehicle, one 100 feet behind and one 200 feet behind the vehicle in the lane the vehicle is stopped in
    C. one triangle 10 feet behind, one triangle 100 feet behind and one 200 feet behind in the lane the vehicle is stopped in
    D. any of the above will meet the regulations

66. Which of the following is countersteering?

    A. turning the wheel to the right
    B. turning the wheel to the left
    C. turning the wheel back in the opposite direction
    D. braking and turning at the same time

67. What is the most important thing to remember about wheel lock-up?

    A. loss of steering will occur
    B. risk of jackknife or spinout will be present
    C. brakes will wear out quicker
    D. both A and B

68. When should stab braking never be used?

    A. on dry roads
    B. on wet or icy roads
    C. in freeway traffic
    D. in city traffic

69. Which of the following is true about braking while traveling down a long or steep grade?

    A. apply and release brakes every 15 seconds in order to maintain proper speed
    B. use only the trailer brakes to control speed
    C. apply brakes on and off, releasing brakes when the vehicle speed is about 5 mph under the "safe speed" and applying again when the vehicle reaches "safe speed"
    D. use stab braking

70. You are traveling down a long grade and you notice your brakes begin to fade, what should you do?

    A. stop as quickly as possible
    B. begin pumping your brake pedal
    C. downshift one gear
    D. check and make sure your insurance policy is paid up

71. If the front steering tires of a straight truck are in a skid:

    A. the vehicle will slide to the left
    B. the rear of the vehicle will swing around
    C. the vehicle will slide in a straight line
    D. the vehicle will slide toward the right shoulder

72. When turning sharply in an evasive maneuver, you should attempt to avoid:

    A. braking
    B. turning too sharply to the right
    C. turning too sharply to the left
    D. accelerating

73. If you experience a tire failure, you may experience which of the following:

    A. a loud pop or a bang
    B. vibration or jerky feeling
    C. the steering may feel heavy and sluggish
    D. all of the above

74. When checking your mirrors, you should look for, or at:

    A. traffic
    B. any cargo securement devices on your vehicle
    C. the tires
    D. all of the above

75. Which of the following is not true about turn signals?

    A. should be used whenever turning or changing lanes
    B. should be used at least 100 feet before the maneuver
    C. should be used to signal other drivers if it is safe to pass
    D. should be cancelled as soon as the maneuver is completed

76. When passing another vehicle at night, you should:

    A. turn on your high beams and keep them on while you are passing
    B. flash high beams quickly and then pass
    C. do nothing, just pass
    D. none of the above

77. Which of these statements about downshifting is true?

A. when you downshift for a curve, you should do so before you enter the curve

B. when you downshift for a hill, you should do so after you start down the hill

C. when double-clutching, you should let the rpms decrease while the clutch is released and the shift lever is in neutral

D. all of the above are true

78. To avoid a crash, you had to drive onto the right shoulder. You are now driving at 40 mph on the shoulder. How should you move back onto the pavement?

A. if the shoulder is clear, stay on it until your vehicle has come to a stop, then move back onto the pavement when it is safe.

B. brake hard to slow the vehicle, then steer sharply onto the pavement

C. steer sharply onto the pavement, then brake hard as you countersteer

D. keep moving at the present speed and steer very gently back onto the pavement

79. If you experience a fire in the engine compartment, you should:

A. open the hood and attempt to put it out

B. leave the hood closed and spray the extinguisher through the grill or from underneath

C. park the truck and go get help

D. head for the nearest fire station

80. An A:B:C fire extinguisher can be used on:

A. gasoline fires

B. electrical fires

C. burning cloth

D. all of the above

81. Which of these statements about driving in areas with strong winds is true?

A. you should drive alongside other vehicles to help break up the wind

B. winds are especially a problem when coming out of tunnels

C. the lighter your vehicle, the less trouble you will have with the wind

D. you can lessen the effect of the wind by letting some air out of your tires

82. If you are being tailgated, you should:

    A. speed up
    B. slow down quickly
    C. increase your following distance
    D. flash your brake lights

83. You are driving a 40-foot vehicle at 35 mph. The road is dry and visibility is good. What is the least amount of space that you should keep in front of your vehicle to be safe?

    Don't add seconds up to 40 miles

    A. 3 seconds
    B. 2 seconds
    C. 5 seconds
    D. 4 seconds

84. When backing you should:

    A. always back toward the driver's side
    B. always back toward the passenger side
    C. use a helper whenever you can
    D. both A and C

85. When using a helper to back, you should:

    A. pay him well
    B. agree on the use of hand signals
    C. give him instructions on where to stand
    D. both B and C

86. The most important instruction for you to give to someone helping you to back is:

    A. the signal to stop
    B. the signal when you're close to the dock
    C. the signal to cut right
    D. the signal to cut left

87. Which of the following is a form of communication?

    A. headlights
    B. brake lights
    C. turn signals
    D. all of the above

88. To determine the total stopping distance of a vehicle, which of the following is used?

    A. perception distance
    B. reaction distance
    C. braking distance
    D. all of the above

89. Which of these is a good thing to do when driving at night?

    A. keep your speed slow enough that you can stop within the range of your headlights
    B. look directly at oncoming headlights only briefly
    C. wear sunglasses
    D. keep your instrument lights bright

90. On snow-covered roads, speed should be reduced by:

    A. 1/4
    B. 1/2
    C. 1/3
    D. 1/6

Answers

1. C	16. A	31. D	46. B	61. D	76. B
2. C	17. C	32. C	47. D	62. A	77. A
3. D	18. D	33. B	48. C	63. D	78. A
4. B	19. C	34. B	49. C	64. C	79. B
5. A	20. A	35. C	50. A	65. A	80. D
6. C	21. C	36. C	51. C	66. C	81. B
7. D	22. D	37. A	52. D	67. D	82. C
8. C	23. A	38. B	53. D	68. B	83. D
9. D	24. A	39. B	54. D	69. C	84. D
10. A	25. B	40. C	55. B	70. A	85. D
11. D	26. B	41. A	56. A	71. C	86. A
12. B	27. A	42. D	57. B	72. A	87. D
13. C	28. B	43. B	58. D	73. D	88. D
14. D	29. A	44. D	59. B	74. D	89. A
15. B	30. D	45. C	60. B	75. C	90. B

dxle - eJe

Part 2: Transporting Cargo

Who must read and learn this chapter?

ALL CDL applicants *ARE* required to know and understand this section in order to pass the General Knowledge Test. Also, all tank vehicle operators wanting to obtain their "N" endorsement must read and understand the section on tank vehicles.

Remember, as you read, take good notes on those items that seem important to you, and pay close attention to the words and phrases written in **BOLD CAPITAL LETTERS AND UNDERLINED.**

This chapter deals with transporting cargo safely. Whether you haul cargo in a dry van, a reefer, a flatbed or bus, you must know how to load and secure it properly. If you load it wrong, it then becomes a danger to you and to all the motorists with whom you are sharing the road. Improperly loaded cargo can cause steering problems. Loosely secured cargo can shift or fall off the truck during sudden stops or turns.

IT MAKES NO DIFFERENCE WHO LOADS THE TRUCK. YOU, THE PROFESSIONAL DRIVER, ARE RESPONSIBLE TO MAKE SURE THAT IT IS LOADED CORRECTLY AND SAFELY. IT IS YOUR RESPONSIBILITY TO:

- **CHECK THAT THE LOAD IS LOADED PROPERLY AND TIED DOWN SECURELY**
- **RECOGNIZE OVERLOADED CONDITIONS**
- **CHECK FOR PROPER WEIGHT DISTRIBUTION**

If you haul hazardous material, you are also required to be familiar with HAZMAT regulations so that you can make sure that your load is properly loaded and properly placarded. In order to obtain your HAZMAT endorsement, you must read Chapter 9 of this manual.

Inspecting Cargo

Inspection of your cargo begins while loading, and continues during the pre-trip inspection and during your trip.

- During loading process—you must load the vehicle in such a way as to properly distribute the weight of the cargo between all axles. Make sure the load is secure.

- During pre-trip—Check to make sure that the load is not overweight, is properly distributed on the axles, and that it is secure.
- During trip—**FEDERAL REGULATIONS REQUIRE THAT YOU IN-SPECT THE CARGO AND ALL LOAD-SECURING DEVICES WITHIN THE FIRST 25 MILES OF THE TRIP.** During this check, make any adjustments necessary. Check your load and securement devices as often as necessary while en route.
- Inspect again—**AFTER YOU HAVE DRIVEN THREE HOURS OR 150 MILES, and AFTER EVERY BREAK YOU TAKE DURING THE TRIP.**

Federal, state and local regulations pertaining to weight, load securement, cover laws and routing differ greatly from place to place. Wherever you travel, the law requires that you be familiar with all of the local rules and regulations. We know it's tough to know all of them, but just keep in mind the old saying, *"ignorance of the law is no excuse."*

Weight and Balance

It is your responsibility not to overload your vehicle. Here are some definitions which you must know:

- GVW—**GROSS VEHICLE WEIGHT**
  The total weight of a single vehicle and its load
- GCW—**GROSS COMBINATION WEIGH**T
  The total weight of a powered unit and its trailer and its load, such as a loaded tractor-trailer
- GVWR—**GROSS VEHICLE WEIGHT RATING**
  The *maximum* GVW specified by the manufacturer for a *single* vehicle and its load
- GCVWR—**GROSS COMBINATION VEHICLE WEIGHT RATING**
  The maximum GCVWR specified by the manufacturer for a specific combination of vehicles and its load
- Axle weight—The weight transmitted to the ground by one axle or a set of axles
- Tire Load—The maximum *safe* weight a tire can carry at a certain tire pressure. This can be found stamped on the side of the tire.
- CG—Center of gravity

● Suspension System—Suspension systems have a manufacturer's suggested weight capacity rating

Legal Weight Limits

You must keep within the legal weight limits. It is your responsibility to know the weights allowed for each state in which you drive. States have maximums for GVW'S and for axle weights.

Bridge Formula

Often you will find that axle weights are set by a bridge formula. **THE BRIDGE FORMULA ALLOWS LESS MAXIMUM AXLE WEIGHT FOR AXLES THAT ARE CLOSER TOGETHER.** The purpose of the bridge formula is to prevent overloading of bridges and roadways.

— Formula

Overloading

OVERLOADING WILL HAVE AN EFFECT ON:

● STEERING—Harder to steer
● BRAKING—More difficult to stop, stopping distance increases
● SPEED CONTROL—Slow on upgrades—Fast on downgrades
● BRAKE FAILURE—More likely to occur with overloads since brakes are working harder

Center of Gravity

The higher a load is loaded on a vehicle, the higher the center of gravity. **THE HIGHER THE CENTER OF GRAVITY, THE MORE LIKELY TO ROLL OVER. A HIGH-CENTER-OF-GRAVITY LOAD IS CALLED A "TOP HEAVY" LOAD.** When loading your vehicle, always attempt to keep the CG as low as possible. Load the heaviest freight on the floor with the lighter freight on top whenever possible. **KEEP IN MIND—IF YOU HAVE A HIGH CG AND ARE "TOP HEAVY," THE TRUCK WILL BE MORE LIKELY TO ROLL OVER ON SHARP CURVES OR WHEN PERFORMING EVASIVE MOVEMENTS LIKE SWERVING TO AVOID HITTING AN OBJECT.** *Be careful.*

Weight Balance

If cargo weight is poorly balanced, it will make handling of the vehicle more difficult and may make it unsafe. Here are a few examples of poor weight balance:

CONDITION	RESULT
Overloaded steering axle	Hard steering—damage to steering axle and tires
Underloaded steering axle (too much weight on rear of vehicle)	Too light to steer properly
Underloaded drive axles	Poor traction
High center of gravity	Rollover

Securing the Cargo

Blocking and bracing is any method used which will prevent the load from moving. Whether a flatbed or dry box—the load must be blocked or braced to prevent movement. When blocking, block all sides of the cargo.

 dmdrre 5

Cargo Tiedowns

Most often used on flatbed trailers or trailers without sides. Tiedowns can be chains, cables, nylon straps, rope, etc. Tensioning devices must be used to secure the tiedowns. Tensioning devices are winches, ratchets, chain binders, etc. When using tiedowns, it is important that the proper type of tiedown be used for the type of cargo being hauled. For example: Don't use nylon straps to tie down a D-9 dozer, or don't use chains and binders to tie down fiberglass insulation panels. Care must be taken to secure the load without damaging it. **ALSO, THE COMBINED STRENGTH OF ALL TIEDOWNS USED MUST BE STRONG ENOUGH TO LIFT ONE-AND-ONE-HALF TIMES THE WEIGHT OF THE CARGO.**

- **CARGO SHOULD HAVE AT LEAST ONE TIEDOWN FOR EVERY 10 FEET.**

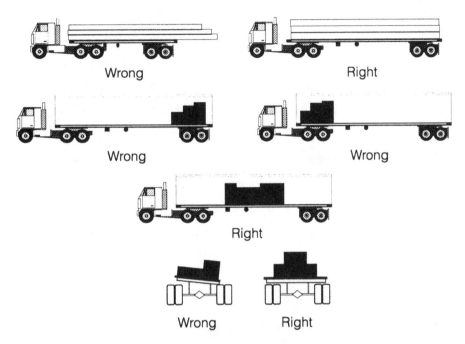

- **NO MATTER HOW SMALL THE CARGO, YOU MUST USE AT LEAST TWO TIEDOWNS.** This will prevent it from shifting or turning.

Header Board

ALSO CALLED HEADACHE RACKS, are mounted at the front of the trailer and **ARE DESIGNED TO PREVENT THE LOAD FROM COMING FORWARD** and crashing into and through the back of the tractor. Make sure the mounts and supports and the header board itself are in good condition and mounted securely.

COVERING CARGO—*WHY DO WE COVER CARGO?*

1. **PROTECT PEOPLE FROM FALLING CARGO**
   and
2. **PROTECT CARGO FROM THE WEATHER**

Many states have cover laws. Make sure you know the laws for the states in which you operate.

When pulling a load that is covered, watch it frequently and check it often. A tarp that comes loose while you're driving 55 mph can tear, blow off, and do a lot of damage very quickly. Check your covers every time you stop and watch them closely in your mirrors.

Containerized Loads

Containerized loads are those that are carried by rail or ship and transported to the railroad or dock by truck. Generally they are a sealed container that you will secure on top of a flatbed. They have several different types of locking and securing devices. Become familiar with how they mount and lock onto the trailer. Many containers have their own axles, frames and tires. These you simply hook up as you would any trailer. Be sure to perform a good pre-trip inspection and be especially watchful for lighting, tire and axle defects.

As most container loads are sealed and cannot be checked by the driver, just assume they are top heavy and drive accordingly. It's always best to assume the worst and then take extra care and precautions.

Other Cargo

Special attention should be given to:

Dry Bulk Tanks

Similar to liquid tankers, dry bulk tankers have a high CG. Always exercise care when driving on curves and when entering or exiting freeway ramps. Always drive under the posted speed limit on curves and ramps.

Swinging Meat

Sides of beef, pork or lamb, hanging from the top of a reefer (refrigerated trailer), **CAN BE EXTREMELY UNSTABLE AND ALWAYS HAS A HIGH CG.** Use the same care and caution as discussed with tankers. Slow down on curves, turns and ramps.

Livestock

Live animals, beef, horses, hogs, sheep, etc., create the same type of problems as liquid loads, plus a few additional ones. Livestock trailers always have a high CG. Livestock will tend to lean as you go around a curve creating a problem similar to the surge effect in a tanker. If you don't have a full load, use portable bulkheads to prevent the animals from moving around. The tighter

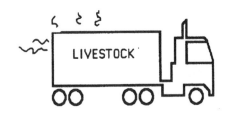

the animals are packed, the less movement. Go slow on ramps, curves and turns—Rollover, due to the high CG is more likely, so—take it easy!

Another problem unique to hauling live animals is what we call the "nose factor." When parking at a truckstop—in order to keep your friends and maintain your popularity, it might be best to park downwind. Of course, if you're looking for some excitement, just park it in the middle of a truckstop; we're sure you'll find all the excitement you can handle.

Over Length, Width and/or Overweight

When transporting these types of loads—special care and attention is needed. Special permits are required; special equipment such as signs, lights, flags, etc. will be needed. Extra driving care is necessary, be especially watchful for overhang and overhead hazards.

WATCH VIDEO—ON GENERAL KNOWLEDGE

☞ LET'S TAKE A TEST

to take turns or ramps 5 - 10 miles under the post and way before taking the ramp

Transporting Cargo Test

Study each question carefully and then indicate your choice by drawing a circle around the letter you have chosen or write the answer in your own words.

1. Ramp speeds are standardized for:

   A. cars
   B. buses
   C. trucks
   D. all of the above

2. Overloading the steering axle will result in:

   A. not enough traction on drive axles
   B. not enough traction on steering axle
   C. improved steering
   D. hard steering

3. Cargo that is not properly loaded or tied down, may cause:

   A. cargo to fall off vehicle
   B. cargo to shift forward
   C. damage to cargo, other motorists or to the driver
   D. all of the above

4. The CG, center of gravity, of a load should be:

   A. as low as possible
   B. as high as possible
   C. doesn't really make a difference
   D. is only a problem if the vehicle has been loaded too heavy

5. Which of the statements about loading cargo is true?

   A. the driver is not responsible for checking the load if it was loaded by someone else
   B. state laws determine the legal weight limits
   C. overloaded vehicles have shorter stopping distances
   D. a truck which is loaded legally is safe in all driving conditions

6. The purpose of cargo covers is:

   A. to protect the cargo
   B. to make work harder for the drivers
   C. to protect people from cargo coming off the truck
   D. both A and C

7. The minimum tiedowns is:

   A. 4
   B. 6
   C. 2
   D. 10

8. Tiedowns are required on certain loads to:

   A. prevent shifting
   B. prevent the driver from seeing the load
   C. increase cost to the driver
   D. none of the above

9. Tiedowns are required every:

   A. 2 feet
   B. 10 feet
   C. 15 feet
   D. 20 feet

10. The center of gravity of a load:

    A. should be kept as high as possible
    B. can make a vehicle more likely to tip over on curves if it is high
    C. is only a problem if the vehicle is overloaded
    D. all of the above

11. A key principle to remember about loading cargo is to keep the load:

    A. to the front
    B. to the rear
    C. as high as possible
    D. balanced in the cargo area

12. You are driving a heavy vehicle. You must exit a highway using an off ramp that curves downhill. You should:

   A. slow down to a safe speed before the curve
   B. slow to the posted speed limit for the off ramp
   C. come to a full stop at the top of the ramp
   D. wait until you are in the curve before downshifting

13. Which of these statements about certain types of cargo is true?

   A. unstable loads such as hanging meat or livestock can require extra caution on curves
   B. oversize loads can be hauled without special permits during times when the roads are not busy
   C. loads that consist of liquids in bulk do not cause handling problems because they are usually very heavy
   D. when liquids are hauled, the tank should always be loaded totally full

14. If a straight vehicle (no trailer or articulation) goes into a front-wheel skid, it will:

   A. slide sideways and spin out
   B. slide sideways somewhat, but not spin out
   C. go straight ahead even if the steering wheel is turned
   D. go straight ahead but will turn if you turn the steering wheel

15. Which of these statements about accelerating is true?

   A. when traction is poor, more power should be applied to the accelerator
   B. rough acceleration can cause mechanical damage
   C. you should feel a "jerking" motion if you are accelerating your vehicle properly
   D. all of the above are true

16. A traffic emergency requires you to leave the road and escape to the shoulder If possible, slow down to _____ mph before using your brakes

   A. 20 mph
   B. 30 mph
   C. 40 mph
   D. 50 mph

17. The best way to take a curve is to slow to a safe speed before entering the curve, then _____ as you go through it.

    A. accelerate slightly
    B. coast
    C. brake lightly
    D. downshift twice

18. Which of these would tell you that a shipment contains hazardous material?

    A. the name of a hazard class on the shipping paper
    B. a four-inch, diamond-shaped hazardous materials label on the container
    C. a hazardous materials placard on the vehicle
    D. all of the above

Answers

1. A	10. B
2. D	11. D
3. D	12. A
4. A	13. A
5. B	14. C
6. D	15. B
7. C	16. A
8. A	17. A
9. B	18. D

If you were able to answer all of the questions correctly—*GOOD JOB!* If you missed any, read it again.

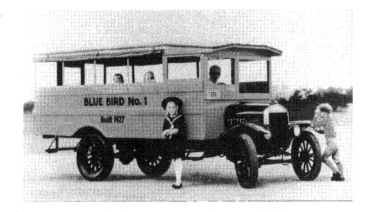

Transporting Passengers

Who Must Study This Section?

ANY DRIVER WHO OPERATES A PASSENGER VEHICLE DESIGNED TO CARRY MORE THAN 15 PASSENGERS INCLUDING THE DRIVER must study this section, and take the *PASSENGER VEHICLE ENDORSEMENT TEST*.

What Other Tests or Endorsements Do You Need?

School Bus

Inter-state Bus

Municipal Bus

Mini-Van

Articulated Bus

If you operate any of the vehicles above,
Any vehicle designed
to carry more than 15 persons

To transport passengers you will need a "Class B" CDL with the proper endorsements.

Tests You Will Need to Take	Chapters You Must Study
The General Knowledge Test	Introduction
Passenger Vehicle Endorsement	Chapter 1—General Knowledge, Part 1and Part 2
Air Brake Endorsement (if your vehicle has air brakes)	Chapter 4—Transporting Passengers
	Chapter 5—Air Brake (If so equipped)

Transporting Passengers

Before driving a bus, it is your responsibility to make sure it is safe to operate. Even though you are not a mechanic, and your company has a shop and mechanic to perform all checks and maintenance, **YOU** still **MUST PERFORM A PRE-TRIP INSPECTION. IF YOU DRIVE FOR AN INTER-STATE CARRIER, YOU MUST ALSO DO AN AFTER-TRIP OR POST-TRIP INSPECTION AND COMPLETE A WRITTEN INSPECTION REPORT FOR EACH BUS YOU DRIVE.**

Step 1 Pre-Trip Inspection

YOU BEGIN your pre-trip inspection **AS YOU WALK TO THE BUS**. Look for any obvious leaks, broken or missing pieces, or to see if the bus is leaning to one side or the other. This may indicate a flat tire or defective suspension.

You then enter the vehicle and **CHECK THE LAST VEHICLE INSPECTION REPORT**. Look at the last report. If the previous driver has listed any defects, you must check to make sure they have been corrected. You will then sign the previous driver's inspection report indicating that either all defects have been repaired, or that none existed.

Step 2 Engine Compartment

All of the items discussed in Chapter 3, Part 1, General Knowledge, must be inspected. If you read that chapter thoroughly and completely, you already know most of the items which have to be checked. What we will cover in this chapter will deal specifically with buses and what must be checked on a bus pre-trip and after-trip inspection.

When checking the engine compartment the key items to look for are:

- Steering mechanism
- Fluid levels (oil, water, transmission)
- Power steering level (if equipped)
- Air connections and lines (if equipped)
- Check belts for tightness and excessive wear
- Check electrical wiring (look for worn or frayed insulation)
- Battery fluid levels
- Leaks of any type

Step 3 Starting the Engine

- Make sure brakes are set
- Start engine (check driver's area and passenger's area)
- Listen for unusual sounds

- Check all instruments and gauges (make sure *all* are in proper operating range)
- Check all controls (look for any loose wires, damage, or sticking)

  —Steering wheel

  —Brake pedal

  —Accelerator

  —Parking brake

  —Transmission controls

  —Dimmer switch

  —Light switches

  —Turn signals

  —Four-way flashers

  —Wipers

  —Horns

  —Mirrors

  —Door controls

  —**RIDER SIGNAL CONTROLS**

- **CHECK EMERGENCY EQUIPMENT**

  —**FIRE EXTINGUISHER (FULLY CHARGED AND SECURED)**

  —**ELECTRICAL FUSES (UNLESS EQUIPPED WITH CIRCUIT BREAKERS)**

  —**THREE EMERGENCY REFLECTORS (TRIANGLES)**

- Check passenger area (to ensure order and safety)

  —Aisles and stairways must be clear

  —Every handhold and railing must be secure

  —Floor covering (properly attached)

  —Rider signaling devices (including restroom buzzer, if equipped, are working in restroom)

  —Emergency exit handles (secure)

  —Seats (securely attached—one exception—**A CHARTER BUS CARRYING FARM WORKERS MAY HAVE UP TO EIGHT TEMPORARY FOLDING SEATS PLACED IN THE AISLE)**

  —Emergency exit signs (clearly visible)

  —Red Emergency Door light working (if equipped)

—Emergency Exit doors, windows, and roof hatches can be opened, and that each is closed and properly secured

Step 4 Turn Off the Engine and Check the Lights

- Set parking brake **(NEVER USE THE BRAKE AND ACCELERATOR INTERLOCK SYSTEM INSTEAD OF THE PARKING BRAKE)**
- Turn on headlights (low beam)
- Turn on 4-way flashers
- REMOVE KEY FROM IGNITION (to make sure no one moves the bus while you are doing pre-trip)
- Stand in front of the bus, check lights and 4-ways
- Return to bus, turn lights on high beams and check
- Turn off headlights and 4-ways, turn on all clearance, parking, marker lights and right-turn signal

Step 5—Walkaround Inspection

The complete pre-trip and walkaround inspection is found in Section 2 of your state's Model Drivers Manual (MDM). You must study these pages in order to become completely familiar with the pre-trip inspection procedures.

The highlights and/or additional items which bus operators need to inspect are:

- Check and close any emergency exits

- Check and close any access panels (baggage, restroom, service, engine, generator, etc.)

- NO RECAPS OR RE-GROOVED TIRES ON STEERING AXLE

- STEERING AXLE TIRES MUST HAVE AT LEAST 4/32-INCH TREAD DEPTH IN ALL MAJOR GROOVES—ALL OTHER TIRES MUST HAVE AT LEAST 2/32-INCH TREAD DEPTH

Step 6 Check brake lights and left turn signals

Step 7 Check braking system

- **TEST HYDRAULIC BRAKES: PUMP BRAKE PEDAL THREE TIMES AND THEN APPLY FIRM PRESSURE TO THE PEDAL AND HOLD FOR FIVE SECONDS. THE PEDAL SHOULD NOT MOVE DURING**

THE FIVE SECONDS. If it does, it probably has a leak somewhere in the system. Get it fixed before beginning your trip.

● TEST AIR BRAKES: *TEST FOR AIR LEAKAGE*

With engine turned off and air system fully charged, **RELEASE SERVICE BRAKE AND TIME THE AIR PRESSURE DROP. AFTER THE IN-ITIAL DROP, IT SHOULD NOT BE MORE THAN:**

> **2 PSI FOR ONE MINUTE—SINGLE VEHICLES,**
> **OR**
> **3 PSI FOR ONE MINUTE—COMBINATION VEHICLES**
> **THEN**

APPLY 90 PSI OR MORE WITH THE BRAKE PEDAL. AFTER THE INITIAL DROP, THE AIR PRESSURE SHOULD NOT DROP MORE THAN:

> **3 PSI FOR ONE MINUTE—SINGLE VEHICLES,**
> **OR**
> **4 PSI FOR ONE MINUTE—COMBINATION VEHICLES**

● **TEST PARKING BRAKES:**
WITH THE VEHICLE FULLY STOPPED, APPLY PARKING BRAKES AND GENTLY ATTEMPT TO MOVE VEHICLE. PARKING BRAKE MUST HOLD THE VEHICLE FIRMLY.

● **TEST SERVICE BRAKES:**
GO THREE TO FIVE MILES PER HOUR
PUSH BRAKE PEDAL FIRMLY
VEHICLE SHOULD STOP IMMEDIATELY. If not—system is faulty—get it repaired before beginning the trip. "Pulling" to one side or the other may mean brake problems. Get it checked.

At the end of the manual is a detachable "Pre-Trip Inspection Checklist." You may use this checklist to help you practice your pre-trip. You will also be permitted to use it when taking your skills test.

IF YOUR BUS IS EQUIPPED WITH SEAT BELTS, ALWAYS WEAR THEM.

The pre-trip portion of this chapter is the toughest part. Congratulations, you've gotten through it without any problems.

Notes:

_____

_____

_____

_____

_____

_____

_____

_____

_____

_____

_____

_____

_____

_____

_____

_____

_____

_____

_____

_____

_____

_____

_____

_____

_____

_____

_____

_____

_____

_____

_____

_____

You are permitted to transport certain hazardous material, but only in quantities so small that is does not require hazardous material placards.

- **YOU MAY TRANSPORT THE FOLLOWING HAZARDOUS MATERIALS:**
  —**DRUGS**
  —**EMERGENCY HOSPITAL SUPPLIES**
  —**SMALL ARMS AMMUNITION LABELED ORM-D.** (The term "ORM" means "Other Regulated Material.")
  —You may also carry small amounts of certain other HM (hazardous material) if the shipper cannot find another method by which to ship them. Check with your company or dispatcher before accepting *any* hazardous material.
- **YOU MAY NOT TRANSPORT:**

  —**CLASS 2 POISON**
  —**LIQUID CLASS 6 POISON**
  —**MORE THAN 100 POUNDS OF CLASS 6 POISONS**
  —**IRRITATING MATERIALS**
  —**TEAR GAS**
  —**LABELED RADIOACTIVE MATERIALS IN THE SPACE OCCUPIED BY PEOPLE**
  —**MORE THAN 500 POUNDS OF ALLOWED HAZARDOUS MATERIAL**

Other Regulations or Safety Rules for Bus Operators:

Prohibited Practices

- **NEVER REFUEL YOUR BUS IN A CLOSED BUILDING WITH PERSONS ON BOARD.**
- Avoid refueling your bus whenever people are on board, unless absolutely necessary.
- Don't talk with any person or engage in any type of distracting activity while driving (driving requires 100% of your attention).

- **DON'T TOW OR PUSH A DISABLED BUS WITH PASSENGERS ON BOARD EITHER VEHICLE, UNLESS ALLOWING THEM TO GET OFF WOULD PLACE THEM IN GREATER DANGER.** For example, you are on a busy inter-state, and the disabled vehicle is sitting in the center lane of three lanes. In such a case, you may tow or push the disabled bus, but only to the nearest safe place, at which point the passengers would be safely discharged. Check with your company to determine what the policy and procedures are governing breakdowns and towing.

- **NEVER USE THE BRAKE AND ACCELERATOR INTERLOCK SYSTEM IN PLACE OF THE PARKING BRAKE.** The interlock system is generally found on mass transit buses because they are boarding and discharging passengers continually. When the rear door is open, the interlock system applies the brake and places the transmission in neutral to provide increased safety to the passengers getting on or off the bus.

- **NEVER ALLOW PASSENGERS TO PLACE CARRY-ON BAGGAGE IN SUCH A WAY AS TO BLOCK THE AISLE, THE DOORS OR THE WINDOWS.**

- **DON'T ALLOW PASSENGERS TO CARRY ON DANGEROUS MATERIALS SUCH AS GASOLINE, KEROSENE, CAR BATTERIES, ETC.** Watch carefully for passengers carrying on hazardous material. Most hazardous materials are not permitted on a bus.

Standee Line:

Buses which are designed to allow passengers to stand, must have a 2-inch line on the floor, or some other means of showing passengers where they can stand. This is called the standee line. **ALL STANDING RIDERS MUST STAND BEHIND THE LINE. NO PASSENGERS ARE PERMITTED TO STAND FORWARD OF THE REAR OF THE DRIVER'S SEAT.**

Passenger Rules

If your company has rules about safety and passenger comfort such as smoking, drinking, playing of radios and TVs, etc., explain the rules to the passengers before beginning the trip.

Passengers may fall or stumble when getting off the bus or when the bus is starting or stopping. Remind passengers to watch their step when exiting the bus, and wait until they are sitting down or bracing themselves before starting.

Passengers should keep their arms and hands inside of the bus at all times. Use your mirrors to scan the interior and exterior of the bus. If you must remind passengers about these and other company rules, do so politely and professionally.

Disruptive or Unruly Passengers

Occasionally you might have an unruly passenger. If you make the decision that he/she be discharged from the vehicle, make sure that you **CHOOSE A SAFE, WELL-LIGHTED AREA, OR THE NEXT STOP. NEVER DISCHARGE AN UNRULY PASSENGER IN AN UNSAFE LOCATION.** Check with your company for the proper method of handling a disruptive passenger.

Before passengers leave the bus, remind them to take all carry-ons with them. Also, if the bus has an aisle that is on a lower level than the seats, remind them to step down. Do this before coming to a complete stop.

Safe Driving

ALWAYS REDUCE SPEED ON CURVES. The speed limit on curves is **STANDARDIZED FOR AUTOMOBILES**, not buses. Even though you may be obeying the speed limit for the curve, you are driving too fast! The best rule of thumb is to always go slower than the posted speed limit, especially on wet, icy, or snow-covered curves when the safe driving speed is drastically reduced.

Railroad Crossings

STOP AT ALL RAILROAD CROSSINGS! The regulations are clear: **STOP NO CLOSER THAN 15 FEET AND NO FARTHER AWAY THAN 50 FEET.** If opening your front door will improve your visibility, do it. Look both ways. Use both your eyes and your ears; look and listen for a train. After the train has crossed, don't even think about moving until you've checked *again* to make sure another train isn't coming from the other direction.

If your bus has a manual transmission, **NEVER SHIFT GEARS WHILE CROSSING THE TRACKS.** Another good safety practice is to turn on your 4-ways when preparing to stop at a RR crossing; this tells the traffic behind you that you are slowing down and will be stopping.

YOU DO NOT HAVE TO STOP, BUT YOU MUST SLOW DOWN, EXERCISE CAUTION, AND LOOK FOR OTHER TRAFFIC WHEN:

- at street car crossings
- at any railroad tracks used only for industrial switching
- within a business district
- where traffic is being directed by a policeman or flagman
- if a traffic signal is located at the crossing and is showing green
- at crossings marked "exempt crossing" (exempt means no longer used)

Avoiding Common Bus Accidents

Know the clearance of your bus—Many accidents occur when pulling away from the bus stop. Look carefully for poles, limbs, overhanging signs, etc.

Intersections are deadly—A major number of accidents occur at intersections. A green light does not mean that you have the right to go through the intersection. A green light means that you have the right to proceed through, with caution, *AFTER* you have thoroughly checked the intersection and have determined that it is safe to do so.

Merging

Accelerating and merging into traffic from a bus stop can be tricky. Know the space your bus will need in order to accelerate and merge safely with traffic. Wait for the space to become available. *Never* try to "bully" your way into traffic. Wait until traffic conditions allow you to enter the traffic stream safely, smoothly and professionally.

Drawbridges

<u>WHEN APPROACHING A DRAWBRIDGE THAT DOES NOT HAVE A SIGNAL LIGHT OR AN ATTENDANT TO DIRECT TRAFFIC, YOU MUST STOP COMPLETELY AT LEAST 50 FEET BEFORE THE DRAW (EDGE) OF THE BRIDGE.</u>

After looking carefully and determining that the bridge is down and completely closed, you may then proceed across. As in the case of the railroad tracks, as you begin to slow down, turn on your 4-ways, and let the traffic behind you see that you are preparing to stop.

You do not need to stop—but you must slow down and exercise caution when:

● a traffic signal is located at the bridge and is showing green
● a traffic attendant or police officer is directing traffic whenever the bridge opens

After-Trip Inspection

IF YOU ARE AN INTER-STATE BUS OPERATOR, YOU MUST COMPLETE A WRITTEN INSPECTION REPORT FOR ALL BUSES DRIVEN. You must identify the bus and list all defects which could affect safety or that may cause a breakdown. If no defects were discovered, you still must complete the report and note that no defects were found.

Even though you may not be an inter-state bus operator, all bus operators should complete a written inspection report for each bus driven and turn the report(s) in to the company at the end of the shift.

WATCH VIDEO—ON TRANSPORTING PASSENGERS

☞ LET'S TAKE A TEST

Transporting Passenger Test

Study each question carefully and then indicate your choice by drawing a circle around the letter you have chosen.

1. How many seats may be placed in the aisle if the bus is a charter and is carrying agricultural (farm) workers?

   A. 0
   B. 8
   C. 6
   D. 4

2. When is it recommended that you wear a seat belt?

   A. never
   B. only at speeds in excess of 25 mph
   C. always
   D. only when traveling on the inter-state highways or turnpikes

3. The standee line is:

   A. a place where passengers wait for the bus to arrive
   B. a location in the bus terminal where the passengers purchase their tickets
   C. a line in the center of the aisle directing passengers to the available seats
   D. a 2-inch line at the front of the bus indicating that no passenger may stand in front of it

4. Recapped tires are permitted on the steering axle provided:

   A. they have at least 4/32-inch of tread depth
   B. they have at least 2/32-inch of tread depth
   C. they have passed a safety inspection
   D. never

5. All of the following are required during your pre-trip inspection, except:

   A. check handholds and railings to see if secure
   B. check cylinder wall thickness
   C. emergency exit handles are secure
   D. check to see if turn signals and brake lights are operating properly

6. When stopping at a railroad crossing, you must stop:

   A. no closer than 15 feet—no farther than 50 feet
   B. no closer than 20 feet—no farther than 60 feet
   C. no closer than 25 feet—no farther than 50 feet
   D. no closer than 10 feet—no farther than 15 feet

7. Which of the following is true about refueling your bus?

   A. you must refuel with all windows opened fully
   B. never refuel with passengers aboard
   C. always use a static cable
   D. never refuel with passengers aboard when in a closed building

8. Which of the following hazardous materials are you permitted to transport?

   A. class 2 poison
   B. small arms ammunition (ORM-D)
   C. tear gas
   D. 1,000 pounds of Organic Peroxide

9. You are approaching a drawbridge and no signal device or attendant is present, you must:

   A. stop at least 50 feet before the draw of the bridge
   B. stop no closer than 75 feet before the draw of the bridge
   C. not stop as that might cause an accident
   D. speed up and cross quickly before the bridge is raised

10. If you must discharge an unruly or disruptive passenger, you should:

    A. stop immediately and discharge the passenger
    B. attempt to offer counseling to him/her before discharging him from the bus
    C. choose a location that is most inconvenient to him
    D. choose a location that is safe and well lighted

11. Passengers may carry gasoline onto the bus:

    A. if it is in an approved container and securely sealed
    B. never
    C. only in case of emergencies
    D. if you secure the gasoline container immediately behind the driver's seat

12. Which of the following emergency equipment is required on your bus?

   A. first-aid kit, tire chains, and tire changing equipment
   B. fire extinguisher, tire chains, and first-aid equipment
   C. fire extinguisher, 3 reflective triangles, spare electric fuses, unless bus is equipped with circuit breakers
   D. fire extinguisher, accident reporting kit, 3 reflective triangles

13. Speed limits on curves are standardized for:

   A. automobiles
   B. buses
   C. tractor-trailers
   D. small straight trucks

14. If your bus is not carrying farm workers, how many aisle seats are you permitted?

   A. 4
   B. 8
   C. 12
   D. 0

15. Which of the following hazardous materials are you permitted to transport?

   A. emergency shipment of drugs
   B. emergency shipment of hospital supplies
   C. small arms ammunition (ORM-D)
   D. all of the above

16. You are driving at night and you must dim your headlights from high to low. What should you do with your speed?

   A. slow down
   B. speed up
   C. drop 5 mph until your eyes adjust
   D. nothing; how well you can see should not affect speed

17. Which of these should be considered a hazard?

   A. an ice-cream truck
   B. a blind intersection
   C. a driver signaling a turn
   D. all of the above

18. You are driving a 40-foot bus at 45 mph. The road is dry and visibility is good. You should keep a safety space in front of your bus that is at least _____ seconds.

A. 8
B. 7
C. 5
D. 3

19. When should you check your mirrors for a lane change?

A. before and after signaling the change
B. right after starting the lane change
C. after completing the lane change
D. all of the above

20. Which of these will result in the best control on curves?

A. brake all the way through curves
B. slow to a safe speed before entering curves, then accelerate slightly through the curves
C. speed up slightly before the curves, then keep speed constant through the curves
D. slow to a safe speed before entering curves, then coast through them

Answers

1. B	6. A	11. B	16. A
2. C	7. D	12. C	17. D
3. D	8. B	13. A	18. C
4. D	9. A	14. D	19. D
5. B	10. D	15. D	20. B

If you were able to answer all of the questions correctly—*GOOD JOB!* If you missed any, re-read the material again until you know it with 100% accuracy.

Air Brakes

Who must read this chapter? All CDL applicants who operate or will be operating equipment that is equipped with an air brake system, must read this chapter and pass the CDL Air Brake Test. All "Class A" CDL applicants and many "Class B" applicants will need to take the Air Brake Test.

If you do not take the air brake test, your license will be marked with the words "**AIR BRAKE RESTRICTION**." You will not be permitted to operate any vehicle that is equipped with air brakes.

In order to successfully pass the air brake test, you must become totally familiar with the parts of an air brake system and how the air brake system works. Many of you are probably thinking to yourselves that this is b— s—t! You are a driver not a mechanic, right? And that's true, but the Federal Government believes that in order to safely operate a vehicle with air brakes, you need to have at least a working knowledge of how they work. Right or wrong, it's the "dealer's choice" and the Federal Government happens to be the "dealer," so, if you want to remove the air brake restriction from your CDL license, you've got to take and pass the air brake test.

The knowledge of air brakes that the government requires you to have is extensive. In this chapter we will cover all of the key parts of the air brake system, what they are and how they work.

Part 1: Air Brake Systems

All air brake systems have three major braking systems which you must know; they are:

Question:

1. **SERVICE BRAKE SYSTEM**
2. **PARKING BRAKE SYSTEM**
3. **EMERGENCY BRAKE SYSTEM**

Service Brake System

This is the system that you use day in and day out—it applies and releases the brakes as you apply and release pressure on the service brake. The service brake system is activated by applying pressure with your foot to the brake pedal.

Parking Brake System

This is the system you use when applying the parking brake.

Emergency Brake System

This system is the one that stops the vehicle in the event of an emergency caused by the failure of the braking system. It uses parts of the service and parking brake system.

Parts of the Air Brake System

Air Compressor

The air brake system uses compressed air to brake the vehicle. **THE AIR COMPRESSOR COMPRESSES THE AIR AND PUMPS IT INTO THE AIR TANKS. THE AIR TANKS ARE ALSO KNOWN AS THE RESERVOIRS OR STORAGE TANKS.**

Many types of air compressors are used in today's trucks. Some are air cooled while others are cooled by the engine cooling system. Some air compressors are connected to the engine with gears, others use V-belts. If V-belts are used in your vehicle, **ALWAYS CHECK THE CONDITION OF THE BELTS DURING YOUR PRE-TRIP INSPECTION**. Failure of the air compressor belts will result in failure of the air compressor which means you'll have no air for your braking system. Again, **ALWAYS CHECK THE AIR COMPRESSOR BELTS DURING THE PRE-TRIP INSPECTION**. Some air compressors have their own oil, while others are lubricated by the engine oil. If it has its own oil supply, always check it during the pre-trip inspection.

Air Compressor Governor

All air compressors have governors. **THE GOVERNOR'S JOB IS TO KEEP AIR IN THE AIR TANKS (RESERVOIRS).** The air compressor governor regulates the air pressure in the air tanks. The governor makes sure the braking system has enough air for proper braking. It does this with the *CUT-IN* and *CUT-OUT* levels. **WHEN THE AIR PRESSURE IN THE AIR TANKS FALLS BELOW A CERTAIN LEVEL, USUALLY 100 PSI, THE CUT-IN STARTS THE AIR COMPRESSOR RUNNING SO THAT THE AIR PRESSURE IS BUILT BACK UP. WHEN THE AIR PRESSURE IN THE TANK REACHES ABOUT 125 PSI, THE CUT-OUT LEVEL IS REACHED AND THE COMPRESSOR TURNS OFF. REMEMBER THESE TERMS:**

100 - cut IN

120
125 - cut out

CUT-IN LEVEL—TURNS AIR COMPRESSOR ON

CUT-OUT LEVEL—TURNS AIR COMPRESSOR OFF

AIR PRESSURE GOVERNOR—THE GOVERNOR MAINTAINS CONSTANT AIR PRESSURE IN AIR TANKS BETWEEN 100 PSI AND 125 PSI.

Air Storage Tanks

ALSO KNOWN AS AIR TANKS OR AIR RESERVOIRS. It is these tanks that hold the compressed air produced by the air compressor. These tanks have enough air to stop the vehicle several times, even if the air compressor has quit working. The size and number of air tanks vary greatly between vehicles.

Air Tank Drains

Air tanks are equipped with drains. Drains are located on the bottom of the air tank. Oil and water accumulate in the tanks and **MUST BE DRAINED DAILY**. Two types of drains are found on air tanks:

at the end of the day

to prevent moisture

1. Manual Drains

   These can be operated by turning a knob (petcock) or by pulling a cable. When turning the knob, turn it a quarter of a turn (see picture).

2. Automatic Drain

   These drains are activated automatically. You can tell if they are working because periodically (every once in awhile) you will hear them blow out the air and any accumulated oil and water.

Manual Reservoir Draining Valve

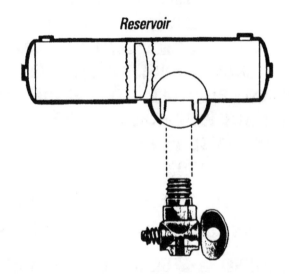

Reservoir

It is very important that these air drains be drained daily, especially in the winter. Below freezing temperatures will cause the moisture in the tanks and lines to freeze. This can seriously affect your braking system. Knowing this, doesn't it make just good common sense to drain your tanks on a daily basis? The government recommends they be drained at the end of each day; we recommend that they also be drained at the beginning of each day—why not do it as you are performing your pre-trip inspection, and then again during your after-trip inspection?

Alcohol Evaporators

Some air brake systems have alcohol evaporators. Alcohol evaporators are designed to automatically inject alcohol into the system to reduce the chance that water in the system will freeze. **EVEN IF THE TRUCK HAS AN ALCOHOL**

EVAPORATOR, YOU STILL MUST DRAIN YOUR AIR TANKS DAILY. During cold weather, you must check and fill the alcohol level daily.

Safety Valve

The safety valve (also known as a pop-off valve) is located in the first tank the air compressor pumps air into. This valve is designed to release excess air. It protects the air system from exceeding psi limitations and possibly damaging the system. Most safety valves are set to release if the pressure reaches approximately 150 psi. If the safety valve pops off (releases), something is probably wrong with the air compressor or the safety valve, and you should have a mechanic check it out as soon as possible.

The Brake Pedal

THE BRAKE PEDAL IS PART OF THE SERVICE BRAKE SYSTEM. THE BRAKE PEDAL IS ALSO KNOWN AS THE FOOT VALVE, FOOT BRAKE OR TREADLE VALVE. When you apply pressure to the brake pedal with your foot, you apply the brakes by forcing the air through the lines to the brakes. The more pressure you apply, the harder the brakes will be applied, and more air will be used. When you take your foot off the pedal, the air that has been used will be released and the amount of air in the air tanks will be reduced. As you can see, the more you press and release the brake pedal, the less air you will have in the system. As discussed earlier, when the air pressure reaches approximately 100 psi, the **CUT-IN LEVEL**, the air compressor governor will allow the air compressor to turn on and pump air into the system to replace the air you used when the brakes were applied. *IMPORTANT*—If you use too much air by repeatedly applying and releasing the brake pedal, you could pump enough air out of the system to render your service brakes useless. Remember, you must have adequate air in your tanks for the service brake system to work properly. Use your brake pedal only when needed.

Low Air Pressure Warning Devices

ALL VEHICLES EQUIPPED WITH AIR BRAKES MUST HAVE A LOW AIR PRESSURE WARNING SIGNAL. LOW AIR PRESSURE WARNING SIGNALS MUST ACTIVATE (COME ON) BEFORE THE AIR PRESSURE

Light comes — before 60 PSI or above

FALLS BELOW 60 PSI. On older vehicles, it must come on at one-half the compressor cut-out pressure level. The warning is usually a red light and sometimes is accompanied by a loud buzzer. **IF THE RED LIGHT AND/OR BUZZER COMES ON, YOU'VE GOT A PROBLEM. IF YOU'RE DRIVING DOWN THE ROAD, STOP IMMEDIATELY WHEN YOU FIND A SAFE SPOT AND ATTEMPT TO DETERMINE WHAT THE PROBLEM IS. DO NOT ATTEMPT TO DRIVE THE VEHICLE UNTIL YOU HAVE FOUND AND FIXED THE PROBLEM.**

THE WIG-WAG—ANOTHER TYPE OF LOW AIR PRESSURE WARNING

The wig-wag is a metal arm which is usually located above the driver's line of sight and is attached at the top of the windshield near the sun visor. When the air pressure reaches about 60 psi, the wig-wag will swing in front of the driver's face and wig-wag in front of his line of sight. Again, if this happens as you are driving down the road, *STOP IMMEDIATELY* and fix the problem. **THE WIG-WAG CANNOT BE RESET UNTIL THE AIR PRESSURE IN THE SYSTEM IS ABOVE 60 PSI.**

Foundation Brakes

THE BRAKES OF EACH WHEEL ARE CALLED FOUNDATION BRAKES. THE FOUNDATION BRAKE USED MOST OFTEN IS CALLED THE "S"-CAM BRAKE. IN ORDER TO PASS THE CDL TEST, YOU MUST LEARN THE PARTS OF THE "S"-CAM BRAKE AND THE CRITICAL PARTS OF THE BRAKING SYSTEM. They are:

- Brake drums
- Brake shoes
- Brake linings
- Slack adjuster
- Push rod
- Return spring
- Brake chamber
- Brake cam shaft

Let's take each part individually:

Brake drum—Is located at the ends of the axle. The brake drum houses (contains) the braking mechanism. The wheels are bolted to the drums.

Brake shoes and linings—When brakes are applied, the brake shoes and linings are pressed against the drum creating friction. It is this friction that causes the vehicle to slow down and/or stop. Friction also creates heat. The longer and harder the brake shoes and linings are held against the brake drum, the more heat is generated. If too much heat is generated, the brakes will begin to fade (lose their stopping ability). Too much heat can also cause the drum to warp or crack.

Brake chamber—When air is applied to the braking system, air is pumped into the brake chamber, the air pressure then pushes out the **PUSH ROD**—which is attached to the **SLACK ADJUSTER**.

Slack adjuster—The **SLACK ADJUSTER** is attached on one end to the **PUSH ROD** and on the other end to the brake **CAM SHAFT**. When the **SLACK ADJUSTER** is pushed out, it will cause the **BRAKE CAM SHAFT** to twist, which will cause the **"S"-CAM** to turn. The **"S"-CAM** is called the **"S"-CAM** because it is shaped like the letter "S." When the **"S"-CAM** turns, it forces the **BRAKE SHOES** away from one another and presses them against the inside of the **BRAKE DRUM**. When you take your foot off the brake pedal, the air is released out of the **BRAKE CHAMBER** and the process reverses itself. The **RETURN SPRING** then pulls the **BRAKE SHOES** away from the **BRAKE DRUM**.

"S" Cam Air Brake

Manual Slack Adjuster

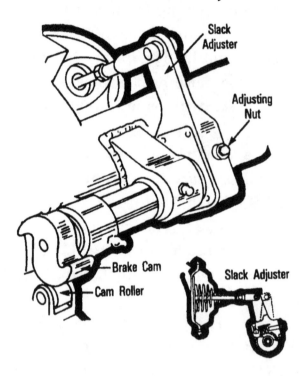

Wedge Brakes and Disc Brakes

Wedge brakes and disc brakes are another form of braking system seen on commercial vehicles. **AS THE "S"-CAM BRAKE IS THE MOST WIDELY USED TODAY**, we will only give a brief explanation of the wedge and disc types.

Wedge—This system works similar to the "S"-cam brake, except a wedge is pushed by the push rod and this wedge is pushed between the ends of the brake shoes, shoving them apart and pressing them against the inside of the brake drum. Wedge brakes may have one or two brake chambers.

Disc—Works the same as the "S"-cam except instead of an "S"-cam, the disc brake has a power screw which is turned when air pressure is applied, causing the power screw to clamp the disc between the brake lining pads of a caliper.

Supply Pressure Gauge

ALL VEHICLES WITH AIR BRAKE SYSTEMS MUST HAVE AN AIR PRESSURE SUPPLY GAUGE. THE AIR PRESSURE SUPPLY GAUGE TELLS THE DRIVER THE AMOUNT OF AIR PRESSURE (PSI) IN THE SYSTEM.

If the vehicle is equipped with a dual air brake system, it will have either one gauge with two needles, (one for each air system) or two separate gauges.

Application Pressure Gauge

[handwritten: look like air pressure gauge but it's different. It sets at 0.]

[handwritten margin: a question?]

THE APPLICATION PRESSURE GAUGE TELLS THE DRIVER HOW MUCH AIR PRESSURE IS BEING APPLIED TO THE BRAKES. The amount of air being applied is determined by the amount of pressure you apply to the brake pedal.

*PLEASE NOTE—***IT IS IMPORTANT THAT YOU UNDERSTAND THE DIFFERENCE BETWEEN THE SUPPLY PRESSURE GAUGE AND THE APPLICATION PRESSURE GAUGE.**

Brake Fade

When applying the service brakes by pressing on the brake pedal, the application pressure gauge tells you how much pressure is being applied. You should look at the application gauge frequently when going down a long grade. If you notice that it is taking more and more pressure to maintain the same speed, your brakes are beginning to heat up and are beginning to fade. You should slow down and use a lower gear to help you maintain your desired speed. You may have to stop and allow your brakes to cool. Using increased pressure to maintain the same speed may also be an indication of brakes that are out of adjustment, have air leaks or other mechanical problems. Poor brake performance is nothing to mess around with. Get the brakes checked as soon as possible.

Stop Lamp Switch

The stop lights are turned on when the brake pedal is applied. **AIR PRESSURE ACTIVATES AN ELECTRICAL SWITCH WHICH TURNS ON THE STOP LIGHTS.**

[handwritten: question]

Front Brake Limiting Valve

Older vehicles manufactured before 1975 have a control switch mounted on the dash called a front brake limiting valve. This valve has two positions: "normal"

Stop Lamp Switch

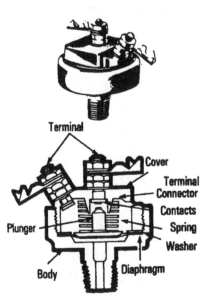

Terminal

Cover
Terminal
Connector
Contacts
Spring
Washer
Diaphragm

Plunger

Body

and "slippery." Putting the valve in the "slippery" position reduces by 50% the normal air pressure to the front brakes, thus reducing the braking power of the front brakes by 50%. Before 1975 it was believed that reducing the braking power to the front axle would help to reduce the chance of front wheel skid on wet or icy roads. We know today that whenever the braking power to the front wheels is reduced, the *ONLY* result is increased stopping distance. **FRONT WHEEL BRAKING IS GOOD UNDER ALL CONDITIONS. UNDER NO CONDITION SHOULD THE "SLIPPERY" POSITION OF THE FRONT BRAKE LIMITING VALVE EVER BE USED. ALWAYS KEEP THE FRONT BRAKE LIMITING VALVE IN THE NORMAL POSITION.**

"Fail Safe" Spring Brakes

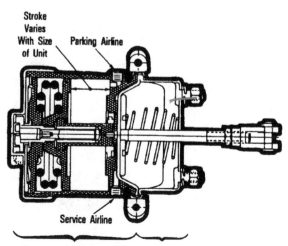

Spring Brake Half   Service Chamber Half

Spring Brakes

Also known as "fail safe brakes." All trucks, truck tractors and buses must have some type of emergency brake and parking brake system. These parking and emergency brakes must be mechanical since air can leak off. **SPRING BRAKES OR "FAIL-SAFE" BRAKES ARE MOST COMMONLY USED.**

When driving, **THE AIR PRESSURE IN YOUR SYSTEM HOLDS THE SPRINGS BACK,** which in turn holds the brake shoes away from the drums. When parking, the parking brakes are applied which allows the air to be released from the brake chamber, allowing the springs to release and apply the brakes.

IN AN EMERGENCY, WHEN THE AIR PRESSURE IN THE SYSTEM FALLS TO A CERTAIN LEVEL, USUALLY AROUND 20 PSI TO 30 PSI, THE SPRING BRAKES WILL AUTOMATICALLY APPLY THEMSELVES. This gets to be very exciting very quickly, especially if you happen to be driving down the road and the brakes lock up. Now you know why you have a low air pressure warning light and/or buzzer or wig-wag. **AT ABOUT 60 PSI, THE WARNING SIGNALS COME ON**—that means you are only 40 to 30 psi away from your spring brakes locking up. When the warning signals come on, you must find a safe place to stop, and you must do it quickly. **THE EFFECTIVENESS OF THE SPRING BRAKES AND THE SERVICE BRAKE SYSTEM IS DEPENDENT ON THE BRAKES BEING PROPERLY ADJUSTED.**

question

WHEN PARKED AND THE PARKING BRAKES ARE APPLIED, NEVER APPLY PRESSURE TO THE BRAKE PEDAL. DAMAGE TO THE BRAKES COULD RESULT BECAUSE OF THE COMBINED FORCE OF THE SPRING BRAKE AND BRAKE PEDAL.

- ojo

Parking Brake Controls

In newer vehicles, you apply the parking brakes (spring brakes) by using a diamond shaped, yellow push-pull control knob. You pull the knob out to apply the parking (spring) brakes, and push it in to release them. In older vehicles, the parking brake will probably be controlled by a lever.

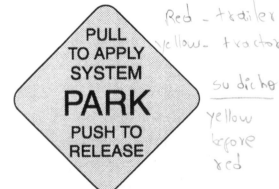

Red - trailer
yellow - tractor

su dicho

yellow
before
red

Whenever you park, always use the parking brakes. By using the parking brakes, you guarantee that you'll never have a roll-off. Most truck-tractors are equipped with a handle attached to, or near, the steering column. This handle is called a "Johnson bar" or "trolley valve." It is used for applying only the trailer brakes. Some drivers, especially those that have been driving for 20 or 30 years, park their vehicles by pulling this handle down and locking the trailer brakes only. This is a dangerous habit and should never be done. **ALWAYS PARK YOUR VEHICLE USING THE PARKING (SPRING) BRAKES ONLY.**

Modulating Control Valve

Some vehicles are equipped with a modulating control valve. This valve is controlled by a handle on the dashboard and can be used to apply the spring brakes gradually. The more you move the handle, the more the spring brakes are applied. Since this handle is spring loaded, you will have a feel for the amount of pressure and braking action being applied. **THE MODULATING CONTROL VALVE IS DESIGNED TO BE USED IN CASE YOUR SERVICE BRAKES FAIL WHILE DRIVING. YOU WILL BE ABLE TO STOP YOUR VEHICLE BY USING THE MODULATING CONTROL VALVE.** Once stopped, lock the handle in the "down" position with the locking device. **DO NOT MOVE THE VEHICLE UNTIL THE SOURCE OF THE SERVICE BRAKE FAILURE HAS BEEN DETERMINED AND REPAIRED.**

Dual Parking Control Valves

As previously discussed, when air pressure falls between 20 to 30 psi, the spring brakes lock-up. **SOME VEHICLES, MAINLY BUSES, HAVE AN AUXILIARY OR SEPARATE AIR TANK THAT CAN BE USED TO RELEASE THE SPRING BRAKES SO THAT THE VEHICLE CAN BE MOVED TO A SAFE LOCATION.** Vehicles with dual parking control valves will have two control knobs on the dash or on the control panel. One is a push-pull type knob which is used to apply the spring brakes for normal parking. The other knob is spring loaded in the "out" position. When pushed in it releases the air from the auxiliary tank and releases the spring brakes. As this knob is spring loaded in the "out" position, it must be held in while moving the vehicle. When released, it pops back "out" automatically and reapplies the spring brakes. It can only be used a few times before running out of air, so plan the move carefully.

Dual Air Brake Systems

Most newer trucks have a dual air brake system. Dual air brake systems offer the driver increased protection against air loss and brake failure.

DUAL AIR BRAKE SYSTEM SIMPLY MEANS THAT THE TRUCK HAS TWO SEPARATE AIR BRAKE SYSTEMS. Now don't get confused, even though it has two completely separate air systems, **IT STILL HAS ONLY ONE SET OF CONTROLS.**

The two air systems are called:

1. **PRIMARY SYSTEM**
2. **SECONDARY SYSTEM**

One system will usually operate the brakes on the rear axle or axles of the unit (truck or truck tractor). The other system will usually operate the brakes on the front axle and maybe one rear axle. Both systems work together to supply air to the trailer or trailers.

Before driving a vehicle that is equipped with a dual system, just as in a vehicle with only one system, you must wait until the air pressure builds up to at least 100 psi. Normally you will have an air gauge for each system, but you might find a vehicle with only one gauge which has two needles in it, one needle for each system.

THE LOW AIR WARNING BUZZER AND LIGHT WORK THE SAME AS IN A SINGLE SYSTEM VEHICLE. IF EITHER SYSTEM FALLS BELOW 60 PSI, THE BUZZER AND LIGHTS WILL COME ON. If this happens, you must stop as quickly as safety will allow. Remember, if only one system has lost air pressure, that means you have lost a portion of your braking ability, so take this into consideration when bringing your vehicle to a stop. Obviously, once you are safely stopped, you should not attempt to drive the vehicle until you get the air system repaired.

Inspecting Air Brake Systems

Inspecting the brake system before driving is nothing but common sense. Why would any professional driver want to drive any vehicle without first checking the brakes? All professionals check the brakes before driving . . . after all, it's your life you're putting on the line.

Listed on the next page are the 10 steps to follow when checking the brake system. Be sure to learn these thoroughly.

Step 1   **CHECK AIR COMPRESSOR BELT AND OIL**

If the compressor is belt driven, check belts for tightness, glazing, fraying and cracks. If compressor has its own lubricating oil, check to see that it's full.

Step 2   **CHECK MANUAL SLACK ADJUSTERS ON "S"-CAM BRAKES**   question

In order to check the slack adjusters, you must **PARK THE VEHICLE ON LEVEL GROUND, PUT VEHICLE IN GEAR, TURN OFF ENGINE, RELEASE THE BRAKES** *AND* **CHOCK THE WHEELS.** This will prevent the truck from moving. When exiting the cab, take the keys with you. **TAKING THE KEYS WILL PREVENT SOMEONE FROM**

ATTEMPTING TO MOVE THE VEHICLE WHILE YOU ARE UNDER IT.

LOCATE THE SLACK ADJUSTERS AND PULL HARD ON THEM. IF THEY MOVE MORE THAN ABOUT ONE INCH WHERE THE PUSH ROD ATTACHES TO IT, IT IS OUT OF ADJUSTMENT and will need to be adjusted before beginning your trip.

OUT-OF-ADJUSTMENT BRAKES ARE THE MOST COMMON PROBLEM FOUND AT STATE AND DOT INSPECTIONS. Protect yourself and your vehicle—*always check the adjustment.*

Step 3   **CHECK BRAKE DRUMS (OR DISCS), LININGS, HOSES**

If brake drums (or discs) have **CRACKS IN THEM LONGER THAN ONE-HALF THE WIDTH OF THE FRICTION AREA, IT IS OUT OF SERVICE.**

LININGS MUST NOT BE LOOSE OR SOAKED WITH OIL OR GREASE. THE LININGS SHOULD NOT BE SO THIN AS TO BE DANGEROUS. Mechanical parts must be in their place, not broken or missing. Check the air hoses connected to the brake chambers. Look for cracks, worn or chafing hoses.

Step 4   **TEST LOW PRESSURE WARNING SIGNAL (LOW AIR WARNING)**
With the air pressure built up to the point that the buzzer and/or warning light has turned off, turn off engine and then turn key switch to "on" position but do not start engine. **BEGIN APPLYING AND RELEASING BRAKES UNTIL LOW AIR BUZZER AND WARNING LIGHT COMES ON. THIS SHOULD HAPPEN AT ABOUT 60 PSI.** If the warning signal doesn't work, get it fixed before driving.

Step 5   **CHECK THAT THE SPRING BRAKES COME ON AUTOMATICALLY**

Using the same procedure as above, except put unit in gear or chock wheels and release parking brake, **CONTINUE PUMPING YOUR BRAKES UNTIL THE PARKING BRAKE CONTROL KNOB POPS**

OUT. THIS SHOULD HAPPEN BETWEEN 20 AND 40 PSI, indicating that the spring brakes have applied.

Step 6   **CHECK RATE OF PRESSURE BUILD-UP**

WITH DUAL AIR SYSTEM AND THE ENGINE IDLING, THE AIR PRESSURE SHOULD BUILD TO BETWEEN 85 TO 100 PSI WITHIN 45 SECONDS. WITH SINGLE AIR SYSTEMS, IT COULD TAKE THREE MINUTES TO BUILD BETWEEN 50 TO 90 PSI. If your air pressure does not build up within these time limits, something may be wrong with the system. Get it checked before driving.

Step 7   **TEST AIR LEAKAGE RATE**

With the air system fully charged (gauge should be showing approximately 125 psi), turn off engine, **RELEASE THE SERVICE BRAKES** and time the air pressure drop (or loss). The loss rate should be:

SINGLE VEHICLE—LESS THAN 2 PSI IN ONE MINUTE

COMBINATION VEHICLE—LESS THAN 3 PSI IN ONE MINUTE

Then **APPLY** 90 psi or more with the brake pedal. After the initial drop (which you do not count), the air loss for **SINGLE VEHICLES SHOULD NOT EXCEED 3 PSI IN ONE MINUTE**, and for a **COMBINATION VEHICLE, AIR LOSS SHOULD NOT EXCEED 4 PSI** in one minute. If your vehicle is losing more than 3 psi for a single or 4 psi for a combination, that's too much! Check the vehicle for air leaks and get them fixed before driving.

☞ **YOU MUST KNOW THESE**

Step 8   **CHECK AIR COMPRESSOR GOVERNOR CUT-IN AND CUT-OUT PRESSURE**
Remember our previous discussion about cut-in and cut-out levels? **THE GOVERNOR SHOULD HAVE COMPRESSOR CUT-IN WHEN AIR PRESSURE GETS TO ABOUT 100 PSI AND SHOULD CUT OUT AT ABOUT 125 PSI.**

With the air gauge reading about 125 psi, begin pumping the brake pedal. When you pump the pressure down to about **100 PSI**, the compressor should kick in. You'll know when this happens because the needle in the gauge will begin to rise, indicating a build-up of air pressure. When the gauge reaches about **125 PSI**, the needle in the gauge should stop rising, indicating that the governor has kicked in and turned off the air compressor. *Conduct this test with your engine idling.*

If the governor is not working properly, it may not maintain the proper air pressure in the system during the trip. Get it checked before starting your trip.

Step 9   **TEST PARKING BRAKE**

With the vehicle fully stopped, apply parking brakes and gently attempt to move the vehicle in 1st gear. Parking brake must hold the vehicle firmly.

Step 10   **TEST SERVICE BRAKES**

After air pressure has built up completely, release parking brakes and begin to move forward slowly. At about 5 mph, firmly apply the brakes using only the brake pedal. Brakes should be sufficient to stop the vehicle firmly. If the vehicle pulls to one side or the other, if the brakes feel spongy, or if you have a delayed stopping action—get them checked before going on the road.

If you are pulling a trailer, check the trailer brakes by beginning to move forward slowly. At about 5 mph, pull down on the trailer hand valve. The trailer brakes should lock firmly. If they don't, get them checked.

Notes:

Part 2: Using Air Brakes

In this part of the chapter we are going to talk about the proper use of air brakes in three different situations:

1. **NORMAL STOPPING**
2. **CONTROLLED BRAKING**
3. **STAB BRAKING**

You must become familiar with these techniques. Be sure to learn the differences between **CONTROLLED BRAKING** and **STAB BRAKING**.

Normal Stopping

Under normal stopping conditions, you simply apply pressure to the brake pedal with a smooth steady movement until the vehicle comes to a stop.

Controlled Braking

Another name for controlled braking is "squeeze" braking because **YOU "SQUEEZE" THE BRAKES FIRMLY WITHOUT LOCKING THE WHEELS**. The important key here is that you **DO NOT LOCK THE WHEELS**. While "squeezing" or applying pressure to the brake pedal, **DO NOT ATTEMPT TO TURN THE WHEELS—THEY MAY LOCK ON YOU**, *and you will lose all steering control*. If you need to turn the wheel, or if you feel the wheels starting to lock up, release the brakes, make your steering adjustment, and then reapply the brakes.

Stab Braking — Freno de puñalada

Stab braking is done in three movements:

1. Apply brakes as hard as you can
2. Release the brakes when wheels lock up
3. When wheels start rolling again, reapply brakes hard—(this process is then repeated as often as necessary).

PLEASE NOTE: If your vehicle is equipped with anti-lock brakes, this section on stab braking may not apply. Read your vehicle's manual for proper emergency braking procedures.

The key point to know in stab braking is that its purpose is **TO LOCK THE WHEELS**. Here are some points to remember about stab braking.

A. When your wheels are locked, you have *NO* steering control

B. When you take your foot off the brake pedal—it will take up to one second before the wheels begin to roll again

C. Keeping the wheels locked too long could result in the vehicle sliding sideways or beginning to jackknife—*BE CAREFUL*—when performing stab braking.

Stopping Distance

Stopping distances in air brake equipped vehicles is different than the stopping distances with hydraulic brake equipped vehicles. With air brakes there is an added delay. This delay is caused by the necessity for the air to travel to the brakes after the brake pedal is applied. The delay isn't much, but it's enough to make a difference.

The stopping distance for air brake equipped vehicles is made up of four factors. **YOU MUST KNOW THESE FACTORS!**

1. Perception distance
2. Reaction distance
3. Brake lag distance   *time the air travels through the tanks*
4. Effective braking distance
   = Total Stopping Distance

Let's discuss each of these factors one at a time.

PERCEPTION DISTANCE is the distance your vehicle will travel from the time you see a hazard, and your mind tells you that it is in fact a hazard, and that you must react to it. **THE AVERAGE DRIVER PERCEPTION TIME IS 3/4 OF A SECOND.** That may not seem like much, but if your vehicle is traveling 55 mph, it will travel approximately 60 feet during that 3/4 of a second.

REACTION DISTANCE is the time it takes for your foot to get off the accelerator, travel to the brake and then "mash" down the brake. **THE AVERAGE DRIVER REACTION TIME IS AGAIN, 3/4 OF A SECOND.** Your vehicle has traveled another 60 feet, and you are just now beginning to brake.

How much total stop distance   32 feet

BRAKE LAG DISTANCE is the distance a vehicle will travel once the brake pedal has been applied and the brakes begin to work. This will take about 1/2 second. In just 1/2 second, at 55 mph, your vehicle will travel another ~~40 feet~~. *(32 feet)*

EFFECTIVE BRAKING DISTANCE is the distance the vehicle will travel once the brakes make contact with the drum. With good braking efficiency (meaning all the brakes are adjusted perfectly) on good dry pavement, the vehicle will travel approximately 150 additional feet until it comes to a stop from 55 mph.

Now let's look at these factors again, using the figures we just calculated—

	At 55 mph
Perception distance	60 ft
Reaction distance	60 ft
Brake lag distance	40 ft
Effective braking distance	150 ft
= Total Stopping Distance *= over 300 ft*	310 ft

About the Length of a Football Field

Can you believe that? At 55 mph, acting as quick as you can, you'll still travel 310 feet. Also, keep in mind that in this example we have perfectly adjusted brakes and a good dry road. Add poorly adjusted brakes or wet roads, and you can see the significance of maintaining a good following distance and looking **12 TO 15 SECONDS DOWN THE ROAD**.

Proper Braking on Downhill Grades

Some drivers get real nervous when you start talking about driving on long mountainous grades. Every "old-timer" has a favorite story about the time he, or a buddy of his, lost it on "Donner's Summit" or "Fancy Gap" or the "Grapevine." While these stories are certainly exciting and entertaining, there is no reason for any professional driver to ever "lose" one on a long downhill.

Brakes get hot when being used. This heat is caused by the friction between the shoes and the drum. It's supposed to happen. The trick is to use your brakes in such a way that they don't get so hot that they begin to "fade," or lose their stopping ability. How do you know when your brakes are beginning to fade? Simple, when brakes begin to fade it takes **MORE PRESSURE ON THE BRAKE PEDAL TO MAINTAIN THE SAME SPEED**. If this happens, you are beginning to experience brake fade. The best thing to do at this point is pull over and allow your brakes to cool. Once cooled, they will regain some of their braking ability, but they might need to be adjusted, depending on how hot they got. If they need adjusting, and if you are qualified to do it, then go ahead and adjust them. If you are not able to adjust them, get a mechanic and get them adjusted before continuing with the trip.

Now, let's talk about how you avoid getting into the above situation. Before starting down a long downgrade, if possible, pull over and make sure that all of your brakes are adjusted and working properly. When starting down the hill, **GET INTO A GEAR THAT WILL ALLOW YOU TO MAINTAIN A SAFE SPEED BY USING THE BRAKING EFFECT OF THE ENGINE.** The braking effect of the engine is greatest when it is close to the governed rpm in the gear that you have chosen. In most cases it will be one or more gears *LOWER* than the one you used to climb the hill. The "**SAFE SPEED**" is the posted speed limit for the type of vehicle you are driving. *NEVER* exceed the posted speed limit. Apply the brakes when you reach the "**SAFE SPEED**." Apply them hard enough that you activate all brakes on the vehicle and you can feel the vehicle slowing down. The amount of braking pressure needed to accomplish this will be at least 20 psi (pounds per square inch). Keep the brakes applied until the vehicle speed has been reduced to about **5 MPH UNDER THE "SAFE SPEED"** and then release the brakes. If you are in the proper gear, the brake application should last about three seconds.

How do you select a gear low enough to help you maintain the "**SAFE SPEED**"? It used to be said that you should go down the hill in the same gear that you used to go up the hill. That may have been true 20 or 30 years ago, but *NOT* today. Many of today's modern engines are so powerful that they can go up steep grades without ever downshifting. For this reason, you will have to choose a gear perhaps *SEVERAL* gears lower than the one you used to climb the hill.

Here's an example: The *"SAFE SPEED"* is 30 mph. You climbed the hill in 9th gear but to be close to the governed rpm's at 30 mph you must use 6th gear to go down the hill. You begin going downhill in 6th gear and when your vehicle reaches 30 mph you apply approximately 20 psi to the brake pedal and noticeably feel the vehicle slowing down. You continue applying the brakes until your vehicle reaches 25 mph at which time you release the brakes. When your vehicle speeds back up to 30 mph you repeat the process and continue to repeat it until you reach the bottom of the hill.

Loss of Air Pressure

What do you do if you begin to lose your air pressure? **YOU MUST STOP YOUR VEHICLE AS QUICKLY AND AS SAFELY AS POSSIBLE.**

When the low air pressure warning comes on, it usually means that you have developed a leak in the air system. The warning buzzer and light will come on when air pressure drops to about 60 psi. The brakes are going to lock up when the air pressure drops to 20 to 45 psi. As you can see, from the time the low air buzzer is activated, until the brakes lock up, is a very short period. **YOU MUST PULL OVER AND STOP AS SOON AS POSSIBLE AFTER THE LOW AIR BUZZER COMES ON.** Failure to stop means that the brakes may lock up as you are traveling down the road—certainly not a good situation, and one that can lead to a loss of control.

THE ONE-WAY CHECK VALVE PREVENTS THE AIR FROM ESCAPING FROM THE AIR SYSTEM in the event a major rupture occurs, such as the trailer separating from the tractor and ripping off the air lines.

Parking Brakes

WHENEVER YOU PARK—USE THE PARKING BRAKE—NEVER USE THE TROLLEY VALVE, also called the trailer hand valve. There will be times when you should not use your parking brake, such as right after coming down a long grade and your brakes are very hot. Excessive heat can damage the brakes. Or, when in freezing temperatures, using the parking brakes may cause them to freeze and lock. If your brakes do freeze up, try this to unstick them. With the engine off, transmission in gear, and wheels chocked, release the parking brake. Get your "tire-checker" or a small metal bar or pipe, and lightly tap the brakes. A light tap may break the ice and allow the brakes to release.

Remember, always park using only your parking brakes. If that is not possible due to hot brakes or freezing temperatures—use chocks—**BUT NEVER USE THE TRAILER HAND BRAKE**.

WATCH THE VIDEO ON AIR BRAKES

☞ LET'S TAKE A TEST

Air Brakes

Study each question carefully and indicate your choice by drawing a circle around
the letter you have chosen.

1. When going down long or steep downgrades you should *always:*

    A. apply light brakes on and off
    B. use the braking effects of the engine
    C. use light steady braking pressure
    D. shift to lower gears when speed is too fast

    calibre

2. The application air gauge shows:

    A. total air pressure in air system
    B. amount of pressure currently being applied by brake pedal
    C. how much air has been used since beginning the trip
    D. none of the above

3. The low air pressure warning will activate at approximately:

    A. 60 psi
    B. 30 psi
    C. 20 psi
    D. 80 psi

4. If you experience a severe air loss and the service brake system is no longer
    working, which brake system is used to stop the vehicle?

    A. parking brake system
    B. interlock air lock system
    C. service brake system
    D. emergency brake system

5. Air tanks should be drained at least:

    A. daily
    B. weekly
    C. after each dispatch
    D. every four hours

GUILHERME
P 757574

6. An alcohol evaporator:

psi — pounds
square
inch

   A. injects alcohol into the air lines to help prevent freezing
   B. is used instead of an air dryer
   C. removes alcohol from air lines
   D. should be used only on hydraulic brake systems

7. The air compressor governor determines:

   A. amount of air sent to brakes when brake pedal is depressed
   B. how fast the air compressor is allowed to run
   C. the cut-in and cut-out pressure
   D. all of the above

8. If you experience a sudden drop in the air system you should:

   A. continue driving and say an effective prayer
   B. continue driving but only to the next repair shop
   C. keep your eye on the gauge and hope it will build the pressure back up
   D. stop immediately when safe to do so

9. At approximately 20-45 psi:

   A. the low air pressure buzzer will activate
   B. spring brakes will apply automatically
   C. nothing unusual will happen
   D. the air compressor governor will quit working

10. Vehicles equipped with air brakes must have:

   A. at least two air tanks, one on tractor and one on trailer
   B. an air pressure gauge — How much pressure is in your tanks
   C. a dual air brake system
   D. automatic air drains

11. When a driver depresses the brake pedal, what air brake system is he using?

   A. service brakes
   B. emergency brakes
   C. parking brakes
   D. both A and B

12. Emergency brakes are activated:

    A. by the brake pedal
    B. by the "S"-Cam
    C. by a loss of air pressure
    D. all of the above

13. Which of the following is the most common foundation brake found on commercial vehicles?

    A. wedge and drum
    B. disc
    C. "S"-Cam drum
    D. none of the above

14. If the air system ruptures, which of the following prevents the air from escaping out of the system?

    A. air compressor
    B. emergency brake system
    C. the emergency relay valve
    D. the one-way check valve

15. The spring brakes, or emergency braking system:

    A. will always work
    B. will work only if the brakes are adjusted properly
    C. cannot be tested by one person during a pre-trip inspection
    D. will work properly, regardless of the brake adjustment

16. A vehicle with a dual air system:

    A. must have two supply pressure gauges
    B. must have two sets of brake controls
    C. will have only one set of controls
    D. will have at least two low air warning buzzers

17. When driving down the road and the air brake system is working properly, the brakes are held away from the drum by:

    A. spring pressure
    B. air pressure
    C. hydraulic pressure
    D. any of the above

18. When air pressure is lost or leaks off:

    A. the vehicle will always roll away
    B. strong springs are released which apply the brakes automatically (these are known as spring brakes)
    C. brakes are always released
    D. the trolley valve can be used to apply brakes

19. A dual parking control valve means:

    A. you can use air pressure from a separate tank to move your vehicle to a safe location
    B. you have two parking brakes
    C. you are required to have two separate brake controls
    D. none of above

20. If you have a dual air brake system and a low air pressure warning is activated, you:

    A. don't have to worry since you have two systems and you can proceed on your trip and get the problem fixed after unloading
    B. should just reduce speed and don't use your brakes unless absolutely necessary
    C. can turn off the buzzer if only one system is affected
    D. stop immediately and get air system repaired

21. The front brake limiting valve should be used:

    A. never
    B. on dry roads only
    C. on wet roads
    D. whenever the driver feels it is necessary

22. A combination vehicle air brake system, with engine off and brakes applied, should not leak more than:

    A. 2 psi in one minute

    B. 3 psi in one minute

    C. 3 psi in 30 seconds

    D. 4 psi in one minute

23. With brakes applied and engine off, air loss in a straight truck or bus should not exceed:

    A. 3 psi in one minute

    B. 2 psi in one minute

    C. 4 psi in one minute

    D. 4 psi in 45 seconds

24. To check for play in the slack adjusters you must:

    A. have two people to do it

    B. park vehicle on flat ground, chock wheels, release brakes and pull hard on slack adjusters

    C. drain all air from system and then pull on slack adjusters

    D. pump air pressure to 20 psi and then look at brake lining gap between drum

25. Combination vehicles with air brakes, engine off and brakes released, cannot lose more than:

    A. 10 psi in one minute

    B. 4 psi in one minute

    C. 2 psi in one minute

    D. 3 psi in one minute

26. Stab braking means:

    A. brake hard until wheels lock up then release until wheels begin to roll again

    B. brake hard, but not enough to lock wheels

    C. light, steady pumping action

    D. none of the above

calibre

27. A supply pressure gauge is:

    A. seldom found on straight trucks or buses
    B. required on all equipment with air brakes
    C. usually not found on combination vehicles
    D. not required

28. On long downhill grades, experts recommend using a low gear and only enough braking pressure to reduce vehicle speed to 5 mph below the "safe speed" for the hill, why?

    A. air usage is less when vehicle is in the proper low gear and brakes are applied only when needed to reduce to speed under the "safe speed"
    B. brake linings should not over heat if in the proper gear
    C. using this method allows you to maintain control of the vehicle
    D. all of the above are true

desoire

29. When is "snubbing" the brakes on a long downgrade acceptable?

    A. if brakes are properly adjusted
    B. if brake linings are made out of asbestos
    C. if brakes are properly adjusted and vehicle is in proper gear
    D. when your company authorizes it

30. Air brakes take more time to work than hydraulic brakes due to:

    A. brake lag — _retraso del freno_
    B. driver's perception time
    C. the working of the one-way check valve
    D. none of the above

31. You lose steering control when:

    A. you have a front tire blowout
    B. your steering tires lock up
    C. you use the controlled braking method
    D. you have more than 9,000 lbs on the front axle

32. Effective braking distance is:

    A. the distance your vehicle travels after you see the hazard
    B. the distance your vehicle travels after you react to the hazard
    C. the distance your vehicle travels after you step on the brake pedal
    D. the distance your vehicle travels after brakes have been applied

33. The most common type of foundation brake found on heavy vehicles is the:

    A. disc
    B. wedge drum
    C. "S"-Cam drum
    D. none of the above

34. A supply pressure gauge shows:

    A. air available in the air tanks
    B. pressure being applied by foot brake
    C. amount of air in brake chamber
    D. amount of air in hydraulic system

35. When going down a long downgrade, and you are driving a "KW" with a 425 "Cat," the gear you should be in is:

    A. the same one you went up the grade in
    B. a higher gear than the one used going up the grade
    C. a lower gear than the one used going up the grade
    D. it doesn't make any difference if your truck is equipped with an engine retarder

36. The brake pedal in an air brake system:

    A. controls the speed of the air compressor
    B. is seldom used, compared to hydraulic systems
    C. controls the air pressure applied to put on the brakes
    D. is connected to slack adjusters by a series of rods and linkages

37. Parking or emergency brakes of trucks and buses can be legally held by _____ pressure.

    A. spring
    B. fluid
    C. air
    D. atmospheric

38. The driver must be able to see a low air pressure warning which comes on before pressure in the service air tanks falls below _____ psi.

    A. 20
    B. 40
    C. 60
    D. 80

39. All air brake equipment vehicles have:

    A. an air use gauge
    B. a supply pressure gauge
    C. at least one brake heater
    D. a backup hydraulic system

40. The braking power of the spring brakes:

    A. increases when the service brakes are hot
    B. depends on the service brakes being in adjustment
    C. is not affected by the condition of the service brakes
    D. can only be tested by highly-trained brake service people

Answers

1. B	16. C	31. B
2. B	17. B	32. D
3. A	18. B	33. C
4. D	19. A	34. A
5. A	20. D	35. C
6. A	21. A	36. C
7. C	22. D	37. A
8. D	23. A	38. C
9. B	24. B	39. B
10. B	25. D	40. B
11. A	26. A	
12. C	27. B	
13. C	28. D	
14. D	29. C	
15. B	30. A	

If you were able to answer all of the questions correctly, *GOOD JOB!* If you missed any, read the material again until you know it with 100% accuracy.

Combination Vehicles

Who Must Study This Section?

"Class A" drivers who operate combination vehicles with GCVWR exceeding 26,000 lbs must take the Combination Vehicle Test. This includes drivers of tractor-trailer, doubles, triples and straight trucks pulling trailers with a GVWR of more than 10,000 lbs. Additionally, tow-truck operators who tow vehicles with a GVWR of more than 10,000 lbs may be required to take the Combination Vehicle Test. Check with your state DMV. Drivers who pull doubles or triples must also study the Double/Triples section in this chapter and take the Double/Triples Endorsement Test.

Section 1: Combination Vehicles Tractor-Trailers

It requires more skill to operate a combination vehicle than it does to operate a single vehicle. Combination vehicles are usually longer, heavier and are articulated (that means they bend at a joint). They require longer distances to stop, tend to roll over more easily, and can jackknife. For these reasons, it is important that drivers be knowledgeable about the risks and hazards associated with combination vehicles.

In this chapter, we will discuss the major differences between single vehicles and combination vehicles. Your attention will be directed to the four major risk factors in driving combinations.

They are:

1. Braking
2. Jackknives—tractor and trailer
3. Rollovers
4. Steering and turning

We will also cover the special skills necessary to operate doubles and triples, and will discuss the proper methods of coupling and uncoupling tractor-trailers and doubles.

Braking

Speed is controlled by either your accelerator or your brake. With combination vehicles, the proper use of the brakes is critical. Any experienced driver will tell you that the less brakes you use, the better off you are. Since combination vehicles are articulated, improper use of brakes can lead to serious problems.

IT TAKES LONGER TO STOP AN EMPTY VEHICLE THAN A LOADED ONE. The stiff suspension on a trailer may make the trailer bounce or skip in an emergency braking situation. **IT IS THE FRICTION BETWEEN THE ROADWAY AND THE TIRES THAT SLOWS, AND ULTIMATELY STOPS, THE VEHICLE.** The bouncing or skipping creates less friction which means more stopping distance. **A HEAVILY LOADED TRUCK WILL STOP IN A SHORTER**

DISTANCE DUE TO THE INCREASED FRICTION BETWEEN THE ROAD-WAY AND THE TIRES.

During emergency braking, when all wheels are locked, the trailer might swing left or right, striking other objects or vehicles.

Rarely are all brakes on a combination vehicle adjusted exactly the same. Therefore, when in a panic stop, some may lock and some may not. This is especially dangerous on wet, snowy or icy roadways. The tire that has stopped rolling will always want to take the lead. In other words, **THE TIRE THAT HAS LOCKED UP WILL ATTEMPT TO COME AROUND AND TAKE THE LEAD.** For example, if you are applying hard brakes and the right rear tandems on the trailer have locked up, but the other tires are still rolling, the trailer is going to come around to the right and try to take the lead. **ONCE THE ANGLE BETWEEN THE TRACTOR AND THE TRAILER REACHES 15 DEGREES**, a jackknife is inevitable. The way to prevent the trailer from coming around is to take your foot off the brake. Once the brakes release, the tires will begin to roll again, causing the trailer to fall back in line. But, **YOU MUST RELEASE THE BRAKES BEFORE THE ANGLE BETWEEN THE TRACTOR AND TRAILER REACHES THE 15-DEGREE MARK.**

"Bobtailing" (driving a tractor without a trailer) can be especially tricky. Bobtails, because of their weight distribution and stiff suspensions, can be especially difficult to stop, and especially easy to slide and to lose control. **TESTS HAVE**

SHOWN THAT IN CERTAIN SITUATIONS, IT TAKES A BOBTAIL LONGER TO STOP THAN A TRACTOR-TRAILER WITH A FULL LOAD.

The first key to operating a combination vehicle is to **ALWAYS MAINTAIN A 12 TO 15 SECOND EYE LEAD TIME.** In other words, always look down the road to a point that would take you 12 to 15 seconds to reach **AT HIGHWAY SPEEDS THAT WOULD BE AT LEAST 1/4 OF A MILE**; in the city, two to three blocks. By always maintaining a 12 to 15 second eye lead time, you will always have plenty of time to react to any situation in a calm and orderly fashion. You eliminate the need to make quick, panic stricken decisions.

The second key is to always maintain a safe following distance. **AT LESS THAN 40 MPH, ALLOW ONE SECOND FOR EVERY 10 FEET OF YOUR VEHICLE LENGTH.** For example, if you are driving a 40-foot vehicle at 35 mph—the proper following distance would be 4 seconds. **AT SPEEDS OVER 40 MPH, YOU ADD ONE SECOND**, so if the same 40-foot vehicle was traveling 55 mph, the safe following distance would be 5 seconds.

Jackknives

THERE ARE TWO TYPES OF JACKKNIVES; TRACTOR JACKKNIFE AND TRAILER JACKKNIFE (see diagram on the next page).

A tractor jackknife is when the tractor comes back toward the trailer.

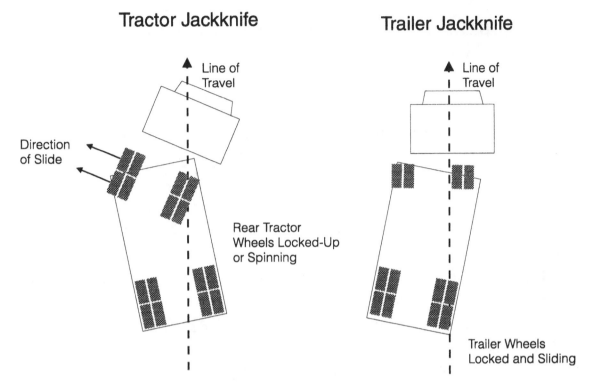

Tractor Jackknife

Line of Travel

Direction of Slide

Rear Tractor Wheels Locked-Up or Spinning

Trailer Jackknife

Line of Travel

Trailer Wheels Locked and Sliding

A trailer jackknife is when the trailer tries to come around or catch up to the tractor.

A JACKKNIFE CAN ONLY OCCUR IF THE BRAKES ARE APPLIED HARD ENOUGH TO LOCK THE WHEELS. This will occur more often with empty or lightly loaded trailers and when driving on wet, snowy or icy roads. Obviously the best way to avoid a jackknife is to avoid using hard brakes. Unfortunately, this is not always possible, so it is important that you recognize the jackknife before it gains control. One of the best defenses against a jackknife is to get into the habit of always checking your mirror whenever you apply the brakes, especially if you apply them hard. Check the rear of your trailer and make sure it is where it's supposed to be. If it isn't, you must get off your brakes quickly in order to pull it back into line where it belongs. **REMEMBER, A JACKKNIFE WILL OCCUR ONCE THE ANGLE BETWEEN THE TRAILER AND THE TRACTOR REACHES 15 DEGREES.**

Once you get "off the brakes" the trailer should pull back in line. Under no circumstances should you pull down the trolley valve (trailer hand valve)! Many drivers believe that by applying the hand valve the trailer will be pulled back in line. *This is absolutely false!* **APPLYING THE HAND VALVE WILL ONLY MAKE THE PROBLEM WORSE.** We repeat, the only way to stop a jackknife is to release the brakes. **ONCE THE WHEELS BEGIN TO GRIP THE ROAD**

AGAIN, THE TRAILER WILL START TO FOLLOW THE TRACTOR and you will then be able to breathe a sigh of relief.

Rollovers

Rollovers are one of the combination drivers biggest enemies. More than half of all truck driver deaths occur from crashes caused by rollovers.

What causes rollovers? A major contributing cause to rollover is improperly loaded trailers. All trucks have a high center of gravity (CG), and will tend to roll over more easily than a car. An improperly loaded truck becomes that much more dangerous. The higher the cargo, the higher the CG, and the greater the risk of rollover. **FULLY LOADED RIGS ARE 10 TIMES MORE LIKELY TO ROLL OVER IN A CRASH THAN EMPTY RIGS.**

What can you do to help prevent rollover? First: **ALWAYS LOAD YOUR LOAD PROPERLY**. If hauling freight, frozen, or flat-bed type products, **LOAD THE LOAD AS CLOSE TO THE GROUND AS POSSIBLE.** Second: **GO SLOWER THAN THE POSTED SPEED LIMITS ON CURVES, EXIT AND ENTRANCE RAMPS.** Third: **KEEP THE LOAD CEN-**

TERED ON THE RIG. Never load only on the rear or drive axle. Never load on one side of the trailer. It may not lean while you're loading it, but it will when you go around a curve. Fourth: Make sure cargo is properly braced, blocked and secured. Fifth: If you're hauling live-stock or liquids or swinging meat, try to pack your loads as tightly or as full as possible, using bulkheads when you can, to minimize sway or surge.

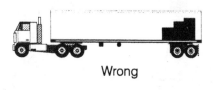

Wrong

Wrong

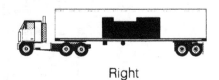

Right

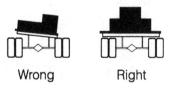

Wrong   Right

Steering

Steering actions with combination vehicles have to be made smoothly and gently. Combination vehicles have a problem that straight trucks don't have. That problem is called **REARWARD AMPLIFICATION**. In truck driver language we call that the "crack-the-whip-effect." When you make a rapid lane change, the movement is amplified (made larger or more powerful) at the rear of the trailer or trailers. Rearward amplification is worse for doubles and triples. Look at the following chart. This chart shows the rearward amplification for various tractor-trailer combinations. The ones at the top of the chart have the least rearward amplification, with the ones at the bottom having the worst. The numbers range from 1.0 to 4.0. A rearward amplification of 3.0 means that the rear trailer is three times more likely to turn over than the tractor. As the chart indicates, a set of triples has a rearward amplification of 3.5. This means that the last trailer is 3.5 times easier to turn over than the tractor. **IT IS ALWAYS THE REAR TRAILER MOST LIKELY TO TURN OVER.**

Influence of Combination Type
on Rearward Amplification

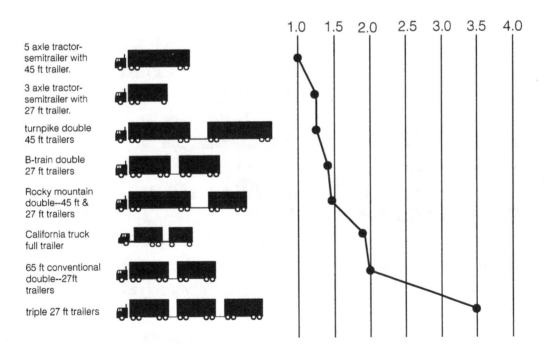

The best advice is to always steer gently and smoothly when pulling trailers, especially when pulling doubles or triples. Always allow yourself a safe following distance, maintain an eye lead time of 12 to 15 seconds, and drive slower than the posted speed limit on curves and ramps.

Turning

Combination vehicles turn different than straight trucks due to their length and points of articulation.

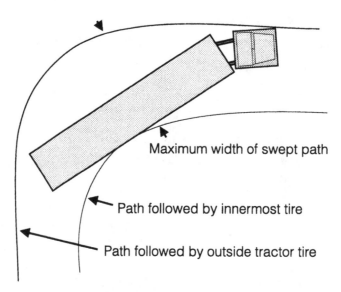

Maximum width of swept path

Path followed by innermost tire

Path followed by outside tractor tire

OFFTRACKING OR "CHEATING" MEANS THAT WHEN YOU TURN A CORNER OR GO AROUND A SHARP TURN, THE TRAILER WILL TAKE A DIFFERENT PATH THAN THE TRACTOR.

Longer trailers will offtrack more than shorter ones, and doubles will tend to offtrack shorter than a tractor pulling a 45-foot van due to the fact that doubles have three points of articulation compared to only one for the tractor-trailer.

When turning at a corner, **STAY IN YOUR LANE AND AS CLOSE TO THE CURB AS LONG AS POSSIBLE**. This will prevent a car or motorcycle from squeezing in between the rear of your trailer and the curb. See the pictures on the next page for the right and wrong way to make a turn.

When making a turn, always watch the rear of your trailer to make sure it is not running over on the curb and possibly striking a pedestrian. If the turn is so sharp that you can't make it without swinging into another lane of traffic, that's OK, just swing wide at the end of your turn instead of at the beginning; that way you'll still miss the curb and prevent another motorist from squeezing between your trailer and the curb.

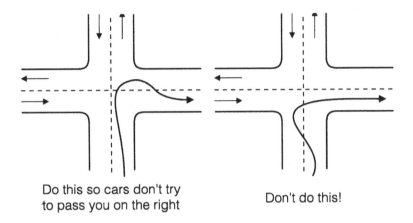

Do this so cars don't try
to pass you on the right

Don't do this!

Offtracking will normally occur on the
inside of the curve. In other words, if the
curve is to the right, the rear wheels of the
trailer will track to the right. *HOWEVER*,
on high-speed curves, such as freeway
ramps, this will not be true. It has been
proven that at higher speeds, the rear
wheels of the trailer will tend to track to
the outside. If the high-speed ramp curves
to the right, the trailer will track to the *left*
of where the tractor tires were tracking.

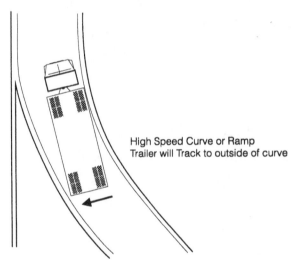

High Speed Curve or Ramp
Trailer will Track to outside of curve

Many rollovers have occurred because
the rear trailer tires have struck the curb on the opposite side of the direction of
the curve, causing the trailer to be "tripped" into a rollover.

Remember—When in a **LOW-SPEED CURVE**, the trailer's **WHEELS WILL
TRACK TO THE INSIDE** of the curve. When in a **HIGH-SPEED CURVE,
THEY WILL TRACK TO THE OUTSIDE.**

Combination Vehicle Air Brake

Before reading this section, you must read Chapter 5, Air Brakes. In this section,
we will discuss the operation of the air brakes and air-braking systems as they
pertain to combination vehicles. In order to understand what we will be talking
about, it is necessary to have a thorough knowledge of the basic air-braking system. So, if you haven't read Chapter 5 yet—do so now before continuing.

All air-brake systems work basically the same way. They all have an air compressor, governor, air lines, brake chamber, etc. The difference in the air-brake system on combination vehicles is that the air must be able to get to the trailer, or trailers, being pulled.

In this section we will discuss the parts found on combination vehicles, their purpose and their proper use. Those parts are:

- Trailer hand valve
- Tractor protection valve
- Trailer air supply control
- Trailer air lines
- Glad hand (hose couplers)
- Trailer air tanks
- Trailer service brakes
- Parking brakes
- Emergency brakes

When we finish our study of the combination vehicle air brake system, we will then spend some time discussing the proper method of coupling and uncoupling various combinations.

Now, let's talk about combination brake systems.

Trailer Hand Valve

As discussed previously, the trailer hand valve goes by many different names, such as trolley valve and Johnson bar. **THE TRAILER HAND VALVE SHOULD ONLY BE USED FOR TESTING THE TRAILER BRAKES. IT SHOULD *NEVER* BE USED WHILE DRIVING OR FOR PARKING.** It is very difficult to control the amount of pressure to the brakes when using the trailer hand valve. Too much pressure will result in trailer skid which may result in a jackknife. Why take the chance—*NEVER USE THE TRAILER HAND VALVE WHEN DRIVING.*

NEVER USE THE TRAILER HAND VALVE FOR PARKING. If the air leaks out of the system, the brakes will release and you might have a rolloff.

Parking Brake Valves

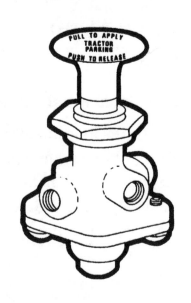

This will occur on trailers without spring brakes. Many older trailers are not equipped with spring brakes. Don't take a chance. **WHENEVER YOU PARK, USE YOUR PARKING BRAKES ONLY.** If your trailer does not have spring brakes, use wheel chocks to keep the trailer from moving.

Tractor Protection Valve

THE PURPOSE OF THE TRACTOR PROTECTION VALVE IS TO KEEP AIR IN THE TRACTOR IN THE EVENT THAT A BAD LEAK DEVELOPS OR THE TRAILER BREAKS AWAY AND RIPS OFF THE AIR LINES. The tractor protection valve is operated by the trailer air supply control valve. The trailer air supply control valve is a push-pull type knob located in the cab. It allows you to open and close the tractor protection valve. **IF AIR PRESSURE IN THE SYSTEM FALLS TO 20-40 LBS, THE TRACTOR PROTECTION VALVE WILL AUTOMATICALLY APPLY.** When this happens, all air is stopped from going out of the tractor. It also permits the air in the trailer air lines to escape, causing the trailer emergency brakes to come on. (More about emergency brakes later.)

Trailer Air Supply Control

On newer trucks, this control is a red, 8-sided knob. **THE TRAILER AIR SUPPLY CONTROL IS USED TO OPERATE THE TRACTOR PROTECTION VALVE.** Push-ing the knob in will supply the trailer with 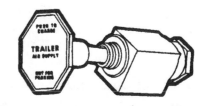 air. **PULLING IT OUT WILL SHUT OFF THE AIR AND CAUSE THE TRAILER EMERGENCY BRAKES TO COME ON. IN THE EVENT OF AN AIR LOSS, THIS VALVE WILL POP OUT WHEN THE AIR SYSTEM REACHES THE RANGE OF 20-40 PSI, CAUSING THE TRAILER EMERGENCY BRAKES TO APPLY.** In older vehicles, the tractor protection valve may not operate automatically. Some older vehicles may have a lever instead of a knob. In the case of a lever, the "normal" position supplies air to the trailer, the "emergency" position turns it off and applies the emergency brakes.

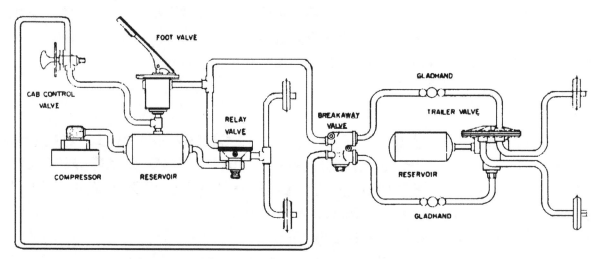

Courtesy of Sealco Air Controls, Inc. City of Industry, Calif.

Trailer Air Lines

All combination vehicles have two air lines. It is through these air lines that air travels from the tank to the trailer, dolly, and other trailer(s). The two lines are called the:

Service air line

Emergency air line (also known as supply line)

IT IS THE SERVICE AIR LINE WHICH IS CONTROLLED BY THE BRAKE PEDAL AND TRAILER HAND VALVE. By applying pressure to the brake pedal or pulling down the trailer hand valve, pressure is increased through the service air line and the brakes are applied in proportion to the pressure being applied by the driver. The service line is connected to **RELAY VALVES ON THE TRAILER. THE RELAY VALVES CONNECT THE TRAILER AIR TANK TO THE TRAILER AIR BRAKES.** When you step on the brake pedal or pull down the trailer hand valve, pressure is sent through the lines to the relay valves. The relay valves then open, sending air pressure to the brake chamber on the trailer, and the brakes are applied in direct proportion to the amount of pressure being applied by the driver.

THE EMERGENCY AIR LINE (also called the supply line) **DOES TWO THINGS**. First, **IT SUPPLIES AIR TO THE AIR TANKS ON THE TRAILER**. Second, **IT CONTROLS THE EMERGENCY BRAKES ON THE TRAILER.** When air pressure is lost due to the trailer breaking away and the air lines being torn off, or because of an air leak, the emergency air line loses air, causing the trailer brakes to lock up and the tractor protection valve to pop out, shutting off the air to the trailer.

TRAILER AIR LINES AND CONNECTIONS ARE OFTEN COLOR CODED; SERVICE AIR LINE IS USUALLY PAINTED BLUE, WHILE THE EMERGENCY LINE WILL BE PAINTED RED.

Glad Hands (Hose Couplers)

Glad hands are the coupling devices which connect the air lines from the tractor to the trailer. They are made out of metal with rubber seals (grommets). It is the rubber grommets that form an air-tight seal and prevent the air from escaping. To attach the glad hands to the connection on the trailer, you simply press the rubber grommets together with the glad hands at a 90-degree angle to each other, and turn or twist downward. By turning the glad hand, which is connected to the air line, the connection is made. In order for the connection to be air tight, the grommets must be clean and the connection must be secure.

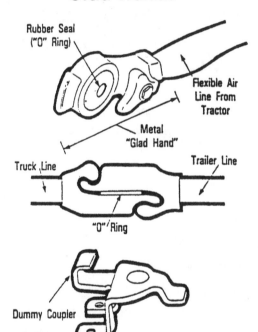

Glad Hands

IT IS IMPORTANT THAT WHEN THE GLAD HANDS ARE NOT ATTACHED TO THE TRAILER THAT THEY BE STORED IN SUCH A WAY AS TO PREVENT WATER AND DIRT FROM GETTING INTO THEM, AS THE WATER AND DIRT WILL END UP IN YOUR AIR SYSTEM. Many tractors have dummy couplers to which the glad hands may be attached. If your vehicle does not have dummy couplers, you may be able to connect your glad hands together. If that is not possible, wrap a plastic bag around each one and secure with a rubber band.

When coupling the glad hands to the trailer, it is necessary that they be coupled to the proper air line. In other words, the glad hand attached to the service air hose *must be* attached to the service glad hand on the trailer. The same is true for the emergency air line. To make identification easier, you will often see color coding being used. <u>**BLUE FOR SERVICE LINE AND RED FOR THE EMERGENCY LINES.**</u>

If you do make a mistake and cross the air lines, you'll discover it as soon as you attempt to release the trailer brakes by pushing in the trailer air supply knob. The parking brakes on the trailer will not release. This is because no air will be getting to the trailer, which is necessary for the spring (parking) brakes to be released. <u>**REMEMBER, IT TAKES AIR PRESSURE TO PULL THE SPRING BRAKES AWAY FROM THE BRAKE DRUM.**</u>

A word of caution. <u>**MANY OLDER TRAILERS DO NOT HAVE SPRING BRAKES. IF YOU ARE HOOKING UP A TRAILER THAT DOES NOT HAVE SPRING BRAKES AND YOU CROSSED YOUR AIR LINES, IT IS POSSIBLE THAT YOU COULD DRIVE AWAY AND NOT HAVE ANY TRAILER BRAKES.**</u> If you couple correctly and do a proper pre-trip inspection, you will never have this problem. Remember, the last step in your pre-trip inspection is to test your brakes. <u>**YOU CHECK YOUR TRAILER BRAKES BY MOVING SLOWLY AND PULLING DOWN THE TRAILER HAND VALVE GENTLY.**</u>

Trailer Air Tank

All trailers and dollies have one or more air tanks. The air tanks on a trailer and dolly are supplied with air from the emergency air line. Once the air tanks are filled, it is the pressure in the service air line which tells the relay valves how much air pressure to send to the brakes.

As discussed in Chapter 5, never allow oil and water to build up in the air tanks. <u>**TRAILER AIR TANKS MUST BE DRAINED EVERY DAY.**</u> If equipped with automatic air drains, they will expel the oil and water regularly. Remember, a build-up of oil and water in the tanks will cause problems, especially in freezing temperatures.

Trailer Service Brakes—Parking Brakes—Emergency Brakes

Before 1975, trailers and converter dollies were not equipped with spring brakes. Many pre-1975 vehicles are still on the road today. In equipment without spring brakes, the emergency brakes are activated by air stored in the tanks in the event of an air loss. Whenever air pressure is lost in the air lines, the emergency brakes will come on. Keep in mind: <u>**TRAILERS OR DOLLIES WITHOUT SPRING BRAKES HAVE NO PARKING BRAKES. THE EMERGENCY**</u>

BRAKES COME ON WHENEVER THE TRAILER AIR SUPPLY KNOB IS PULLED OUT OR WHENEVER THE TRAILER IS DISCONNECTED FROM THE TRACTOR. But, here's the problem. When the air leaks out of the air tanks, and it will—the brakes will release, since they have no springs to keep them applied against the brake drum. Therefore, **YOU MUST USE CHOCKS WHEN PARKING A TRAILER WITH NO SPRING BRAKES.**

Two final points:

1. **A MAJOR LEAK** or rupture **IN THE EMERGENCY AIR LINE** will cause the **EMERGENCY BRAKES TO BE APPLIED WHEN THE AIR PRESSURE FALLS BETWEEN 20 TO 40 PSI.**

2. **A MAJOR LEAK OR RUPTURE IN THE SERVICE AIR LINE MAY NOT BE NOTICED UNTIL THE BRAKE PEDAL IS APPLIED.** Air will then be rapidly pushed out of the system, lowering the air pressure in the tank very quickly, and causing the trailer brakes to come on.

Coupling and Uncoupling Combination Vehicles

The ability to correctly couple and uncouple combination vehicles is critical for the safe operation of any combination vehicle.

This section will deal first with the coupling of a tractor semi-trailer; you must become familiar with each step of the coupling and uncoupling process. We will also then discuss the coupling and uncoupling of doubles/triples. Only those drivers who operate doubles/triples and will be obtaining the double/triples endorsement will need to study this section.

Coupling Tractor Semitrailers

Step 1. Inspect Fifth Wheel

- Check for damaged/missing parts.
- Check to see that mounting to tractor is secure, no cracks in frame, etc.
- Be sure that the fifth wheel plate is lubricated as required. Failure to keep the fifth wheel plate lubricated could cause steering

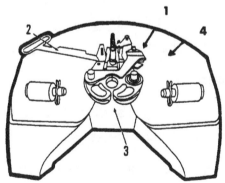

Blowup of Fifth Wheel Components

1. Coupler Arm
2. Release Handle
3. Locking Jaws
4. Skid plate
   (also called lower coupler)

problems because of friction between the tractor and trailer.

- Check if fifth wheel is in proper position for coupling.
  —Wheel tilted down towards rear of tractor.
- Jaws open and fifth wheel handle in automatic lock position.
- If your trailer has a sliding fifth wheel, make sure it is locked.
- Make sure the trailer kingpin is not bent or broken.

Step 2. Inspect Area and Chock Wheels

- Make sure area around the vehicle is clear of debris, vehicles or people.
- **<u>BE SURE TRAILER WHEELS ARE CHOCKED OR SPRING BRAKES ARE ON.</u>**
- Check that cargo (if any) is secured against movement which may occur as tractor and trailer are being coupled.

Step 3. Position Tractor

- **<u>POSITION THE TRACTOR DIRECTLY IN FRONT OF THE TRAILER. (NEVER BACK UNDER THE TRAILER AT AN ANGLE, BECAUSE YOU MIGHT PUSH THE TRAILER SIDEWAYS AND BREAK THE LANDING GEAR.)</u>**
- Check tractor position, using outside mirrors, and look down both sides of the trailer.

Step 4. Back Slowly

- **<u>BACK UNTIL THE FIFTH WHEEL JUST TOUCHES THE TRAILER.</u>**
- **<u>DON'T HIT THE TRAILER.</u>** If the trailer has no spring brakes and is not chocked, hitting it may send it rolling backwards.

Step 5. Secure Tractor

- Apply parking brake.
- Place transmission in neutral.

Step 6. Check Trailer Height

- **<u>THE TRAILER SHOULD BE LOW ENOUGH THAT IT IS RAISED SLIGHTLY BY THE TRACTOR WHEN THE TRACTOR IS BACKED UNDER IT. RAISE OR LOWER THE TRAILER AS NEEDED. (IF TRAILER IS TOO LOW, TRACTOR MAY STRIKE AND DAMAGE NOSE OF</u>**

TRAILER; IF TRAILER IS TOO HIGH, IT MAY NOT COUPLE COR-RECTLY. This is called a "high hook.")

- Make sure the kingpin and fifth wheel are aligned.

Step 7. Connect Air Lines to Trailer

- Check and clean glad hand seals and connect tractor emergency air line to trailer emergency glad hand.
- Check and clean glad hand seals and connect tractor service air line to trailer service glad hand.
- Make sure air lines are safely supported where they won't be crushed or caught while tractor is backing under the trailer.

Step 8. Supply Air to Trailer

- From cab, push in "air supply" knob or move tractor protection valve control from the "emergency" to the "normal" position to supply air to the trailer brake system.
- Wait until the air pressure is normal, 90 to 120 lbs.
- **CHECK BRAKE SYSTEM FOR CROSSED AIR LINES.**
  - **—SHUT ENGINE OFF SO YOU CAN HEAR THE BRAKES.**
  - **—APPLY AND RELEASE TRAILER BRAKES. LISTEN FOR SOUND OF TRAILER BRAKES BEING APPLIED AND RELEASED. YOU**

SHOULD HEAR THE BRAKES MOVE WHEN APPLIED AND AIR ESCAPE WHEN THE BRAKES ARE RELEASED.

—Check air brake system pressure gauge for signs of air loss. If any, check glad hands. Correct all air leaks before beginning trip.

- When you are sure trailer brakes are working, start engine.
- Make sure air pressure is up to normal.

Step 9. Lock Trailer Brakes

- **PULL OUT THE "AIR SUPPLY" KNOB, OR MOVE THE TRACTOR PROTECTION VALVE CONTROL FROM "NORMAL" TO "EMERGENCY."** This reapplies the trailer brakes and prevents trailer from moving during the coupling process.

Step 10. Back Under Trailer

- Use lowest reverse gear.
- Back tractor *slowly* under trailer to avoid hitting the kingpin too hard.
- Stop when the kingpin is locked into the fifth wheel and you hear the sound of the fifth wheel locking into place.

Step 11. Check Connection for Security

- Raise trailer landing gear slightly off ground. Use low gear on dolly crank.
- **PULL TRACTOR GENTLY FORWARD WHILE THE TRAILER BRAKES ARE STILL LOCKED TO CHECK THAT THE TRAILER IS LOCKED ONTO THE TRACTOR.**

Step 12. Secure Vehicle

- Put transmission in neutral.
- Apply parking brakes.
- **TURN OFF ENGINE AND TAKE KEY WITH YOU SO SOMEONE ELSE WON'T MOVE TRUCK WHILE YOU ARE UNDER IT.**

Step 13. Inspect Coupling

- Use a flashlight if necessary.
- **MAKE SURE THERE IS NO SPACE BETWEEN UPPER AND LOWER FIFTH WHEEL. IF THERE IS SPACE, SOMETHING IS WRONG (KINGPIN MAY BE ON TOP OF CLOSED FIFTH WHEEL JAWS; TRAILER WOULD COME LOOSE VERY EASILY).** Again, this

is called a "high hook."

Please note: The "upper" fifth wheel refers to the plate on the bottom of the trailer that the kingpin is attached to. The "lower" fifth wheel is the actual fifth wheel on the tractor.

- **<u>GO UNDER TRAILER AND LOOK INTO THE BACK OF THE FIFTH WHEEL. MAKE SURE THE FIFTH WHEEL JAWS HAVE CLOSED AROUND THE SHANK OF THE KINGPIN.</u>**
- Check that the locking lever is in the "lock" position.
- **<u>CHECK THAT THE SAFETY CATCH IS IN POSITION OVER THE LOCKING LEVER</u>**. (On some fifth wheels, the catch must be put in place by hand.)
- **<u>IF THE COUPLING ISN'T RIGHT, DON'T DRIVE THE COUPLED UNIT; GET IT FIXED.</u>**

Upper Coupler

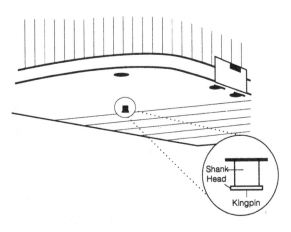

Step 14. Connect the Electrical Cord and Check Air Lines

- Plug the electrical cord into the trailer and fasten the safety catch located in the cover of the electrical plug.
- Check both air lines and electrical line for signs of damage.
- Make sure air and electrical lines will not hit any parts of the vehicle. This will cause chafing which can put you out of service.

Step 15. Raise Front Trailer Supports (Landing Gear)

- Use low gear range (if so equipped) to begin raising the landing gear by turning the crank handle. Once free of weight, switch to the high gear range. Pulling out on the crank handle will place landing gear in high range. Pushing in will put it into low range.

- **RAISE THE LANDING GEAR ALL THE WAY UP. (NEVER DRIVE WITH LANDING GEAR ONLY PART WAY UP, AS IT MAY CATCH ON RAILROAD TRACKS OR OTHER THINGS.)**
- After raising landing gear, secure the crank handle safely.
- When full weight of trailer is resting on tractor:
  —Check for enough clearance between rear of tractor frame and landing gear. (When tractor turns sharply, it must not hit landing gear.)
  —Check that there is enough clearance between the top of the tractor tires and the nose of the trailer.

Step 16. Remove Trailer Wheel Chocks

- Remove and store wheel chocks in a safe place.

Uncoupling Tractor Semitrailers

The following steps will assist in uncoupling safely.

Step 1. Position Rig

- Make sure surface of parking area can support weight of trailer. If you have any doubt, choose another location or place supports under the landing gear.
- Have tractor lined up straight with the trailer. **(PULLING OUT AT AN ANGLE CAN DAMAGE LANDING GEAR.)**

Step 2. Ease Pressure on Locking Jaws

- Shut off trailer air supply to lock trailer brakes.
- Ease pressure on fifth wheel locking jaws by backing up gently (this will remove the tension on the fifth wheel locking lever).
- Apply parking brakes while the tractor is pushing against the kingpin. This will hold rig with pressure off the locking jaws.

Step 3. Chock Trailer Wheels

- **CHOCK THE TRAILER WHEELS IF THE TRAILER DOESN'T HAVE SPRING BRAKES OR IF YOU'RE NOT SURE.** (The air could leak out of the trailer air tank, releasing its emergency brakes. The trailer could then move if it didn't have chocks.)

Step 4. Lower The Landing Gear

- If trailer is empty—lower the landing gear until it makes firm contact with ground.
- If trailer is loaded—after the landing gear makes firm contact with the ground, turn crank in low gear a few extra turns; this will lift some weight off the tractor. (Do not lift trailer off the fifth wheel.) This will:
—make it easier to uncouple the fifth wheel;
—make it easier to couple next time.

Step 5. Disconnect Air Lines and Electrical Cable

- Disconnect air lines from trailer. Connect air line glad hands to dummy couplers at back of cab, or couple them together.
- Hang electrical cable with plug down to prevent moisture from entering it. Some tractors have holders designed for this purpose.
- Make sure lines are supported so they won't be damaged while driving the tractor.

Step 6. Unlock Fifth Wheel

- Raise release handle lock.
- Pull the release handle to "open" position.
- **KEEP LEGS AND FEET CLEAR OF THE REAR TRACTOR WHEELS TO AVOID SERIOUS INJURY IN CASE THE VEHICLE MOVES.**

Step 7. Pull Tractor Partially Clear of Trailer

- Pull tractor forward until fifth wheel comes out from under the trailer.
- **STOP WITH TRACTOR FRAME UNDER TRAILER (PREVENTS TRAILER FROM FALLING TO GROUND IF LANDING GEAR SHOULD COLLAPSE OR SINK).** If this happens and the tractor frame is still under trailer, you may be able to back under the trailer, thus avoiding an accident.

Step 8. Secure Tractor

- Apply parking brake.
- Place transmission in neutral.

Step 9. Inspect Trailer Supports

- Make sure ground is supporting trailer.
- Make sure landing gear is not damaged.

Step 10. Pull Tractor Clear of Trailer

- Release parking brakes.
- Check the area and proceed away from trailer.

Combination Vehicle Brake Check

In addition to the following items, when checking air brake systems, you must also check items which were discussed in Chapter 5, Air Brake Systems.

After hooking up doubles and triples, it is necessary that you check their air systems to determine that air is traveling through the system properly. Secure the tractor with the parking brakes and/or wheel chocks. After air pressure has reached the "normal" stage (90-120 lbs), push in the red "trailer air supply" knob. This will supply air to the emergency (supply) lines, then pull down and secure the trailer hand valve which will provide the service line with air. You then walk back to the rear of the last trailer and open and close first the supply line (usually painted red) and then the service line (usually painted blue). **WHEN YOU OPEN THEM, YOU SHOULD HEAR AIR ESCAPING**. That tells you that the air lines are open and that each trailer is receiving air. **IF YOU DO NOT HEAR AIR ESCAPING, CHECK THE OTHER TRAILER(S) AND DOLLY(S) TO MAKE SURE THAT THE SHUT-OFF VALVES ARE OPEN.** You must have air to all trailers in order for the brakes to work.

TEST TRACTOR PROTECTION VALVE. With the air system fully charged, turn off the engine. Turn key switch back on, push in the "air supply" knob and then begin to pump and release the brake pedal. At approximately 60 psi, the low air warning buzzer should come on. **CONTINUE PUMPING THE BRAKE PEDALS UNTIL AIR PRESSURE REACHES 20-40 PSI, AT WHICH POINT THE AIR SUPPLY KNOB (ALSO KNOWN AS THE TRACTOR PROTECTION VALVE) SHOULD POP BACK OUT.** If this doesn't happen, or if the alarm buzzer doesn't come on, get the system checked before driving.

TEST TRAILER EMERGENCY BRAKES. With the air system completely charged, release the brakes and make sure the units roll easily. Then **STOP AND PULL OUT THE TRAILER AIR SUPPLY KNOB OR PLACE IT IN THE EMERGENCY POSITION, TUG GENTLY ON THE TRAILER TO TEST THAT THE BRAKE ARE HOLDING.** If not, get the system checked and/or brakes adjusted.

TEST TRAILER SERVICE BRAKES. With air system fully charged, **BEGIN ROLLING SLOWLY AND THEN PULL DOWN THE TRAILER HAND VALVE (TRAILER VALVE), IF SO EQUIPPED. BRAKES SHOULD COME ON FIRMLY AND STOP THE VEHICLE FROM MOVING.** If not, get brakes adjusted. **REMEMBER—*NEVER* USE THE TRAILER HAND VALVE WHEN DRIVING.**

STOP

WATCH VIDEO ON COMBINATION VEHICLES

☞ LET'S TAKE A TEST

Combination Vehicle Test

Study each question carefully and indicate your choice by drawing a circle around the letter you have chosen. Any questions with an asterisk (*) should only be answered by the person taking the doubles/triples test (see Chapter 7).

1. Which of the following statements is true?

    A. it takes longer to stop a loaded vehicle
    B. it takes longer to stop a empty vehicle
    C. it takes the same amount of time to stop a loaded vehicle as it does to stop an empty one.
    D. none of the above are true

2. Jackknife will occur once the angle between the tractor and trailer reaches:

    A. 10 degrees
    B. 25 degrees
    C. 15 degrees
    D. 5 degrees

3. Your 60-foot vehicle is traveling 45 mph; what is the proper following distance?

    A. 7 seconds
    B. 5 seconds
    C. 4 seconds
    D. 6 seconds

4. How far down the road should you look when driving? (This is called eye-lead time.)

    A. 5-8 seconds
    B. 12-15 seconds
    C. 3-5 seconds
    D. 17-20 seconds

5. The trailer air supply control:

    A. is used for parking for short periods of time
    B. connects the trailer air tank to the trailer air brakes
    C. connects the tractor air supply to the trailer
    D. operates the tractor protection valve, in the event of a rapid air loss, will cause the emergency brakes on trailer to be applied

6. The emergency air line is:

   A. also called the supply line which supplies air to the trailer and controls the trailer emergency brakes
   B. always painted blue for easy identification
   C. a red 8-sided push/pull knob
   D. used only in emergency situations

7. You should use wheel chocks when:

   A. trailer is not equipped with spring brakes
   B. you're not sure if trailer has spring brakes
   C. always
   D. both A and B

8. Name the two types of jackknives.

   1. tractor
   2. trailer

9. Which is true concerning the use of the trailer hand valve?

   A. it should be used in order to save wear and tear on tractor brakes.
   B. it should be applied with a light steady pressure when going down a long grade.
   C. it should never be used for braking when driving.
   D. both A and B.

10. If you are using the proper eye-lead time, the distance down the road at which you will be looking, at highway speeds will be approximately:

    A. two blocks
    B. 1/2 mile
    C. 800 feet
    D. 1/4 mile

11. In order to prevent rollover, which of the following is most helpful?

    A. go slow around turns
    B. never accept high center-of-gravity loads
    C. load cargo as close to the ground as possible
    D. both A and C

12. The service air line:

    A. allows air to travel from air compressor governor to the air compressor
    B. pops off when air pressure falls below 20 psi
    C. is used only when pulling doubles
    D. is operated by the brake pedal and trailer hand valve

13. When coupling to the trailer, the fifth wheel must:

    A. be properly lubricated
    B. be tilted down towards rear of tractor
    C. have unlocking handle in automatic lock position
    D. all of the above

14. It is OK to use the trailer hand valve to straighten out a jackknifing trailer:

    A. only if on dry roads
    B. never
    C. if used with slight, steady pressure
    D. only if you are an experienced driver

*15. When pulling doubles, which unit is more likely to turn over?

    A. lead trailer
    B. both trailers equally
    C. rear trailer
    D. converter dolly

16. When cranking up the landing gear, which statement is true?

    A. landing gears should be cranked up just high enough to clear the ground
    B. landing gears should be cranked up as high as they will go and crank handle secured
    C. landing gears should be cranked up as high as they will go
    D. landing gears should be cranked up and then removed for safekeeping

*17. When pulling triples, the heaviest trailer should be the:

    A. rear trailer
    B. lead trailer
    C. middle trailer
    D. doesn't make any difference

18. Offtracking can best be described as:

 A. the rear wheels of the trailer will track further to the inside of a turn than the wheels of the tractor

 B. the rear wheels of the trailer will track further to the outside of a turn than the wheels of the tractor

 C. the tractor wheels will track further to the outside of a turn than the wheels of the trailer

 D. the tractor wheels will track further to the inside of a turn than the wheels of the trailer

*19. A converter dolly is:

 A. a toy to be given to a little girl

 B. a device used to connect two trailers together

 C. a device that is used to convert a semitrailer into a full trailer

 D. a device used to convert the single air system to a dual air system

20. If trailer is carrying a load, when you crank down the landing gear, you should:

 A. lower it until it just touches the ground

 B. after it has touched ground, crank a few extra turns

 C. lower it until it almost touches the ground

 D. none of the above

21. When uncoupling and you are pulling tractor away from trailer, you should:

 A. pull out quickly

 B. pull out slowly

 C. pull out smoothly and slowly, stop when fifth wheel is free but tractor frame is still under trailer

 D. pull out as fast as possible so that if landing gear collapses, the trailer will not crush the tractor tires

22. When bobtailing, the glad hands should be secured in such a way as to:

 A. prevent water from getting in them

 B. prevent dirt from getting in them

 C. prevent rubbing and chafing against other tractor parts

 D. all of the above

23. If glad hands, after connected properly to trailer, leak air, you should:

   A. replace them
   B. sand or grind down the metal parts in order to form a better connection
   C. hook-up to a different trailer
   D. check and clean the rubber grommets and then re-connect and test

24. It is OK to use the trailer hand valve to park when:

   A. it is only for a short time
   B. if the trailer does not have spring brakes
   C. if the tractor brakes are not working
   D. never

25. Air tanks should be drained:

   A. daily
   B. hourly
   C. once each trip
   D. weekly

26. After coupling to a trailer, you should:

   A. raise landing gear slightly off the ground and then tug gently with the tractor to test connection
   B. not check coupling since you heard the jaws latch
   C. crawl under trailer and visually check the connection
   D. both A and C

27. How much space is permitted between the upper and lower fifth wheel plates?

   A. none
   B. up to 1/4 inch
   C. up to 1/2 inch
   D. up to 1 inch

*28. When pulling doubles, the heaviest trailer should be:

   A. the rear trailer
   B. the lead trailer
   C. doesn't make a difference
   D. each state has separate regulations covering it

*29. The shut-off valves must be in what positions when pulling doubles?

    A. lead trailer *open*; rear trailer *closed*; dolly air tank *closed*

    B. lead trailer *closed*; rear trailer *open*; dolly air tank *closed*

    C. lead trailer *closed*; rear trailer *closed*; dolly air tank *open*

    D. lead trailer *open*; rear trailer *closed*; dolly air tank *open*

*30. When dropping the rear trailer, you must:

    A. leave dolly under rear trailer for support

    B. pull dolly out from under rear trailer before disconnecting from front trailer

    C. do either A or B; it doesn't matter

    D. check with the state regulations which govern how they must be dropped

Answers

1. B	11. D	21. C
2. C	12. D	22. D
3. A	13. D	23. D
4. B	14. B	24. D
5. D	15. C	25. A
6. A	16. B	26. D
7. D	17. B	27. A
8. Trailer, Tractor	18. A	28. B
9. C	19. B	29. A
10. D	20. B	30. B

If you were able to answer all of the questions correctly—*GOOD JOB!* If you missed any, read the material again until you know it with 100% accuracy.

Doubles and Triples

Who Must Study This Chapter?

Any driver who intends to pull doubles or triples must study this chapter and take the doubles and triples endorsement test.

You must use extra caution when pulling doubles and triples. The safety record in the trucking industry for doubles and triples is excellent. The reason for such a good safety record is that professional drivers take extra care when pulling doubles and triples.

Doubles and triples are less stable than a regular tractor semi-trailer combination. Because of the **"CRACK-THE-WHIP EFFECT,"** also known a **REARWARD AMPLIFICATION. THE LAST TRAILER IN THE COMBINATION IS MUCH MORE LIKELY TO TURN OVER. A FAST OR SUDDEN MOVEMENT WITH THE STEERING WHEEL, ESPECIALLY AT HIGHWAY SPEEDS, CAN RESULT IN THE REAR TRAILER TIPPING OVER.** Also, because a double or triple combination has more articulation points they tend to wiggle a bit as they go down the highway. In other words, they can tend to be a bit "squirrely." This is why you will hear professional drivers refer to them as "wiggle wagons."

Since doubles and triples tend to be less stable than regular combination vehicles, you must make adjustments when pulling them. The four points to remember when pulling doubles and triples are:

1. Inspect completely
2. Look far ahead
3. Manage space
4. Extra caution in adverse conditions

Inspect Completely

Doubles and triples have more articulation points and more parts which need to be checked. You must check these additional items before leaving on a trip and make sure they are in good working order. You will check these items in addition to all of the other items that must be checked during your 7-point walkaround inspection:

1. **Converter dolly(s)** Check that fifth wheel is securely mounted to frame, no missing parts, sufficient grease, no space between fifth wheel and plate on bottom of trailer, jaws have locked around the shank properly, release arm is properly seated and safety latch is locked and kingpin is not bent.

2. **Air and electric lines** Make sure pigtail (light cord) is plugged in and secure, air lines and rubber grommets are clean and properly connected so no air is leaking. Check that all lines and cords are not damaged and have enough slack to make turns.

3. **Spare tire (if equipped)** Make sure spare tire is inflated and properly secured.

4. **Landing gear** Must be fully raised, no parts missing or damaged. Crank handle must be properly secured

5. **Safety chains** Make sure safety chains are secure, not damaged and connected in such a way as to allow turns; must not be dragging on ground.

6. **Pintle eye and hook** Must be connected properly and working properly.

7. Service and emergency lines shut-off valves in proper position. **THE SHUT-OFF VALVES ON THE FRONT TRAILER (AND THE MIDDLE TRAILER IF PULLING TRIPLES) MUST BE OPEN.** This allows air to travel back to the rear trailer(s). **THE SHUT-OFF VALVES AT THE REAR TRAILER MUST BE CLOSED.** This prevents the air from escaping from the system.

8. Petcock on dolly must be closed in order for air tank to fill.

Look Far Ahead

Since doubles and triples are less stable when going down the highway, you must look farther ahead. Remember what we learned in the General Knowledge chapter about **EYE-LEAD TIME**. It is critical that you look down the road at least **12–15 SECONDS**. At highway speeds, this will be at least **1/4 OF A MILE**. Be on the lookout for anything that may affect your path of travel. This will allow you to respond to an emergency more smoothly and *WITHOUT* sharp steering movements. Remember, **A SHARP STEERING MOVEMENT CAN RESULT IN THE REAR TRAILER TIPPING OVER.** Also, it is impossible to back up a set of doubles or triples. When driving in city traffic, looking far ahead may prevent you from getting into a situation where backing is necessary. Looking down the road **12-15 SECONDS** in the city means you will be looking at least *two to three city blocks* ahead.

Manage Space

Double and triple combinations take up more space. You must manage your space more efficiently than if you were driving a regular tractor-trailer combination. **ALWAYS ALLOW MORE FOLLOWING DISTANCE WHEN PULLING DOUBLES AND TRIPLES. DOUBLES AND TRIPLES CANNOT BE TURNED SHARPLY OR STOPPED QUICKLY. IF YOU TURN OR STOP QUICKLY, THEY MAY JACKKNIFE OR TIP OVER . . . OR BOTH**.

Managing your space means checking your mirrors frequently. You must always know where you are in relationship to all the other vehicles around you. This will allow you to make all steering and braking movements smoothly.

Adverse Conditions

Since double and triple combinations have more articulation points they are likely to lose traction and skid or spin out. This is especially true on wet, snow-covered and icy roads. Another reason they are likely to lose traction is because most doubles and triples are pulled by a tractor with a single axle, and because the total weight of the vehicle is distributed between many single axles.

When you encounter slippery road conditions or when driving in the mountains, you must exercise extra caution. Remember this: always apply power and brakes in moderation. If you are driving on a slippery road surface and you apply the brakes too hard . . . this can result in a skid. **IF A SKID DOES RESULT, THE ONLY WAY TO STOP IS TO RELEASE THE BRAKES.** If you don't take your foot off the brakes fast enough, it may result in a trailer jackknife. A spin-out can occur only on slippery surfaces if you apply too much pressure to the drive axle. In other words, you step on the accelerator too hard. If this occurs the only action you can take is to take your foot off the accelerator. If a spin-out occurs and you don't take your foot off the accelerator fast enough, it may result in a tractor jackknife.

One last thought about braking. **IT IS ILLEGAL AND UNSAFE TO DISCONNECT OR IN ANY WAY DISABLE THE BRAKES ON THE FRONT AXLE.** To do so *WILL* result in longer stopping distances and will *NOT* prevent a jackknife. Remember, a jackknife occurs when the wheels stop rolling and start skidding. It will *ALWAYS* be the skidding wheel that attempts to come around and take the lead.

Coupling and Uncoupling

Doubles and Triples

We will now discuss the proper coupling and uncoupling procedures for a twin trailer. If you are not going to apply for the doubles/triples endorsement, you will not be tested on coupling and uncoupling twin trailers.

Coupling Twin Trailers

Step 1. Secure Second (Rear) Trailer

- If the second trailer doesn't have spring brakes or if you are not sure, **DRIVE THE TRACTOR CLOSE TO THE TRAILER, CONNECT THE EMERGENCY LINE, CHARGE THE TRAILER AIR TANK**, and disconnect the emergency line. This will set the trailer emergency brakes (if the slack adjusters are correctly adjusted). Chock the wheels if you have any doubt about the brakes.

Step 1
Position Rear
Trailer

Step 2. Couple Tractor and First Semitrailer as Described Earlier.

- **CAUTION: FOR SAFE HANDLING ON THE ROAD, THE MORE HEAVILY LOADED SEMITRAILER MUST ALWAYS BE IN FIRST POSITION BEHIND THE TRACTOR. THE LIGHTER TRAILER SHOULD BE IN THE REAR.***

* Check with your company to see if they have a policy governing this.

Step 3. Position Converter Dolly in Front of Second (Rear) Trailer

- Release dolly brakes by opening the air tank petcock.** (Or, if the dolly has spring brakes, use the dolly parking brake control.)
- If distance is not too great, push dolly into position by hand so it is in line with the kingpin.
- Or, use tractor and first semitrailer to pick up the converter dolly (many tractors have pintle hooks on rear of tractor allowing dolly to be placed into position with tractor).

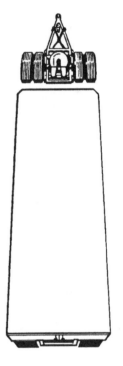

  —Position combination as close as possible to converter dolly.
  —Move dolly to rear of first semitrailer and couple it to the trailer.
  —Lock pintle hook.
  —Secure dolly support in raised position.
  —Pull dolly into position as close as possible to nose of the second semi-trailer.
  —Lower dolly support.
  —Unhook dolly from first trailer.
  —Push dolly into position in front of second trailer in line with the kingpin.

Step 3

** On dollies not equipped with spring brakes, opening the petcock allows all of the air to be drained out of the tank and releases brakes so that dolly can be moved into position.

Step 4. Connect Converter Dolly to Front Trailer

- Back first semi-trailer into position in front of dolly tongue.
- Hook dolly to front trailer.
—Lock pintle hook
—Secure converter gear support in raised position

Step 5. Connect Converter Dolly to Rear Trailer

- Make sure trailer brakes are locked and/or wheels chocked.
- Make sure trailer height is correct. (It must be slightly lower than the center of the fifth wheel, **SO TRAILER IS RAISED SLIGHTLY WHEN DOLLY IS PUSHED UNDER.**)
- Back converter dolly under rear trailer.
- Raise landing gear slightly off ground to prevent damage if trailer moves.

Step 4

Step 5

- Test coupling by pulling against kingpin of number two semitrailer.
- Make visual check of coupling. (No space between upper and lower fifth wheel; locking jaws closed on kingpin.)
- Connect safety chains, air hoses and light cords.
- Close converter dolly air tank petcock, and *SHUT-OFF VALVES** at rear of second trailer (*SERVICE AND EMERGENCY SHUT-OFFS*).
- Open shut-off valves at rear of first trailer (and on dolly if so equipped).
- Raise landing gear completely.
- Charge trailers (push "air supply" knob in) and **CHECK FOR AIR AT REAR OF SECOND TRAILER BY OPENING THE EMERGENCY LINE SHUT-OFF**. If air pressure isn't there, something is wrong and the brakes won't work.

---

* Shut-off valves are located at the rear of trailers used to tow other trailers. They permit the service and supply air lines to be opened or closed. They must all be open on the lead or middle trailer so that air can be supplied to the rear trailer. The shut-off valve must be closed on the rear trailer to prevent air from escaping.

Uncoupling Twin Trailers

Uncouple Rear Trailer

- Park rig in a straight line on firm level ground.
- Apply parking brakes so rig won't move.
- Chock wheels of second trailer if it doesn't have spring brakes.
- Lower landing gear of second semitrailer enough to remove some weight from dolly.
- Close air shut-offs at rear of first semitrailer (and on dolly if so equipped).
- Disconnect all dolly air and electric lines and secure them.
- Release dolly brakes.
- Release converter dolly fifth wheel latch.
- Slowly pull tractor, first semitrailer and dolly forward to pull dolly out from under rear semitrailer.

Uncouple Converter Dolly

- Lower dolly landing gear.
- Disconnect safety chains.
- Apply converter gear spring brakes or chock wheels.
- Release pintle hook on first semi-trailer.
- Slowly pull clear of dolly.

Caution: **NEVER UNLOCK THE PINTLE HOOK WITH THE DOLLY STILL UNDER THE REAR TRAILER. THE DOLLY TOW BAR MAY FLY UP, POSSIBLY CAUSING INJURY, AND MAKING IT VERY DIFFICULT TO RE-COUPLE.**

Coupling and Uncoupling Triple Trailers

Couple Second and Third Trailers

- Couple second and third trailers using the method for coupling doubles.
- Uncouple tractor and pull away from second and third trailers.

Couple Tractor/First Semi-Trailer to Second/Third Trailers

- Couple tractor to first trailer. Use the method already described for coupling tractor semitrailers.

- Move converter dolly into position and couple first trailer to second trailer using the method for coupling doubles. Triples rig is now complete.

Uncouple Triple-Trailer Rig

- Uncouple third trailer by pulling the dolly out, then unhitching the dolly, using the method for uncoupling doubles.
- Uncouple remainder of rig as you would any double-bottom rig using the method already described.

Inspecting a Combination Vehicle

Use the seven-step procedure as described in Chapter 1. Combination vehicles have more items to check. During your walkaround inspection the following items must be checked, in addition to the items which are checked on a single vehicle:

Coupling System Areas

- Check fifth wheel (lower)
  —Securely mounted to frame
  —No missing, damaged parts
  —Enough grease
  —**<u>NO VISIBLE SPACE BETWEEN UPPER AND LOWER FIFTH WHEEL</u>**
  —**<u>LOCKING JAWS AROUND THE SHANK, NOT THE HEAD OF KINGPIN</u>**
  —Release arm properly seated and safety latch/lock engaged
- Fifth wheel (upper)
  —Glide plate securely mounted to trailer frame
  —Kingpin not damaged
- Air and electric lines to trailer
  —Electrical cord firmly plugged in and secured
  —Air lines properly connected to glad hands, no air leaks, properly secured with enough slack for turns
  —All lines free from damage
- Sliding fifth wheel
  —Slide not damaged or parts missing
  —Properly greased
  —All locking pins present and locked in place

—If air powered—no air leaks.

—Check that fifth wheel is not so far forward that tractor frame will hit landing gear, or cab hit the trailer, during turns

Landing Gear

- *FULLY RAISED*, no missing parts, not bent or otherwise damaged
- Crank handle in place and secured
- If power operated, no air or hydraulic leaks
- <u>**SHUT-OFF VALVES (AT REAR OF TRAILERS, IN SERVICE AND EMERGENCY LINES):**</u>
  <u>**—REAR OF FRONT TRAILERS: OPEN**</u>
  <u>**—REAR OF LAST TRAILER: CLOSED**</u>
- Be sure air lines are supported and glad hands are properly connected.
- If spare tire is carried on converter gear (dolly), make sure it's secured.
- Be sure pintle-eye of dolly is in place in pintle hook of trailer(s).
- <u>**MAKE SURE PINTLE HOOK IS LATCHED.**</u>
- Safety chains should be secured to trailer(s). Chains should be crossed in order to form a "cradle" for the converter dolly tongue in the event the pintle hook comes unlatched.
- Be sure light cords are firmly in sockets on trailers.

Brake Check

In addition to the following items, when checking air brake systems, you must also check items which were discussed In Chapter 5, Air Brake Systems.

After hooking up doubles and triples, it is necessary that you check their air systems to determine that air is traveling through the system properly. Secure the tractor with the parking brakes and/or wheel chocks. After air pressure has reached the "normal" stage (90-120 lbs), push in the red "trailer air supply" knob. This will supply air to the emergency (supply) lines, then pull down and secure the trailer hand valve which will provide the service line with air. You then walk back to the rear of the last trailer and open and close first the supply line (usually painted red) and then the service line (usually painted blue). <u>**WHEN YOU OPEN THEM, YOU SHOULD HEAR AIR ESCAPING.**</u> That tells you that the air lines are open and that each trailer is receiving air. <u>**IF YOU DO NOT HEAR AIR ESCAPING, CHECK THE OTHER TRAILER(S) AND DOLLY(S) TO**</u>

MAKE SURE THAT THE SHUT-OFF VALVES ARE OPEN. You must have air to all trailers in order for the brakes to work.

TEST TRACTOR PROTECTION VALVE. With the air system fully charged, turn off the engine. Turn key switch back on, push in the "air supply" knob and then begin to pump and release the brake pedal. At approximately 60 psi, the low air warning buzzer should come on. **CONTINUE PUMPING THE BRAKE PEDALS UNTIL AIR PRESSURE REACHES 20-40 PSI, AT WHICH POINT THE AIR SUPPLY KNOB (ALSO KNOWN AS THE TRACTOR PROTECTION VALVE) SHOULD POP BACK OUT.** If this doesn't happen, or if the alarm buzzer doesn't come on, get the system checked before driving.

TEST TRAILER EMERGENCY BRAKES. With the air system completely charged, release the brakes and make sure the units roll easily. Then **STOP AND PULL OUT THE TRAILER AIR SUPPLY KNOB OR PLACE IT IN THE EMERGENCY POSITION. TUG GENTLY ON THE TRAILER TO TEST THAT THE BRAKES ARE HOLDING.** If not, get the system checked and/or brakes adjusted.

TEST TRAILER SERVICE BRAKES. With air system fully charged, **BEGIN ROLLING SLOWLY AND THEN PULL DOWN THE TRAILER HAND VALVE (TRAILER VALVE), IF SO EQUIPPED. BRAKES SHOULD COME ON FIRMLY AND STOP THE VEHICLE FROM MOVING.** If not, get brakes adjusted. **REMEMBER—*NEVER* USE THE TRAILER HAND VALVE WHEN DRIVING.**

STOP

WATCH VIDEO ON DOUBLES AND TRIPLES

☞ LET'S TAKE A TEST

Doubles and Triples

Study each question carefully and indicate your choice by drawing a circle around the letter you have chosen.

1. While driving a set of doubles you must make a quick stop in order to avoid a crash. You should:

   A. push the brake pedal as hard as you can and hold it there
   B. use controlled or stab braking
   C. use light, steady pressure on the brake pedal
   D. use only the trailer brakes

2. You are driving a set of triples. Which trailer is most likely to turn over in an emergency maneuver?

   A. front trailer
   B. middle trailer
   C. rear trailer
   D. all are as likely to turn over

3. How can you check if air is going to the rear trailer in the combination?

   A. step on the brake pedal and watch for brake lights to come on
   B. you will hear air escaping if you open the emergency line shut-off on rear trailer
   C. watch the air gauge for a 30 psi drop in pressure
   D. open the petcock on the dolly and see if the unit rolls forward

4. If you are in a skid you should:

   A. steer counterclockwise
   B. pull down the trailer hand valve
   C. Jump!
   D. take your foot off the brake and restore traction to the tires

5. On slippery road you must avoid:

   A. braking too hard
   B. accelerating too hard
   C. rural roads
   D. both A and B

6. When pulling doubles and triples you should always look at least 12-15 seconds ahead. At highway speeds this will be:

   A. about 3/4 mile
   B. about 1/4 mile
   C. about 1 mile
   D. about 1/2 mile

7. Before hooking the dolly to the rear trailer, how do you tell if the trailer height is correct?

   A. it will be slightly lower than the center of the fifth wheel
   B. the center of the kingpin will line up with the locking jaws
   C. the kingpin will be resting on the fifth wheel
   D. the fifth wheel will be touching the trailer lip

8. Converter dollies:

   A. often do not have spring brakes
   B. have little braking power because they are small
   C. usually need a glad-hand converter
   D. all of the above

9. It is 12 noon and you are driving in a rainstorm. What should you do to make sure you are maintaining the proper following distance?

   A. allow the same amount of space you would allow at night
   B. allow much more space that is needed for ideal driving conditions
   C. allow one second to the space needed in good driving conditions
   D. allow one car length for every 10 mph

10. When is it okay to disconnect the steering axle brakes on your vehicle?

   A. never
   B. when the roads are slippery
   C. when driving in very heavy traffic
   D. when towing a trailer that has properly adjusted brakes

11. When making a lane change, when should you check your mirrors?

    A. after signaling the change
    B. right after starting the lane change
    C. after completing the lane change
    D. all of the above

12. Which of these statements is true?

    A. empty trucks have *SHORTER* stopping distances than full ones
    B. empty trucks may have less traction due to bouncing and wheel lockup
    C. you should always downshift while stopping an empty truck
    D. empty trucks should be stopped using *ONLY* the trailer hand valve

13. "Spot," convex or "bug-eye" mirrors:

    A. are not as good as regular flat mirrors
    B. make objects appear larger and closer than they really are
    C. are illegal in many states
    D. make objects appear small and farther away

14. You are doing a walkaround inspection of a set of doubles. You should be sure that the converter dolly air tank drain valves are _____ and the pintle hook is _____.

    A. open; free
    B. closed; latched
    C. open; latched
    D. closed; free

15. What is the best way to keep your brakes from overheating when going down hill?

    A. use the air brake coolers
    B. drive fast enough that the wind keeps them cool
    C. use only the trailer brakes
    D. never exceed the "safe speed." When "safe speed" is reached, apply brakes firmly until vehicle speed has dropped to about 5 mph under the "safe speed" and then release brakes.

16. You're visually checking the coupling of a converter dolly to the rear trailer. How much space should be between the upper and lower fifth wheel?

   A. it depends on how the vehicle is loaded
   B. none
   C. 1/2 inch to 3/4 inch
   D. drivers are not able to visually check this coupling point

17. You are driving a 73-foot long double trailer combination at 35 mph. Pavement is dry and visibility is excellent. How much following distance in seconds should you maintain at all times?

   A. 4 seconds
   B. 8 seconds
   C. 7 seconds
   D. 9 seconds

18. What is likely to happen if you disconnect the dolly from the front trailer while it is still under the rear trailer?

   A. the trailer brakes will unlock and the dolly will roll away
   B. the air lines will rupture
   C. the dolly tow bar may fly up and injure you
   D. nothing will happen

19. What is the best way to make sure that you supplied air to the rear trailer?

   A. open the emergency line shut-off
   B. open the hand valve with the rig securely parked
   C. watch for a drop of at least 30 psi on the air gauge
   D. apply the hand valve while traveling at 10 mph; it will stop in the same distance as one trailer traveling at 5 mph

20. When pulling more than one trailer, which of the following is correct?

   A. the heaviest trailer must be in the first position behind the tractor
   B. the lightest trailer must be in the first position behind the tractor
   C. you don't pull the trailers unless they are the same weight
   D. the short trailer goes in the front of the long one

Answers

1.	B	11.	D
2.	C	12.	B
3.	B	13.	D
4.	D	14.	B
5.	D	15.	D
6.	B	16.	B
7.	A	17.	C
8.	A	18.	C
9.	B	19.	A
10.	A	20.	A

Tank Vehicles

Who Must Study This Chapter?

Any driver who will be pulling a tanker used to carry liquid or liquid gas in a quantity of 1,000 or more gallons must study this chapter and take the Tank Vehicle Endorsement Test.

Pulling a tank vehicle requires special driving skills. It also requires that the driver be familiar with the particular type of tanker he/she will be pulling.

Tank vehicles come in all sizes and shapes but the one thing they have in common is a high center of gravity and the fact that they transport items which move. Liquid moves . . . Because liquid moves, it has a dramatic effect on the ride and stability of the vehicle. The liquid moves not only front to back, but also side to side. This movement is called **SURGE**. When **SURGE** is combined with a high-center-of gravity vehicle it is an altogether different experience than pulling a flatbed or reefer with freight sitting on the floor.

Tankers also have special requirements for loading and unloading and for protecting the material inside the tank. Special requirements are also necessary to protect the driver and the public. Because of all of this . . . it does take special skills to safely operate a tanker.

This chapter is designed to assist you in obtaining those skills and to give you the knowledge necessary to obtain your tank vehicle endorsement.

Tank Designs

As discussed previously, all tankers have a high center of gravity (CG). In the chapter on General Knowledge we discussed the importance of keeping the center of gravity of the load as low as possible. In a tanker this is not possible because the load sits higher than in other vehicles, therefore, the CG is *ALWAYS* high. **HIGH CG VEHICLES ARE MORE PRONE TO ROLL OVER IN CERTAIN SITUATIONS,** such as curves, interstate ramps and during evasive movements.

Tanks come in three basic designs:

1. Bulkhead
2. Baffled
3. Unbaffled or "smooth bore"

Bulkhead

Some tankers, such as gasoline tankers, are equipped with bulkheads. A bulkhead is simply a **SOLID STEEL DIVIDER WITHIN THE TANK WHICH CREATES SEPARATE COMPARTMENTS**. The advantage of having separate compartments means that you can haul different types of products in the same tanker at the same time. For example:

Compartment One	1,750 gallons of regular gas
Compartment Two	2,250 gallons of unleaded gas
Compartment Three	2,250 gallons of super unleaded gas
Compartment Four	1,750 gallons of regular gas

Being able to transport several different products at the same time allows the company and the driver to meet the needs of the customer by bringing the products he desires.

Bulkheads reduce the front-to-back surge and help to reduce the side-to-side surge.

Bulkhead Tanker

Baffles

Baffles are dividers, similar to bulkheads, but with one exception: *BAFFLES HAVE HOLES IN THEM.* If you can imagine taking a soup can and putting a donut in it, you have a baffle. Baffles are *NOT* designed to create separate compartments. **BAFFLES ARE DESIGNED TO SLOW DOWN THE FRONT-TO-BACK SURGE. THEY DO NOT HAVE MUCH OF AN EFFECT ON SIDE-TO-SIDE SURGE.** Because the side to side surge is still present and powerful even with baffles, you must still exercise caution and reduce speed on curves and ramps. The holes in the baffles allow the product in the tank to move, but slows down the movement.

Baffled Tanker

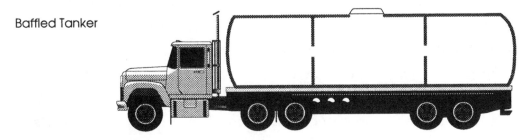

Unbaffled or "Smooth Bore"

Just like the name implies, **A SMOOTH BORE TANK HAS NO BAFFLES OR BULKHEAD. THE SURGE EFFECT IS MOST POWERFUL IN THIS TYPE OF TANK.** When driving a smooth bore tank you must be extra careful. This is especially true when starting, stopping, turning or using on and off ramps. It is most common to find these types of tanks hauling food products and certain chemicals. Baffles and bulkheads make the inside of a tank difficult to clean and sanitize. Therefore, tankers involved in the transportation of food products will almost always be smooth bore.

Smooth Bore Tanker

Surge

What is surge and how does it affect your vehicle? **SURGE IS MOVEMENT OF THE LIQUID FROM THE FRONT TO THE BACK AND FROM SIDE TO SIDE.** The amount of surge is determined by two major factors:

1. **AMOUNT OF LIQUID IN THE TANK.** For example, if the tank has a 9,000 gallon capacity and is only half full . . . the surge will be greater and more powerful than if the tank were loaded to capacity.
2. **DESIGN OF THE TANK.** We have already seen that if the tank has baffles or bulkheads installed, the surge will be reduced. Smooth bore tanks have the most surge.

When stopping at a traffic light the momentum of the truck shifts toward the front. This causes the surge to travel toward the front of the tank. Once the vehicle is stopped the surge will then go rushing towards the back of the tank. Once it hits the back of the tank it will then reverse, just like a wave and travel back to the front. This will continue with each wave getting less and less powerful until it stops. One thing to keep in mind, when it travels to the front the second time, if your foot is not firmly on the brake pedal, the force of the surge can be strong enough to push you into the intersection. If you are on icy or snow-covered roads and stop suddenly at a light, the situation becomes much worse. It is because of this surge that a tanker operator must plan all of his/her movements carefully. Slow down more slowly, **MAINTAIN A 12–15 SECOND EYE LEAD TIME**, time the traffic lights to avoid stopping and use engine speed and downshifting when appropriate to reduce the effects of surge. When approaching curves, **ALWAYS SLOW DOWN BEFORE ENTERING THE CURVE AND THEN ACCELERATE GENTLY THROUGH IT. IT IS POSSIBLE THAT A TANKER CAN ROLL OVER WHEN TRAVELING AT THE POSTED SPEED LIMIT IN A CURVE. THE POSTED SPEED LIMITS ARE FOR CARS, NOT TRUCKS, AND CERTAINLY NOT TANKERS. SIDE-TO-SIDE SURGE IS A MAJOR CAUSE OF TANKER ROLLOVER.**

Outage

Liquids expand as they warm. When loading a cargo tanker you must leave room for the liquid to expand. Because of this you never load a tanker completely full. **THE SPACE YOU LEAVE FOR EXPANSION IS CALLED OUTAGE.** Since different liquids expand by different amounts, **YOU MUST KNOW THE OUTAGE REQUIREMENTS OF EACH PRODUCT YOU HAUL.**

Product Weight

You must always know the weight of the product you are hauling. Weights of liquids vary a great deal. Acids tend to weigh much more than other liquids. Since the weight of each liquid varies, it is necessary for you to know how much a particular liquid weighs so that you know how much you can load and still be within the legal weight limits. So, prior to loading any liquids you must know the following:

1. **THE AMOUNT THE LIQUID WILL EXPAND**
2. **THE WEIGHT OF THE LIQUID PER GALLON**
3. **THE LEGAL WEIGHT LIMITS**

Unloading Requirements

When loading a tanker which has bulkheads, you must keep in mind how you will be unloading, especially if you will have more than one stop. Proper weight distribution is critical when pulling a tanker. As an example, let's use a tanker that has four separate compartments which are separated by bulkheads. Let's say that at your first stop you will be unloading three of the compartments. You would load the tanker in such a way that you unload the last three compartments at your first stop. This means that as you are traveling to your second and final stop, all of the weight of the remaining liquid is in the front of the tanker, giving you maximum control and traction on the drive axle. If you were to unload the first three compartments at the first delivery, then all of the weight would be on the rear tandems giving you much less control and traction. It would kind of be like "the tail wagging the dog." Knowing your unloading requirements becomes even more critical when driving in inclement weather.

A Few More Tips

Drive Smart . . . Drive Smooth. When starting, stopping and shifting *BE SMOOTH*. The smoother you are the less the effect of the surge will be. When turning and changing lanes . . . do it smoothly!

If you drive smooth, you can avoid most problems. Keep in mind the **THREE FACTORS THAT CAN CAUSE A SKID: OVERSTEERING, OVERBRAKING AND OVERACCELERATION**. If you drive smooth . . . you avoid all three. If the worst happens and you find yourself in an emergency situation and you must take quick action, remember this, **IT IS ALMOST ALWAYS BETTER TO STEER TO AVOID AN EMERGENCY THAN TO BRAKE TO AVOID ONE. ABOVE ALL, DON'T BRAKE WHILE MAKING AN EMERGENCY TURNING MANEUVER.** If you have to brake don't panic! **USE STAB OR CONTROLLED BRAKING.** Using stab or emergency braking allows you to maintain control of your vehicle. Remember that when using stab braking, you must release the brakes as soon as the wheels lock up, and then apply the brakes hard again. If

you simply "slam" on the brakes and hold them down, a jackknife may result if the trailer wheels or drive wheels lock up. **IF THE STEERING TIRES LOCK UP YOU WILL CONTINUE ON IN A STRAIGHT LINE REGARDLESS OF HOW YOU TURN THE STEERING WHEEL.**

IF BECAUSE OF AN EMERGENCY YOU MUST LEAVE THE ROADWAY, SLOW TO 20 MPH BEFORE APPLYING THE BRAKES. Better yet, don't get yourself into a situation where you have to make emergency maneuvers. How do you do it? Simple . . .

1. <u>**ALWAYS MAINTAIN A PROPER FOLLOWING DISTANCE. ONE SEC-OND FOR EVERY 10 FEET OF YOUR VEHICLE LENGTH FOR SPEEDS UP TO 40 MPH. ADD A SECOND FOR SPEEDS OVER 40 MPH.**</u>
2. <u>**DOUBLE YOUR FOLLOWING DISTANCE ON WET ROADS.**</u>
3. <u>**EMPTY TANK VEHICLES WILL TAKE LONGER TO STOP THAN LOADED ONES BECAUSE THE TRAILER MAY BOUNCE AND LOSE TRACTION, AND BECAUSE . . . THE LESS WEIGHT ON THE VEHICLE, THE LESS FRICTION BETWEEN THE TIRES AND THE ROAD SURFACE.**</u>

And finally . . .

Many operators of tank vehicles have lost their lives because their brakes overheated while going down a steep grade. Their lives could have been saved if they used the truck escape ramps . . . but, because they were driving a tanker they thought it was not safe to enter an escape ramp. <u>**IF YOU LOSE YOUR BRAKES WHILE GOING DOWN A STEEP GRADE, USE THE TRUCK ES-CAPE RAMP!!**</u> Truck escape ramps have saved many lives, equipment and cargo. They can save your life. You should <u>**ALWAYS**</u> use it if necessary.

WATCH VIDEO ON TANK VEHICLES

☞ LET'S TAKE A TEST

Tank Vehicles

Study each question carefully and indicate your choice by drawing a circle around the letter you have chosen.

1. When loading a cargo tank with liquid, you must consider which of the following?

    A. the legal weight limits in the states in which you will be operating
    B. the amount the liquid will expand during transportation
    C. the weight of the liquid
    D. all of the above

2. You need to be extremely careful when driving smooth bore tanks. This is especially true when you are:

    A. going up or downhill
    B. starting or stopping
    C. loading and unloading
    D. hauling milk or other food products

3. When you unload the smaller compartments of a tanker with bulkheads, be careful to check your:

    A. weight distribution
    B. air-to-fuel ratio
    C. water content
    D. power usage

4. When should a driver of a tank vehicle who has lost their brakes use a truck escape ramp?

    A. never
    B. only when the tanker is empty
    C. only when the tank has bulkheads
    D. always

5. Because of a high center of gravity in tankers, which of the following is important to remember?

   A. tankers can roll over at the posted speed limits for curves and ramps
   B. most tankers have a high center of gravity
   C. curves, exit and entrance ramps have speed limits which are safe for cars but may not be safe for tankers and other high center-of-gravity vehicles
   D. all of the above

6. Ramp speeds are standardized for:

   A. cars
   B. buses
   C. trucks
   D. all of the above

7. You are driving a loaded tanker and are exiting a highway using an off ramp that curves downhill and to the right. You should:

   A. observe the posted speed limit for the off ramp
   B. slow down to a safe speed before exiting
   C. come to a full stop at the stop of the ramp and then proceed cautiously
   D. wait until you are in the turn before downshifting

8. You are driving a tank truck and the front wheels begin to skid. What do you think will occur?

   A. you will continue in a straight line and keep moving forward regardless of how much you steer
   B. the liquid surge will pull the tanker to the right or to the left
   C. the truck will roll over
   D. the truck will stop in the shortest distance because the surge is at the rear of the tank

9. A liquid tanker with baffles can still have what kind of surge?

   A. side to side
   B. top to bottom
   C. front to back
   D. quick

10. A traffic emergency requires you to the leave the roadway and escape to the shoulder. If possible, you should slow down to what speed before applying your brakes?

    A. 20 mph
    B. 30 mph
    C. 40 mph
    D. 50 mph

11. Which of the following statements about emergency steering and tankers is true?

    A. a tanker is easier to countersteer than most vehicles
    B. when making a quick steering movement, do not apply the brakes
    C. you should wrap your thumbs around the steering wheel before starting a quick steering movement
    D. all of the above are true

12. A smooth bore tank which is loaded to 50% capacity will:

    A. have *LESS* surge
    B. will have *THE SAME AMOUNT* of surge as one loaded to 100% capacity
    C. make the vehicle handle better
    D. have *MORE* surge

13. A smooth bore tank will:

    A. have *LESS* surge than a baffled tank
    B. have *LESS* surge that a tank with bulkheads
    C. have *MORE* surge that a baffled tank
    D. all tanks have the same amount of surge if carrying the same amount of liquid

14. Side-to-side surge can cause what to happen?

    A. suspension system failure
    B. overspeeding
    C. rollover
    D. tank failure

15. The center of gravity of a load:

    A. should be kept as *HIGH* as possible
    B. can make a vehicle more likely to roll over on curves
    C. is only a problem if the vehicle is overloaded
    D. all of the above

16. You must know the outage needed for the liquids you load because:

    A. you must unload some liquids at a faster rate than others
    B. tank baffles are not always legal with outage
    C. some liquids expand more than others as they warm up
    D. size of the delivery hose is determined by outage requirements

17. You are driving a tank vehicle and you must stop quickly to avoid a crash. You should:

    A. use light, steady pressure on the brake pedal
    B. push the brake pedal as hard as you can and hold it there
    C. use only the rear or trailer brakes
    D. use controlled or stab braking

18. The best way to maneuver through a curve is to slow to a safe speed before entering the curve, and then _____ as you go through it.

    A. accelerate slightly
    B. coast
    C. brake slightly
    D. downshift twice remembering to double clutch as you downshift

19. Which of the following can cause a vehicle to go into a skid?

    A. oversteering
    B. overbraking
    C. overacceleration
    D. all of the above

20. An approaching vehicle drifts into your lane of travel. Which of the following is the correct course of action to take?

    A. immediately move to the left
    B. immediately move to the right
    C. use emergency hard braking and come to a complete stop in your lane
    D. blow horn, flash lights and come to a complete stop in your lane

Answers

1.	D	11.	B
2.	B	12.	D
3.	A	13.	C
4.	D	14.	C
5.	D	15.	B
6.	A	16.	C
7.	B	17.	D
8.	A	18.	A
9.	A	19.	D
10.	A	20.	B

Hazardous Material

Who Must Study This Chapter?

Any driver who transports hazardous material in such an amount that hazardous material placards must be displayed on the vehicle, must study this chapter and take the Hazardous Material Endorsement Test.

The CMVSA/86 requires that all persons holding the hazardous material endorsement must re-take the hazardous material endorsement test every time their license is renewed.

Currently, some states are now requiring drivers to comply with the two-year testing regulations, others are not. Those states that are not currently complying must comply or obtain a temporary wavier. Check with your state to see if they are currently requiring the re-testing.

Since the first edition of this book was written in 1989, the hazardous material regulations have changed substantially. Those changes are covered in this edition. All that you need to know is in this chapter. In fact, we have included much of the new regulations as they are found in HM-181 and HM 126-F. Even though much of this material will not be on the CDL HAZMAT endorsement test, it is important for you to know and it will help your employer to comply with those regulations for driver training.

A Note to Employers:

HM-181 and 126-F Training Guidelines

HM-126-F requires that HM training, covering HM-181, be given to all drivers involved in the transportation of hazardous material. The regulation further requires that a record of such current training be kept on file while the driver is employed with the company and for 90 days after the driver leaves the employment of the company. The record must contain the following:

1. The employee's name
2. The most recent training completion date
3. A description copy or the location of the training materials which were used to meet the requirements in paragraph (a) of this section
4. The name and address of the person providing the training
5. Certification that the employee has been trained *AND* tested in accordance with these regulations

The HM-126-F regulations require that drivers who are involved in the transportation of hazardous material be trained in four separate areas:

1. General awareness
2. Function specific
3. Safety training
4. Driver training

This Study Manual helps to meet the requirements for general awareness, safety training and driver training of hazardous materials drivers. The manual includes tests at the end of each chapter which can, when put into the driver's files, serve as having tested the drivers in accordance with the HM regulations. In order to certify that the training and testing was done, the trainer must teach the general awareness portion of the training from the Hazardous Material chapter. The Safety Training and Driver Training certification can be obtained by using the General Knowledge, Tanker, Combination Vehicles, Doubles and Triples (if applicable) and the Air Brake chapters contained in this manual, along with the appropriate tests.

The Hazardous Material Regulations (HMR) can be found in parts 171-180 of Title 49 of the Code of Federal Regulations. They are commonly referred to as 49 CFR 171-180.

Hazardous material regulations require that *ALL* drivers involved in the transportation of hazardous material receive training and testing. Your employer or his representative is required to provide this training to you. The employer is required to keep a log, or record, of this training for each employee for as long as that employee is working for the company and for 90 days after the employee leaves the employment of the company. The regulations also require that the employee receive update hazardous material training every two years.

Employees who transport **FLAMMABLE CRYOGENIC LIQUIDS AND CERTAIN ROUTE CONTROLLED QUANTITIES OF RADIOACTIVE MATERIAL MUST RECEIVE SPECIAL TRAINING EVERY TWO YEARS. THEY MUST ALSO CARRY WITH THEM A DATED CERTIFICATE SHOWING THE DATE OF THE TRAINING.** Employees who pull cargo tanks and portable tanks must meet the same two-year training requirement.

Sometimes special routing is required for certain hazardous material and states may require a special permit before certain materials may be transported. Make sure you become familiar with the special rules or regulations in the area in which you will be driving. Check with your company or the local authorities to ensure that you are in compliance.

The Intent of the Hazardous Material Regulations

Since many hazardous materials are dangerous, can kill or injure people, the intentions of the regulations is to provide rules which lessen the danger. Rules exist for shippers of HAZMAT as well as for the drivers and carriers. These rules spell out very clearly how the material must be packaged, loaded, transported and unloaded. The rules are known as **CONTAINMENT RULES. CONTAINMENT RULES ARE THE PROCEDURES USED TO MAKE SURE THE HAZMAT IS CONTAINED PROPERLY AND TO MAKE SURE THERE ARE NO LEAKS AND NO SPILLING.**

Shippers and drivers are required to **COMMUNICATE THE RISK**. *SHIPPERS* must warn *DRIVERS* and others about the hazardous qualities of the material. Drivers must take steps to warn motorists and others that they are transporting HAZMAT. Drivers are also required to warn others in the event of an accident or spillage of any amount. One way that shippers warn others is by making sure that all HAZMAT is packaged with the appropriate (correct) HAZMAT labels. Drivers **COMMUNICATE THE RISK** through the use or proper placards on **ALL FOUR SIDES OF THE VEHICLE**. Drivers also communicate the risk by ensuring the proper placements of the shipping papers during transit. So, as you can see, "communicate the risk" simply means to let others know that you are carrying HAZMAT.

ALL DRIVERS TRANSPORTING HAZMAT MUST HAVE THE HAZARDOUS MATERIAL ENDORSEMENT ON THEIR CDL. Failure to comply with this rule *WILL* result in fines and possible jail terms. Don't break the rules. They are designed for your safety and the safety of others.

Who Does What?

Hazardous material regulations (HMR) divide the responsibility of proper handling into these categories:

1. The shipper
2. The carrier
3. The driver

The Shipper

- Is the person or company sending the HAZMAT from one place to another. This can be done by truck, rail, ship or aircraft.
- He must understand and use the HAZMAT regulations in order to decide the products:
  —Proper shipping name
  —Hazard class
  —Identification numbers
  —Correct type of packing
  —Correct label and marking on package
  —Correct placard(s)
- Is required to properly package HAZMAT, provide proper labeling and identification on the package and supply the placards.
- **CORRECTLY PREPARES THE SHIPPING PAPERS**

—SHIPPER MUST CERTIFY ON THE SHIPPING PAPERS THAT HE HAS PREPARED THE SHIPMENT ACCORDING TO THE RULES. THE ONLY EXCEPTION TO THIS IS WHEN THE SHIPPER IS A PRIVATE CARRIER TRANSPORTING ITS OWN PRODUCTS.

The Carrier

- Transports the shipment to its destination
- Must check and make sure that the shipper correctly named, labeled and marked the shipment
- Must report to the proper government agency any accident or incident involving HAZMATS

The Driver

- Must make sure the shipper has properly identified, marked and labeled all HAZMATS
- **MUST REFUSE LEAKING SHIPMENTS**
- Attaches appropriate placards when loading
- Delivers the products as safely and quickly as possible while obeying all rules concerning the transportation of HAZMATS
- Is required to keep all HAZMAT shipping papers in the proper place

Communicating the Risk

Communication rules mean simply *COMMUNICATING THE RISKS*; letting others know that you are hauling hazardous material. In order to know the best methods for communicating this risk, we must first know what a *HAZARD CLASS* is, and what it means.

The *HAZARD CLASS* indicates the risks associated with a hazardous material. There are nine different hazard classes. A hazard class means the category of hazard assigned to a hazardous material. They can be found under the definitional criteria of Part 173 of the HMR and the provisions of Section 172.101. Don't worry, this won't be on the test. And, you won't need to memorize the hazard classes.

There used to be 22 hazard classes. The new regulations changed them to just nine. What follows are the nine new hazard classes. So that they will be easier to understand we have also listed the old classes. We thought this might make it easier for you to learn them and to understand the new classes of hazards. These changes were brought about by the new HM-181 Regulations. Instead of using a description such as "Explosives A," the new system now uses a numbering system. For example, "Explosives A" is now Class 1.1. "Class 1" means explosives; the ".1" means "Explosives A." Seems like maybe the government just wants to keep us on our toes.

HM 181 CLASSES AND DIVISIONS	OLD CLASSES
Class I (Explosive)	**Explosives**
1.1	Explosive A
1.2	Explosive A or B
1.3	Explosive B
1.4	Explosive C
1.5	Blasting Agent
1.6	
Class 2 (Gases)	**Gases**
2.1	Flammable Gas
2.2	Non-Flammable Gas
2.3	Poison Gas
Class 3 (Flammable Liquids)	**Flammable Combustible Liquids**
3	Flammable Liquid
	Combustible Liquid
Class 4 (Flammable Solids)	**Flammable Solids**
4.1	Flammable Solid
4.2	Flammable Solid or Flammable Liquid (spontaneously combustible or pyroforic)
4.3	Flammable Solid—dangerous when wet
Class 5 (Oxidizing Substances)	**Oxidizing Substances**
5.1	Oxidizer
5.2	Organic Peroxide

Class 6 (Poisons)	Poisons
6.1	Poison B
6.2	Etiologic Agents (infectious substances)

Class 7 (Radioactive Materials)	Radioactive Material

Class 8 (Corrosive Material)	Corrosive Material

Class 9 (Miscellaneous Material)	ORM (Other Regulated Material)

A little explanation. The first number in the sequence tells you the class of the hazardous material; the second number tells you the division. For example "1.3." The "1" tells you that it is an explosive; the "3" tells you the division, which is Explosive B.

Now, let's look at the definitions of each class, and remember, this will not be on the CDL tests but it is important that you have a reasonable understanding of what each of these materials are and the threat they represent to you and to others during loading, unloading and transportation. Also, this material can serve to assist your employer to comply with the training requirements found in HM-181.

Class 1 Explosives

An explosive is any material or substance or item, including an explosive device, which is designed to function by explosion, or by a chemical reaction by itself. Or can function in a similar manner even if it is not designed to explode.

Class 1 is divided into six divisions:

Division 1.1   Are explosives that have a mass explosion hazard. A "mass explosion" is one which can affect the entire load immediately. In other words, it's dangerous as hell.

Division 1.2   Are explosives that have a projection hazard but not a mass explosion hazard.

Division 1.3   Are explosives which have a fire hazard. Also, explosives which have either a minor blast hazard or a minor projection hazard, or even both, but they do not have a mass explosion hazard.

Division 1.4   Are explosive devices which present a minor explosion hazard. Also, no device in Division 1.4 can contain more than 25 grams (0.9 ounces) of a detonating material.

Division 1.5   These are very insensitive explosives. The items found in this division do have a mass explosion hazard but it is usually very remote. Under normal conditions the materials found in this division would not make the transition from being on fire to exploding.

Division 1.6   This division consists of items that do not have a mass explosion hazard. The articles in this division contain only very insensitive detonating substances and have demonstrated almost no chance of accidental fire or explosion.

Class 2 Gases

Class 2 is divided into three divisions.

Division 2.1   Is any material which is a gas at 20 degrees centigrade (68 degrees fahrenheit) or less, and 101 ka (14.7 psi) of pressure and can ignite when in a mixture of 13% or less by volume with air, or has a flammable range with air of at least 12% regardless of the lower limit.

Division 2.2   Materials found in this division are non-flammable and non-poisonous compressed gases. This includes compressed gas, liquefied gas, pressurized cryogenic gas and compressed gas which is in solution. This means any material or mixture which exerts an absolute pressure on the packaging of 200 kpa (40 psia) at 20 degrees C (68 degrees F). Any material in this division does not meet the definition of Division 2.1 and 2.4.

Division 2.3   Are known to be poisonous and are known to be so toxic to humans as to pose a health hazard during transportation, or they are presumed to be toxic to humans, even though adequate data does not exist. The materials found in this group are presumed to be toxic to humans because when tested on laboratory animals they were toxic. The scientific jargon says that they have an LC 50 value not more than 5000 ppm.

Class 3 Flammable Liquids

Class 3 is not divided into divisions.

A flammable liquid is defined as any liquid which has a flash point of not more than 60 degrees C (140 degrees F). This is true except for materials meeting the definition of any Class 2 material. It also includes a mixture having one or more components that have a flash point greater than 60.5 degrees C (141 degrees F) or higher, if it makes up at least 99% of the total volume of the mixture. Or a distilled spirit of 140 proof or lower is considered to have a flash point of lower than 23 degrees C (73 degrees F).

A flash point is the point (or temperature) where the liquid will catch on fire, detonate, explode or combust (catch on fire).

Class 4 Flammable Solids

Class 4 is divided into three divisions:

Division 4.1   This division includes three types of flammable solid materials. They are:

Wetted explosives that when dry are explosives of Class 1, except those of compatibility group A.

Self-reactive materials that may undergo, at normal or elevated temperatures, a decomposition which might make them ignite. This can happen at excessively high transport temperatures or by contamination.

Any readily combustible solids which can cause a fire through friction. This material must show a burning rate faster than 2.2 mm (0.087 inches) per second. Also includes metal powder that can ignite and react over the whole length of a test sample in ten minutes or less.

Division 4.2   Materials in this division are liquid or solid which, even in small quantities, can ignite within five minutes of exposure to air under certain test procedures.

Division 4.3   Materials in this division are those that upon contact with water can become spontaneously flammable, or material that can give off flammable or toxic gases at a rate greater than 1 liter per kilogram per hour.

Class 5 Oxidizing Substances

Division 5.1   Material in this class, because they give off oxygen, can cause or enhance the combustion of other materials.

Division 5.2   Organic peroxide is included in this class, which is a derivative or hydrogen peroxide.

Class 6 Poisons

Class 6 is divided into two divisions.

Division 6.1   Materials in this class are those that are known to be toxic to humans, or those that are so toxic that they pose a health hazard during transportation or those that are presumed hazardous to humans because of tests done in laboratories. This class also includes irritants such as tear gas.

Division 6.2   Materials found in this class are infectious substances which may cause disease or death in humans or animals. Substances such as excreta, secreta, blood, tissue and tissue components are found in this division.

Class 7 Radioactive Material

Radioactive material is any material which has a specific activity greater than 0.002 microcuries per gram. (You know, it's the stuff that makes you glow in the dark.)

Class 8 Corrosive Material

Corrosive materials are those that can cause visible destruction and irreversible damage to human skin tissue at the point of contact. It can be either liquid or solid. It also has a severe corrosion rate on steel or aluminum.
PLACARDS ARE REQUIRED WHEN THE AMOUNT EXCEEDS 1,000 POUNDS

Class 9 Other Regulated Material

This division includes material which presents a hazard during transportation but is not included in any of the other classes but is subject to the hazardous material regulations.

The **SHIPPING PAPER** is the document that describes the HAZMAT. It is required that each item description on the shipping paper show the hazardous materials hazard class. **SHIPPING ORDERS, BILLS OF LADING AND MANIFESTS ARE ALL SHIPPING PAPERS.**

Contains Hazardous Materials						

Shipping Paper

Trailer #	From	To	Revenue	XXxX	Date	Bol#

Deliver To: CTTS/Safety Products, Inc. 1026 Monroe Drive, NE Atlanta, GA 30303-3648	Shipping Papers page 1 of 3
Shipper ABC Factories	

Qty	HM	Description	Weight	Total
10	RQ	Drums, Methyl Ethyl Ketone, 3 (Flammable), UN 1193	5,500 lbs	
26	X	Cylinders, Nitrogen - Compressed Nonflammable Gas, UN 1066	650 lbs	
15		Boxes, light bulbs	30 lbs	
12		Cases, shoes	65 lbs	

I/we hereby certify that the above-named materials are properly classified, described, packaged, marked and labeled, and are in proper condition for transportation according to the applicable regulations of the Department of Transportation.

Emergency Response Telephone Number   1 (800) 424-9300

Shipper: ABC Factories

Per:

Date:

Carrier: Safe Freight

Per:

Date:

Contains Hazardous Materials	

The shipping paper must include:

- page numbers if more than one page—the first page must tell the total number of pages
- proper description of any hazardous materials
- shipper's certificate signed by shipper's representative. Certification must say that the shipment has been prepared according to all applicable regulations.

PLEASE NOTE: WHEN THE SHIPPER IS A PRIVATE CARRIER CARRYING THEIR OWN PRODUCT, THEY DO NOT NEED TO SIGN A SHIPPER'S CERTIFICATION.

If the shipping papers have a mixture of hazardous and non-hazardous products, those that are hazardous must be marked in a special way. That is done by:

1. Can be described first
2. Can be printed or highlighted in a different color
3. Can be identified by an "X" placed before the shipping name in the column marked "HM." Instead of an "X," the letters "RQ" may be used if the shipment is a *reportable quantity*.

This is very important: the description of the hazardous product **MUST INCLUDE** the **PROPER SHIPPING NAME**, the **HAZARD CLASS OR DIVISION** and the **IDENTIFICATION NUMBER. THEY MUST BE WRITTEN IN THAT ORDER!** The shipping name, hazard class, and ID number **MUST NOT BE ABBREVIATED**. The description must also show:

- the total quantity and unit of measure (an example of a unit of measure would be drums, cylinders, etc.)
- if a reportable quantity, the letters "RQ" must be on the shipping paper under "HM"

THE PROPER SHIPPING NAME, HAZARD CLASS AND THE IDENTIFICATION NUMBER MUST BE LISTED IN THIS ORDER—WITH NO ABBREVIATIONS.

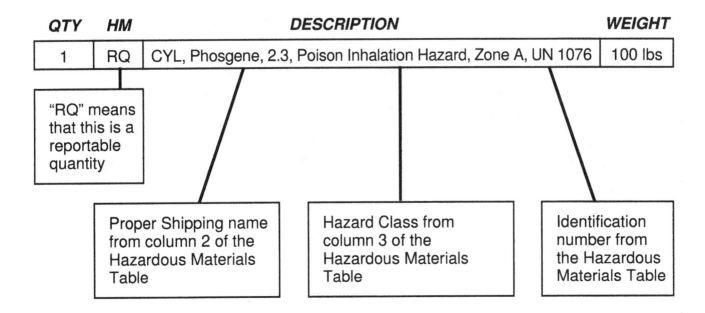

The only abbreviation permitted is for the packaging type and the unit of measurement. Also, it can appear *before* or after the description.

If the shipper is shipping hazardous waste, the word *"waste"* must appear before the name of the material.

NEVER, UNDER ANY CIRCUMSTANCES, CAN A NON-HAZARDOUS MATERIAL BE DESCRIBED BY USING A HAZARD CLASS OR ID NUMBER.

One of the primary purposes of the shipping paper is to **COMMUNICATE** what is being shipped and what risks are involved. If you are in an accident or involved in a hazard material incident, you may be injured and/or unable to talk to law enforcement officers. In that case, the shipper's papers can communicate to the officers what hazardous material is on the vehicle and in what quantity. After obtaining this information from the shipping papers, the officers can then take whatever actions are necessary to provide for the safety of everyone involved. You can readily see why it is so important that the shipping papers be filled out correctly. Your life or the lives of others may depend on it.

In the event of an accident, it is also necessary that law enforcement officers obtain information quickly. For that reason, additional rules apply. They:

● Require that the shipping papers describing hazardous material be **TABBED OR TAGGED** and that they be **PLACED ON TOP** of any other shipping papers. **THIS IS THE RESPONSIBILITY OF THE CARRIER AND THE DRIVER.**

- **WHEN THE DRIVER IS OUT OF THE TRUCK, SHIPPING PAPERS MUST BE PLACED ON DRIVER'S SEAT, OR IN POUCH ON DRIVER'S DOOR.**
- **WHILE DRIVING, SHIPPING PAPERS MUST BE IN A POUCH ON THE DRIVER'S DOOR, OR IN CLEAR VIEW OF DRIVER WHEN SEAT BELT IS IN USE.**

Proper Packaging

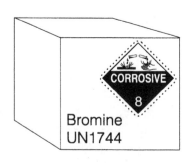

Another responsibility of the shipper is to make sure that the package is labeled properly. Shippers must apply diamond-shaped labels indicating the hazardous material in the package.

If a label cannot be affixed to the package, as in the case of a cylinder, the shipper must then attach a tag or decal indicating the hazard. A DOT chart is located at the back of this manual showing proper labels and placards.

Placards

As mentioned earlier, placards are another form of **COMMUNICATING THE RISK**. Placards are diamond-shaped signs that are affixed to the four sides of the vehicle. The placards show the hazard class of the product being shipped. The rules require that the placards be readable from all four directions. Placards must be affixed to the rear of the trailer, both sides and to either the front of the trailer or tractor. Placards must read from left to right and be at least three inches away from any other markings. If you're pulling a tanker, the ID number of the hazardous material must be shown. They can be shown inside the placard or on an orange panel.

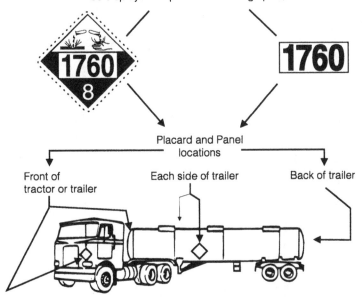

Hazardous Material identification numbers may be displayed on placards or orange panels.

Placard and Panel locations

Front of tractor or trailer

Each side of trailer

Back of trailer

Don't forget, **IT IS THE DRIVER'S RESPONSIBILITY TO MAKE SURE THE VEHICLE IS PROPERLY PLACARDED. IT IS ALSO THE DRIVER'S RESPONSIBILITY TO REMOVE THE PLACARDS WHEN THE HAZARDOUS MATERIALS HAVE BEEN UNLOADED.**

Hazardous Material Lists

Since it is impossible for shippers, carriers and drivers to memorize all of the hazardous materials in existence, **THREE MAIN LISTS** are available to help us determine the proper handling of any hazardous material.

These lists are:

1. The **HAZARDOUS MATERIAL TABLE**
2. The **LIST OF HAZARDOUS SUBSTANCES AND REPORTABLE QUANTITIES**
3. List of marine pollutants

BEFORE TRANSPORTING ANY UNFAMILIAR PRODUCTS, LOOK FOR ITS NAME ON EACH LIST. You'll find the proper shipping name, hazard class, identification number and proper labeling required.

Let's look at each of these lists individually:

Hazardous Materials Table—The example on the next page shows a portion of a Hazardous Material Table. Column 1 shows which shipment the entry affects.

Columns 2-4 shows each material's shipping name, hazard class, identification number and which label(s) are required.

§172.101 Hazardous Materials Table

(1) Symbol	(2) Hazardous materials descriptions and proper shipping names	(3) Hazard class or Division	(4) Identification Numbers	(5) Packing Group	(6) Label(s) required (if not excepted)	(7) Special Provisions	(8) Packaging Authorizations (§173.101)			(9) Quantity limitations		(10) Vessel stowage requirements	
							(8A) Exceptions	(8B) Non bulk packaging	(8C) Bulk packaging	(9A) Passenger aircraft or railcar	(9B) Cargo aircraft only	(10A) Vessel stowages	(10B) Other stowage provisions
	Accelterene, see p-Nitrosodimethylantine												
	Accumulators, electric, see Batteries, wet etc.												
D	Accumulators, pressurized, pneumatic or hydraulic (containing non-flammable gas)	2.2	NA1956		NONFLAMMABLE GAS		306	306	None	No Limit	No Limit	A	
	Acetol	3	UN1088	II	FLAMMABLE LIQUID	17	150	202	242	5L	60 L	E	
	Acetaldehyde	3	UN1089	I	FLAMMABLE LIQUID	A3, B16, T20, T26, T29	None	201	243	Forbidden	30 L	E	
A	Acetaldehyde ammonia	9	UN1841	III	CLASS 9		156	204	241	200 kg	200 kg	A	34
	Acetaldehyde oxima	3	UN2332	II	FLAMMABLE LIQUID	T8	150	202	242	5L	60 L	A	
	Acetic acid, glacial or acetic acid solution, more than 80% per cent acid, by mass	8	UN2789	II	CORROSIVE	A3, A6, A7, A10 B2, T8	154	202	242	1L	30 L	A	12, 21, 48
	Acetic acid solution, more than 10 percent but not more than 8- percent acid, by mass	8	UN2790	II	CORROSIVE	A3, A6, A7, A10 B2, T8	154	202	242	1L	30 L	A	112
	Acetic anhydride	8	UN1715	II	CORROSIVE	A3, A6, A7, A10 B2, T8	154	202	242	1L	30 L	A	40
	Acetone	3	UN1090	II	FLAMMABLE LIQUID	T8	150	202	242	5L	60 L	B	

The symbols in column 1 each have a specific meaning. They are:

"+"   indicates that the designated proper shipping name and hazard class must always be shown, even if the product doesn't match the hazard class definition.

"D"   means the proper shipping name is appropriate for describing materials for domestic transportation, but may not be proper for international transportation.

"A"   is subject to the regulations only when transported by air, unless the material is a hazardous substance or a hazardous waste.

"W"   is subject to the regulations only when transported by water unless the material is a hazardous substance or a hazardous waste or marine pollutant.

Column 2 shows the name of the regulated materials in alphabetical order. The proper shipping name is *always* shown in *regular* type. All shipping papers must show **THE PROPER SHIPPING NAMES**. The names shown in italics are not proper shipping names and can only be used along with the **PROPER SHIPPING NAME**.

Column 3 shows the hazardous material's hazard class or division, or may have the word "forbidden." **NEVER TRANSPORT A MATERIAL THAT IS "FORBIDDEN."** The material's hazard class is your key to using the proper placards. **IN CHOOSING THE PROPER PLACARDS—YOU ONLY NEED TO KNOW THREE THINGS:**

1. **MATERIAL'S HAZARD CLASS**
2. **AMOUNT BEING SHIPPED**
3. **AMOUNT OF ALL HAZARDOUS MATERIALS OF ALL CLASSES ON YOUR VEHICLE**

If you know these three things, you can always select the proper placard. **ONE NOTE ABOUT PLACARDS—IF THE WORD "INHALATION HAZARD" IS ON THE SHIPPING PAPERS OR PACKAGE—YOU MUST USE A "POISON" PLACARD IN ADDITION TO ANY OTHERS THAT ARE REQUIRED.**

Column 4 lists the identification number for each proper shipping name. The numbers are preceded by the initials "UN" or "NA." The letters "NA" are only used in shipments traveling between the United States and Canada.

The identification number **MUST APPEAR ON THE SHIPPING PAPER AND ALSO APPEAR ON THE PACKAGE. IT MUST ALSO APPEAR ON CARGO TANKS** and all other bulk packagings.

Column 5 identifies the packing group which is assigned to a material.

Column 6 shows the hazard label which shippers must put on packages of hazardous materials. Often products will require more than one label. If the word *"NONE"* appears in this column, no label is required.

Column 7 lists any additional provisions which apply to this material. If you see an entry in this column you must refer to the federal regulations for specific information.

Column 8 is a three-part column which shows the section numbers covering the packaging requirements for each hazardous material.

Columns 9 and 10 do not apply to highway transportation.

List of Hazardous Substances and Reportable Quantities

The Department of Transportation (DOT) and the Environmental Protection Agency (EPA) want to know about spills or leaks of certain products. **"RQ" STANDS FOR REPORTABLE QUANTITIES.** The Hazardous Substances and Reportable Quantities List will tell you if the material is a reportable quantity. The type of product and the amount spilled determines if it is reportable. Look at the example for Phosgene below. The (*) next to the name indicates that this

The name "Phosgene" is starred (*) because the name also appears in the hazardous materials table.

Spills of 10 pounds or more must be reported.

LIST OF HAZARDOUS SUBSTANCES AND REPORTABLE QUANTITIES — continued		
Hazardous Substance	Synonyms	Reportable Quantity (RQ) Pounds (Kilograms)
Phenyl mercaptan	Benzinethiol	100 (45.4)
	Thiophenol *	100 (45.4)
Phenylmercuric acetate	Mercury, (acetato-O) phenyl	100 (45.4)
N-Phenylthiourea	Thourea phenyl	100 (45.4)
Phorate	Prosphorodithioic acid, o,o-diethyl S-(ethylthio),methylester	10 (4.54)
Phosgene *	Carbonyl chloride	10 (4.54)
Posphine *	Hydrogen phosphide	100 (45.4)
Phosphoric acid *		5000 (2270)
Phosphoric acid, diethyl p-nitrophenyl ester	Diethyl p-nitrophenyl phosphate	100 (45.4)
Phosphoric acid, lead salt	Lead phosphate	1 (0.454)

product also appears in the hazardous material table. To the right of the chart the numbers 10 (4.54) appear. The 10 stands for 10 lbs, the 4.54 stands for 4.54 kilograms. If 10 pounds or more are spilled, the employer **MUST** report the spill. The driver **MUST** report the spill to his employer.

Rules for Package Marking and Labels

It is the shipper's responsibility to properly mark or label the package. The hazardous material name on the package must be the same name as on the shipping paper. When required by the regulations, the shipper must also put the following on the package:

- the name and address of shipper or consignee
- the hazardous material's shipping name and ID number
- any labels required

If the regulations require that the words **INHALATION HAZARD** be on the package, the shipper must put them on. **THIS IS ALSO AN INDICATION TO THE DRIVER THAT POISON PLACARDS MUST BE PLACED ON ALL FOUR SIDES OF THE VEHICLE.** If a leak or spill occurs, it must be reported to the employer.

In some cases, more than one label may be required. In such case, all labels will be close to each other and near the proper shipping name.

Driver's Responsibility in Recognizing Hazardous Materials

It is the driver's responsibility to recognize that he is loading and will be transporting hazardous materials. Always look at the shipping papers and determine if hazardous materials are being shipped. If so, the driver must make sure that the proper shipping name, hazard class and ID number are listed in that order. The driver must also look for a highlighted entry or the letters "RQ" or "X" in the HM column. This will indicate that HAZMATS are being shipped. When accepting delivery for shipment, the driver must be absolutely sure that the shipping papers are correct, the packages are labeled correctly, and the vehicle is loaded properly and displaying the proper placards. If the driver is not 100% certain that every step of this process is correct, he should contact his dispatcher and *MAKE SURE*. **NEVER ACCEPT DAMAGED OR LEAKING HAZARDOUS MATERIAL.**

When in doubt, contact your dispatcher for instructions.

More Details About Proper Placarding

As it is usually the driver's responsibility to make sure his vehicle is properly placarded. Let's review some of the rules.

1. **MUST BE ON ALL FOUR SIDES OF THE VEHICLE**
2. **PLACED SO WORDS ARE LEVEL AND READ FROM LEFT TO RIGHT**
3. **MUST BE AT LEAST THREE INCHES AWAY FROM ANY OTHER MARKINGS**
4. **MUST BE REMOVED AS SOON AS HAZARDOUS MATERIALS HAVE BEEN UNLOADED**

The only time you can ever drive an improperly placarded vehicle is in an emergency in order to protect life or property.

How do you determine which placards to use? We'll admit it does get confusing, but if you follow the steps listed here, it'll make things a little easier for you.

Step 1.   Check the shipping papers and look for the **HAZARD CLASS, AMOUNT SHIPPED** and the **TOTAL WEIGHT OF ALL HAZARDOUS MATERIALS IN THIS SHIPMENT.** You need all three to determine which placard(s) must be used.

Step 2.   Check the packages being shipped and make sure they match the hazard class on the shipping papers.

Step 3.   Once you have made sure that the labels on the packages agree with the shipping papers, and you know:
- the hazard class
- the weight
- the total weight of all HAZMATS being shipped

You check the placard tables to determine which placard or placards to use.

There are two placard tables. One table requires placards for *any amount* of the material being shipped, the other requires placards if the amount exceeds 1,000 lbs or more. Let's look at these two tables.

PLACARD TABLE 1
ANY AMOUNT

Category of material (hazard class or division number and additional description, as appropriate)	Placard name	Placard design section reference (§)
1.1	EXPLOSIVES 1.1	172.522
1.2	EXPLOSIVES 1.2	172.522
1.3	EXPLOSIVES 1.3	172.522
2.3	POISON GAS	172.540
4.3	DANGEROUS WHEN WET	172.548
6.1 (PG 1. inhalation hazard only)	POISON	172.554
7 (Radioactive yellow 111 label only)	RADIOACTIVE	172.556

If the shipment you are picking up contains *any amount* of these materials, the appropriate placard must be displayed on all four sides of the vehicle.

PLACARD TABLE 2
1,001 LBS. OR MORE

Category of material (hazard class or division number and additional description, as appropriate)	Placard name	Placard design section reference (§)
1.4	EXPLOSIVES 1.4	172.523
1.5	EXPLOSIVES 1.5	172.524
1.6	EXPLOSIVES 1.6	172.525
2.1	FLAMMABLE GAS	172.532
2.2	NON-FLAMMABLE GAS	172.528
3	FLAMMABLE	172.542
Combustible liquid	COMBUSTIBLE	172.544
4.1	FLAMMABLE SOLID	172.546
4.2	SPONTANEOUSLY COMBUSTIBLE	172.547
5.1	OXIDIZER	172.550
5.2	ORGANIC PEROXIDE	172.552
6.1 (PG 1 or 11, other than PG 1 inhalation hazard)	POISON	172.554
6.1 (PG 111)	KEEP AWAY FROM FOOD	172.553
6.2 (None)	(None)	
8	CORROSIVE	172.558
9	CLASS 9	172.560
ORM-D	(None)	

The hazard classes in Table 2 only require placards if the amount transported is **1,001 LBS OR MORE**, including the packaging. If you picked up hazardous materials from another location, add the weight of the product you picked up to the weight of the product you are picking up. If the combined weight for a Table 2 product is 1,001 lbs or more, then you know you'll have to display the appropriate placard.

Hazardous Waste Manifest

WHEN TRANSPORTING HAZARDOUS WASTE YOU MUST SIGN AND CARRY A HAZARDOUS WASTE MANIFEST. THE SHIPPER PREPARES THE MANIFEST. YOU TREAT IT AS YOU WOULD ANY SHIPPING PAPER.

IT IS THE RESPONSIBILITY OF THE TRANSPORTER (CARRIER) OF HAZARDOUS WASTE TO MAKE SURE THAT THE HAZARDOUS WASTE MANIFEST IS PROPERLY COMPLETED. IT IS THE RESPONSIBILITY OF THE SHIPPER TO ALWAYS PLACE THE WORD "WASTE" BEFORE THE PROPER SHIPPING NAME ON THE SHIPPING PAPERS. A SHIPMENT WHICH IS LABELED AS HAZARDOUS WASTE MAY ONLY BE DELIVERED TO ANOTHER REGISTERED TRANSPORTER OR TO A FACILITY AUTHORIZED TO HANDLE HAZARDOUS WASTE.

THE TRANSPORTER OF HAZARDOUS WASTE MUST KEEP A COPY OF THE HAZARDOUS WASTE MANIFEST FOR THREE YEARS.

ONCE DELIVERED TO A FACILITY AUTHORIZED TO HANDLE HAZARDOUS WASTE, IT IS THE FACILITY OPERATOR WHO MUST SIGN FOR THE SHIPMENT.

If you have two or more of a Table 2 product, say 1,000 lbs of a material requiring a flammable placard and 1,000 lbs of a material requiring a combustible placard, instead of using two separate placards, you are permitted to use a *DANGEROUS* placard. Here are two exceptions to that rule: (1) If you have loaded 5,000 lbs or more at one location, you must use the specific placard for that material. (2) If the words *INHALATION HAZARD* are on the shipping papers, you must use that material's specific placard required by its hazard class *AND* a placard saying *POISON*. **YOU MUST ALWAYS USE THE HAZARD CLASS PLACARD AND THE POISON PLACARD WHENEVER THE WORDS "INHALATION HAZARD" APPEAR ON THE SHIPPING PAPERS, REGARDLESS OF THE AMOUNT.**

Division 1.6 *blasting agents,* Division 5.1 *oxidizer* and *dangerous* placards do not have to be used if a vehicle contains Class 1 explosives *and is placarded Divi-*

sion 1.1 or Division 1.2 or Division 1.3. If your vehicle is displaying a Division 2.1 *Flammable Gas* placard or an *Oxygen* placard, you do not need to display a Division 2.2 *Non-flammable Gas* placard if you were to pick up a material that called for it.

When determining what placards to use, some drivers, if they are not sure, will put placards on the vehicle "just to make sure." The rules state that you must always display the **PROPER** placard. Displaying the wrong placard is as bad as not displaying any placard. Never display placards unless you are absolutely sure they are correct. If you're not sure, check with your dispatcher. **NEVER DISPLAY A PLACARD ON A VEHICLE THAT CONTAINS NON-HAZARDOUS MATERIAL.** Remember, the intent of the hazardous material regulations are:

1. **SAFE DRIVERS AND EQUIPMENT**
2. **CONTAINMENT**
3. **COMMUNICATE THE RISK**

Displaying the wrong placard, or displaying a placard when none is needed, is communicating the wrong message.

Required Notification

We have mentioned that if a reportable quantity (RQ) of a material is spilled or leaked, it must be reported by the carrier. Who does the carrier report it to?

It is reported to the **NATIONAL RESPONSE CENTER** (NRC). The NRC has the ability to contact the proper law enforcement officers quickly if necessary. In the event an RQ is spilled or leaked, the carrier, and/or maybe the driver, must call immediately . . .

NATIONAL RESPONSE CENTER
(800) 424-8802

. . . if any of the following occur:

1. a person is killed
2. a person receives injuries requiring hospitalization
3. property damage is estimated to exceed $50,000
4. the general public is evacuated for one hour or more
5. one or more major roadways are closed or shut down for one hour or more
6. fire, breakage, spillage or suspected radioactive contamination occurs
7. fire, breakage, spillage or suspected contamination of etiologic agents occur

The person making the call must be ready to give the NRC the following information:

- their name
- name and address of the carrier they work for
- phone number where they can be reached
- date, time, and location of incident
- the extent of injuries, if any

- classification, name, and quantity of hazardous materials involved, if such information is available
- type of incident and nature of hazardous material involvement
- if a reportable quantity of hazardous substance was involved, the caller should give:
  —the name of the shipper
  —the quantity of the hazardous substance discharged

This call would be made in addition to any other calls which may have been made to local law enforcement officers in the locality where the incident occurred.

We would suggest that the driver not make the call to the NRC unless instructed to do so by his employer or local law enforcement officials.

In addition to the call to the NRC, **A DETAILED WRITTEN REPORT MUST BE FILED WITH THE NRC WITHIN 30 DAYS OF WHEN THE SPILL OCCURRED.** Since the driver's help will be needed, it is advisable for the driver to write out a report as soon as possible explaining what took place.

The Chemical Transportation Emergency Center (CHEMTREC), in Washington, also has a 24-hour toll-free line. CHEMTREC was created to provide emergency personnel with technical information about the physical properties of hazardous products. The National Response Center and CHEMTREC are in close communication. If you call either one, they will tell the other about the problem when appropriate.

```
CHEMTREC
(800) 424-9300
```

Loading, Unloading and Driving Hazardous Materials

We've talked so far about the rules and regulations concerning the paperwork, placarding and reporting. Let's talk now about actually handling and transporting the products from one point to another.

Loading and Unloading

First a few common sense rules:

- Park and set brakes on vehicle and chock wheels
- Never load damaged or leaking packages or containers
- Do everything you can to protect the public
  - —don't use any device when loading that may damage the package, such as hooks
  - —block or brace firmly, taking special care with cylinders, drums, etc.
  - —load away from heat sources
- No smoking
  - —when loading certain HAZMATS, you must not smoke or have any fire or heat source around. **YOU MUST NEVER LOAD EXPLOSIVES (CLASS 1), OXIDIZERS (CLASS 5) OR FLAMMABLES (CLASS 3 OR 4 OR DIVISION 2.1) WHILE SMOKING OR AROUND ANY TYPE OF HEAT SOURCE.**
- Do not open any packages during transport. If a spill or leak develops, call your company immediately.
- Cargo Heater Rules
  - —The rules generally forbid the use of cargo heaters or air-conditioning units. Unless you know the related rules for the cargo you'll be hauling— check with your company before loading.
  - —**NEVER LOAD EXPLOSIVES (CLASS 1), FLAMMABLE LIQUIDS (CLASS 3) OR FLAMMABLE GAS (DIVISION 2.1) INTO A TRAILER WITH A CARGO HEATER/AIR-CONDITIONING UNIT**
- No overhangs or tailgate loads are permitted for:
  - —Explosives—Class 1
  - —Flammable solids—Class 4
  - —Oxidizing materials—Class 5

This must be loaded in a closed cargo space unless their packages are fire and water resistant or covered with a fire and water resistant tarp.

- EXPLOSIVES—Class 1

  Before loading or unloading explosives, you must:

  —Turn engine off

  —**DISABLE CARGO HEATERS (DISCONNECT HEAT POWER SOURCES AND DRAIN HEATER FUEL TANKS)**

  —**CHECK INSIDE OF TRAILER OR TRUCK FOR ANY SHARP POINTS WHICH MAY DAMAGE CARGO**

  —**CHECK FLOORBOARDS AND SIDE WALLS**

  —**YOU MUST USE A FLOOR LINING WITH DIVISIONS 1.1, 1.2 OR 1.3 EXPLOSIVES—THE LINER MUST NOT CONTAIN STEEL OR IRON**

  —Never transfer Class 1.1, 1.2 or 1.3 (Class A or B) explosives from one vehicle to another on a public highway, except in an emergency.

  —**NEVER ACCEPT DAMAGED PACKAGES OR PACKAGES WITH AN OILY STAIN OR DAMPNESS**

  —**NEVER TRANSPORT DIVISION 1.1 EXPLOSIVES IN TRIPLES**

  —**NEVER TRANSPORT DIVISIONS 1.2 AND 1.3 EXPLOSIVES IN VEHICLE COMBINATIONS IF:**

    - **THERE IS A PLACARDED CARGO TANK IN THE COMBINATION, OR any other of the combination contains:**

      —initiating explosives

      —radioactive materials labeled "yellow," Class 7

      —Class 6 poisons

      —hazardous materials in a portable tank, spec. 106A of 110A tank

- CORROSIVE LIQUIDS

  If loading breakable containers by hand—load one at a time.

  —Don't drop

  —Don't turn over

  —Don't top load unless weight can be held by freight on bottom

  —Keep right side up

  —Never load nitric acid above anything else and never more than 2 stacks high

—NEVER LOAD CORROSIVES NEXT TO DIVISIONS 1.1, 1.2 AND 1.3 EXPLOSIVES, CLASS 4 FLAMMABLE SOLID OR CLASS 5 OXIDIZING MATERIAL

- Cylinders (compressed gases—cryogenic liquids—Class 2)

—If vehicle has no racks—cylinders must be kept upright or braced laying down, or in boxes that will prevent them from turning over

- Poisons (poison—poison gas or *IRRITANT*)

—Never load with foodstuffs

—Never load in driver's cab or sleeper

Radioactive Materials

Regardless of how well packaged and insulated, all radioactive material will have radiation which escapes through the packaging. **RADIOACTIVE II AND RADIOACTIVE III (CLASS 7) MATERIALS WILL HAVE A NUMBER ON THE PACKAGE.** *THIS NUMBER IS CALLED THE TRANSPORT INDEX.* Radiation will surround these packages and travel through all other packages. To make sure that too many of these packages are not loaded together, the number of radioactive II and III packages permitted on a vehicle is controlled. **THE TRANSPORT INDEX TELLS THE DEGREE OF CONTROL NEEDED DURING TRANSPORTATION. THE TOTAL TRANSPORT INDEX OF ALL PACKAGES IN A SINGLE VEHICLE CANNOT EXCEED 50.**

Mixed Loads

The regulations demand that certain hazardous materials be loaded separately. This regulation is called the **SEGREGATION AND SEPARATION CHART**. Following is an example of some materials which must be separated.

DO NOT LOAD . . .	*IN THE SAME VEHICLE WITH . . .*
POISON labeled material—Class 6	Animal or human food, unless the poison package is overpacked in an approved way. Foodstuff is anything you swallow. However, mouthwash, toothpaste, and skin creams are not foodstuff.
Poison—Division 2.3	Oxidizers, flammables, corrosives, organic peroxides
Charged storage batteries—Division 1.1	Explosives
Detonating primers	Any other explosives unless in authorized containers or packagings

Cyanides or cyanide mixtures	Acids, corrosive materials, or other acidic materials which could release hydrocyanic acid from cyanides. Cyanides are materials with the letters "cyan" as part of their shipping name. For example:
	     Acetone cyanohydrin
	     Silver cyanide
	     Trichloroisocyanuric acid, dry

Nitric acid	Other corrosive liquids in carboys, unless separated from them in an approved way

Driving Rules

Here we go! We've checked the shipping papers and properly placarded and loaded the truck. Now we can finally get down to doing what we do best, driving. Yes, that's right, it's time to get on the road, start grabbing gears and get those tires hummin'. But first, we'd better go over a few more rules.

Whenever you're transporting HAZMAT, you've got a whole different set of rules to play by. They're not that complicated, but you've got to know them! So, let's get started.

Parking with Explosives—Divisions 1.1, 1.2 and 1.3

<u>**NEVER PARK WITH DIVISION 1.1 EXPLOSIVES OR DIVISIONS 1.2 AND 1.3 EXPLOSIVES WITHIN FIVE FEET OF THE TRAVELED PART OF THE ROAD.**</u>
   <u>**DO NOT PARK WITHIN 300 FEET OF A BRIDGE, TUNNEL OR BUILDING, A PLACE WHERE PEOPLE GATHER OR AN OPEN FIRE.**</u>

Someone must be in attendance of the vehicle at all times. That can be you, or some one else, if your vehicle is:

on the shipper's property
on the carrier's property
on the consignee's property

Vehicle can be unattended only if it is in a government-approved safe haven. <u>**A GOVERNMENT-APPROVED SAFE HAVEN IS A LOCATION THAT HAS BEEN APPROVED FOR PARKING UNATTENDED VEHICLES LOADED WITH EXPLOSIVES.**</u>

Parking for Vehicles Not Carrying Explosives

- may be parked within 5 feet of roadway only if job requires it and someone is with it at all times, and that person is aware of the hazards involved
- never uncouple a trailer and leave it on a public street
- when parked along side roadway set out reflective triangles within 10 minutes

Never Park Within 300 Feet of an Open Fire

Attending Parked Vehicles

- <u>**IF YOU HAVE SOMEONE WATCH THE VEHICLE FOR YOU—THAT SOMEONE MUST**</u>
    - <u>**—BE IN THE VEHICLE (NOT THE SLEEPER) AND MUST BE AWAKE, OR**</u>
    - <u>**—BE WITHIN 100 FEET AND HAVE IT WITHIN CLEAR VIEW**</u>
    - <u>**—MUST KNOW WHAT TO DO IN AN EMERGENCY**</u>
    - <u>**—MUST BE ABLE TO MOVE THE VEHICLE IF NECESSARY**</u>

Flares—(Fusees)

- <u>**NEVER USE FUSEES OR ANY BURNING SIGNAL DEVICE AROUND**</u>
    - <u>**—TANKER USED FOR FLAMMABLES**</u>

—DIVISION 1.1 EXPLOSIVES, DIVISIONS 1.2 OR 1.3 EXPLOSIVES, CLASS 3 FLAMMABLE LIQUID OR DIVISION 2.1 FLAMMABLE GAS.

Route Restrictions

Some states and counties require permits and special routing when transporting certain material. It is your responsibility as the driver to find out about these special regulations. Check with your company. Always check your routes before beginning a trip and make sure you are permitted to travel on them.

WHEN TRANSPORTING DIVISIONS 1.1, 1.2 OR 1.3 EXPLOSIVES, YOU ARE REQUIRED TO HAVE A WRITTEN ROUTE PLAN AND YOU MUST FOLLOW THAT PLAN.

When transporting placarded radioactive materials, the carrier must choose the safest route. The carrier is responsible for telling the driver that he is transporting radioactive material and showing the route to him.

Smoking

Never smoke within 25 feet of a placarded tank used for flammables.

ALSO—DON'T SMOKE OR CARRY LIGHTED MATERIAL WITHIN 25 FEET OF ANY VEHICLE CONTAINING: CLASS 1 EXPLOSIVES—CLASS 5 OXIDIZERS—CLASS 3 AND 4 FLAMMABLES.

Fires on the Roadway

WHENEVER YOUR VEHICLE IS PLACARDED, DO NOT DRIVE RIGS BY OPEN FIRE UNLESS YOU CAN SAFELY PASS WITHOUT STOPPING.

Tire Checks

WHILE EN-ROUTE, YOU ARE REQUIRED TO STOP AT LEAST EVERY TWO HOURS OR 100 MILES AND CHECK YOUR TIRES.

- **REMOVE ANY OVERHEATED TIRE.**
- Never drive on a leaking or flat tire except to the nearest safe place to repair it.

Refueling

- Turn off engine before refueling
- Someone must be in control of the fuel flow, at the nozzle

Shipping Papers While Driving

- **MUST BE IN POUCH ON DRIVER'S DOOR, OR . . .**
- **WHERE DRIVER CAN REACH THEM WHILE HIS SEAT BELT IS BUCKLED AND IS IN CLEAR VIEW.**
- Shipping papers containing HAZMAT must be tabbed or tagged and on top of all other shipping papers.
- **WHEN DRIVER IS OUT OF TRUCK—SHIPPING PAPERS MUST BE PLACED ON DRIVER'S SEAT OR IN DRIVER'S DOOR POUCH.**

Divisions 1.1, 1.2 and 1.3 Explosives

Drivers must be familiar with, and have in his possession while driving, the:

- shipping papers
- written emergency instructions
- **WRITTEN ROUTE PLAN**
- **A COPY OF THE FMCSR, PART 397**

Chlorine

ANY DRIVER TRANSPORTING CHLORINE MUST HAVE AN APPROVED GAS MASK IN THE VEHICLE. THE DRIVER MUST ALSO HAVE, AND KNOW HOW TO USE, AN EMERGENCY KIT FOR CONTROLLING LEAKS IN DOME LID PLATE FITTINGS ON THE TANK.

Railroad Crossings

You must stop vehicle if:

- **VEHICLE IS PLACARDED**
- **CARRYING ANY AMOUNT OF CHLORINE**

- **HAS CARGO TANKS, LOADED OR EMPTY, USED TO TRANSPORT HAZMAT**

YOU MUST STOP NO CLOSER THAN 15 FEET AND NO FURTHER AWAY THAN 50 FEET. DON'T SHIFT GEARS WHILE CROSSING. A good safety practice is to turn on your 4-way flashers when stopping. **NEVER SHIFT GEARS WHILE CROSSING RAILROAD TRACKS.**

Those are the rules for driving, now let's talk about hazardous materials emergencies.

Emergency Response Guidebook (ERG)

THE EMERGENCY RESPONSE GUIDEBOOK IS A GUIDEBOOK FOR FIRE FIGHTERS, POLICE OFFICERS AND INDUSTRY PERSONNEL ON WHAT TO DO IN THE EVENT OF AN EMERGENCY INVOLVING HAZARDOUS MATERIALS. It is available through the Department of Transportation.

Whenever an emergency occurs, police and fire officials must first determine what type of hazardous material is on the truck. They do this by looking at the shipping papers, looking at the placards and talking with the driver. However, in some accidents, because of their severity, they may not be able to talk to the driver or locate the shipping papers. If this happens, the only thing they can do is look at the placards. Once they determine what type of hazardous material is involved, they can then take the proper steps to protect life and property. You can now see why it is so important that the shipping papers always be filled out correctly, the driver be aware of what he is transporting, and that the proper placards be displayed on all four sides of the vehicle.

Accidents/Incidents Involving Hazardous Materials

As a professional driver—what is your responsibility at the scene of an accident involving hazardous materials?

- *Keep people away.* Warn them of the danger, keep people away and upwind from the spill
- **CONTAIN** the spill. You should attempt to contain the hazardous material *only if you can do so safely*.
- **COMMUNICATE.** Contact the appropriate emergency response personnel and inform them of what has happened.

Be prepared to tell them . . .

    —the product's shipping name, hazard class, and ID number

    —extent of the spill

    —location

    —when it happened

    —phone number where you can be reached

    —let them hang the phone up first. Often, drivers will hang up to rush
      back to the truck before giving all the information necessary.

    —contact your company—and follow their instructions.

Here are a few common sense rules about dealing with hazardous material incidents or accidents.

IF A VEHICLE CARRYING EXPLOSIVES CRASHES INTO ANOTHER OBJECT—THE EXPLOSIVES MUST BE REMOVED AND PLACED AT LEAST 200 FEET AWAY BEFORE ATTEMPTING TO SEPARATE THE VEHICLE FROM THE OTHER OBJECT.

Fires

- Never attempt to fight a hazardous material fire *unless you have received specific training on how to do it*. HAZMAT fires can create numerous problems that may kill you. Explosions, poisonous fumes and flash fires are just a few examples.

- **THE POWER UNIT OF A PLACARDED VEHICLE MUST HAVE A FIRE EXTINGUISHER WITH A UL RATING OF AT LEAST 10 BC.**

Leaks or Spills

If something has spilled, or is leaking, *DON'T TOUCH IT*—certain hazardous materials can kill you just by touching or breathing them. Attempt to determine what the material is by looking at your shipping papers, but under no circumstances should you go near it or allow anyone else to. Contact your company and the local authorities as quickly as possible. Do not attempt to move the vehicle unless you have to due to safety concerns.

- If you are driving down the road and notice something is leaking from the vehicle, **STOP IMMEDIATELY**—pull as far off the road as you can safely, obtain your shipping papers, get away from the vehicle and then send someone else for help. Stay away from the truck, but keep it in sight, so you can keep others away. Do not drive to a phone if you spot something leaking out of the vehicle. You will be making the situation much worse. Remember—you must do everything you can to *CONTAIN* the spill, but only if safety permits.

- When sending someone else for help, be sure to write down on a piece of paper:
  —your location
  —description of the emergency
  —your name, your carrier's name, and your carrier's phone number
  —the shipping name, hazard class and ID number

Whenever an emergency occurs involving hazardous materials, the **EMERGENCY RESPONSE TEAM (ERT)** will need to know what material is involved. The driver must be able to give that information, or if he is unable to speak, then the shipping papers or the placarding must be able to provide it. This is what we call **COMMUNICATING THE RISK**.

It is safe to say, except in very rare instances, in the event of an emergency involving hazardous materials, the driver should never attempt to handle the materials involved. He should keep others away. Never smoke or allow smoking—and only attempt to move the vehicle away from people or property if absolutely safe to do so.

If, while unloading the vehicle, you discover that a package containing hazardous materials has been damaged, *get out of the vehicle* quickly and contact your company immediately. Do not touch or inhale the material.

Bulk Tank Marking

There are two type of bulk tanks.

1. **CARGO TANKS**—These are **ATTACHED PERMANENTLY** to the vehicle. Loading and unloading takes place with the tank on the vehicle.
2. **PORTABLE TANKS**—These are portable, **NOT PERMANENTLY MOUNTED** to the vehicle, and loading and unloading takes place with the tanks off the vehicle.

With cargo tanks, the placard requirements are a little different. The rules require that the *ID NUMBER* must appear on the vehicle. This requirement can be met in several ways. The rules require that the numbers be black 4-inch numbers on an orange panel; a *DOT* placard on a white, diamond-shaped background. Specification cargo tanks must also show re-test date markings.

Tank Cargo Markings

Portable tanks must also show the owner's or leaser's name. The shipping name and ID number must be on *opposing* sides. If the tank holds 1,000 gallons or more, then the ID number must be on *all four sides*. The numbers and letters must be in black ink and at least two inches high.

Loading and Unloading

When loading or unloading a tank vehicle, certain additional rules must be followed. The person unloading must:

- be within 25 feet and have a clear view
- be aware of the hazards
- know procedures to follow in an emergency
- be authorized and able to move the cargo tank if necessary

When loading and unloading tanks with flammables or gases:

- don't smoke
- turn off engine—use engine only to run pump if necessary
- **<u>ENGINE SHOULD BE TURNED ON ONLY AFTER PRODUCT HOSE IS HOOKED UP AND TURNED OFF BEFORE UNCOUPLING HOSE</u>**
- secure truck against movement
- secure ground correctly (if required); have ground attached before and after opening fill hole

Following the test at the end of this chapter is Appendix A: Table of Hazard Class and Division Definitions. (You do not need to memorize this, it will not be on your CDL test.)

STOP

WATCH VIDEO ON HAZARDOUS MATERIALS

☞ LET'S TAKE A TEST

Hazardous Materials

All applicants seeking the Hazardous Material Endorsement for their Commercial Drivers License must take this test.

1. Who is responsible for safely transporting hazardous material and keeping the shipping papers in their proper location?

    A. the carrier
    B. the driver
    C. the consignee
    D. the shipper

2. If you are hauling a hazardous material which is noted as "Flammable Liquid" and the description also says "Poison Inhalation," you should:

    A. affix placards to your vehicle for "Poison" only
    B. affix placards to your vehicle for "Flammable Liquid" only
    C. affix placards to your vehicle for "Dangerous" only
    D. affix placards to your vehicle for both "Poison" and the hazard class for flammable liquids

3. If you are involved in a hazardous material emergency you should first:

    A. get as far away from the emergency as you can
    B. seek help
    C. take steps to protect yourself and the public
    D. hose the material down with water and try to dilute it as much as possible

4. When transporting hazardous materials which of the following is required?

    A. stop and check your dual tires once every 2 hours or 100 miles
    B. stop and check your dual tires once every 3 hours or 150 miles
    C. stop and check your dual tires once every 4 hours or 200 miles
    D. stop and check your dual tires the first 25 miles of the trip

5. If you discover a hazardous materials leak, you should:

   A. drive to the nearest safe haven and call for assistance
   B. identify the hazardous material which is leaking
   C. remove the leaking material and place it a safe distance away from the vehicle
   D. smell the leaking material to determine what it is

6. How do you determine if a load contains hazardous material(s)?

   A. inspect each package and/or container
   B. ask the dispatcher
   C. review the shipping papers
   D. ask the shipper

7. Your vehicle is carrying a Class/Division 8 hazardous material. When must you properly placard the vehicle?

   A. when the amount exceeds 10 pounds
   B. when the amount exceeds 100 pounds
   C. when the amount exceed 1,000 pounds
   D. you never use placards for Class/Division 8 hazardous materials

8. Your vehicle is not equipped with racks to hold cylinders. You can load them onto your vehicle provided:

   A. they are placed in the driver's compartment and secured
   B. they are loaded upright or braced laying down flat
   C. are properly labeled as "non-flammable gas"
   D. bundled together with steel or rubber strapping

9. What is the shape of the hazardous material label that the shipper places on most hazardous material packages?

   A. diamond
   B. round
   C. oval
   D. square

10. Whose responsibility is it to determine the proper routing and permits needed to haul hazardous materials?

    A. carrier
    B. consignee
    C. shipper
    D. driver

11. Your load contains 500 lbs of Explosives 1.1 and 500 lbs of Explosives 1.2. Which placard or placards must you use?

    A. explosives 1.1
    B. explosives 1.1 and explosives 1.2
    C. dangerous
    D. explosives and dangerous

12. The symbol "D" in column 1 of the Hazardous Material Table means that the proper shipping name of the hazardous material is:

    A. appropriate for describing material for domestic transportation
    B. describes hazardous material that can be shipped overseas by air in all cases
    C. not subject to the hazardous material regulations when shipped to Europe
    D. appropriate for all international shipments of hazardous materials

13. It is the responsibility of the shipper of hazardous waste to:

    A. give the driver all necessary MSDS's
    B. place the word "Waste" before the proper shipping name on the shipping papers
    C. require the driver to load the material onto the vehicle
    D. plan out the route to be traveled

14. Your vehicle is improperly placarded for the hazardous material you are transporting, when can you move the vehicle?

    A. never
    B. anytime as long as you are driving directly back to your terminal to obtain the correct placards
    C. only in the event of an emergency when necessary to protect life and property
    D. if the amount of the hazardous material is less than 1,001 lbs

15. When can you transfer flammable liquids from one cargo tanker to another on a public roadway?

    A. never
    B. between the hours of midnight and 5 P.M. when traffic is light
    C. anytime
    D. only in an emergency

16. You have just discovered a hazardous material leaking from a package but not leaking from the vehicle, you should:

    A. drive to the nearest safe place and call emergency personnel
    B. remove the material from the vehicle and place it safely off the roadway and call for help
    C. repack the material with anything that will contain it
    D. do nothing as long as it is NOT leaking from the vehicle and complete your trip in a normal manner

17. When must the quantity of a hazardous material appear on the shipping paper?

    A. always
    B. when the amount is more that 10 lbs or 100 gallons
    C. when the reportable quantity (RQ) box is checked
    D. when the amount transported exceeds 500 lbs or 1,001 gallons

18. It is "OK" to transport Nitric Acid (Class 8) hazardous material with other hazardous material provided it is not stacked more than two levels high, and:

    A. the quantity does not exceed 1,000 lbs
    B. the transport index does not exceed 1.5
    C. the quantity is not marked "RQ" (reportable quantity)
    D. it is never loaded above any other material

19. If a hazardous material spill occurs, it must be reported to the National Response Center (NRC) within:

    A. 24 hours
    B. 30 days
    C. 15 days
    D. 36 hours

20. A hazard class name or ID number must not be used to describe a:

    A. hazardous waste
    B. reportable quantity of a hazardous substance
    C. non-hazardous material
    D. hazardous material

21. The intention of the hazardous material regulations are to ensure safe drivers and equipment, to communicate the risk, and:

    A. determine proper taxes to be charged to the shipper
    B. to contain the material
    C. to allow for state enforcement of hazardous material regulations
    D. none of the above

22. The power unit of a placarded vehicle is required to have a fire extinguisher with a UL rating of at least:

    A.   5 B:C
    B. 10 B:C
    C. 15 B:C
    D. 20 B:C

23. You may not park a vehicle carrying hazardous material within how many feet of an open fire?

    A.   300 feet
    B.   400 feet
    C.   500 feet
    D. 1000 feet

24. Before loading or unloading any explosives, you must check the cargo space for:

    A. a cargo heater that could start
    B. sharp point that might damage the cargo
    C. loose floor boards or plates
    D. all of the above

25. Which of the following shipping paper descriptions is in the correct order?

    A. hydrogen bromide, non-flammable gas, UN 1048
    B. UN 1787, corrosive material, hydriotic acid
    C. corrosive material, hydrochloric acid, UN 1789
    D. hexane, UN 1208, flammable liquid

26. When hauling Class 7 (radioactive) material in a single transport you cannot:

    A. haul explosive 1.1 in the same transport
    B. cannot stop every 2 hours and check your tires and cargo
    C. load the vehicle yourself
    D. haul ORM-D in the same transport

27. If a vehicle carrying explosive crashes with another vehicle, you must not separate the vehicles from one another until:

    A. at least 30 minutes has passed and no fire or smoke is visible
    B. a firefighting crew is standing by
    C. the explosives have been removed and placed at least 200 feet away
    D. bomb experts have checked the explosives for stability

28. After loading hazardous material into a cargo tanker you must do what before moving the tanker?

    A. have the shipper check for leaks
    B. sign all paperwork
    C. call your dispatcher and ask for instructions for proper placarding
    D. close all manholes and valves and check for leaks

29. How much "Poison Gas" can you transport before you must placard the vehicle with "Poison Gas" placards

    A. 100 lbs
    B. 500 lbs
    C. more than 1,000 lbs
    D. any amount

30. You may briefly park within five foot of the roadway when hauling most hazardous material if your work requires it. Which of the following are the exception and do not allow parking near a road?

    A. ORM C, D or E
    B. explosives 1.1 and 1.2
    C. corrosives
    D. poisons

31. In the event of a hazardous materials emergency, you should:

    A. warn others of the danger
    B. contact the appropriate authorities
    C. prevent smoking and keep any open flame away
    D. all of the above

32. If you transport route controlled radioactive material—you must have received specialized training within the past:

    A. 2 years
    B. 12 months
    C. 3 years
    D. 5 years

33. If you break down on the highway, and are transporting gasoline, flammable liquid, UN1203, which of the following warning devices are you permitted to use?

    A. fusees
    B. flares
    C. reflective triangles
    D. smudge pots

34. If you are transporting Division 1.2 or 1.3 Explosives, how close to a bridge, tunnel or building can you park?

    A. 100 feet
    B. 200 feet
    C. 500 feet
    D. 300 feet

35. When transporting Division 1.1, 1.2 or 1.3 Explosives, the driver is required to have a written route plan.

    True   False

36. If your vehicle is hauling hazardous material and you've broken down along the highway, you may leave your vehicle briefly if you can get someone else to watch it. What are the requirements of the person watching the vehicle in this case?

    A. must be on the vehicle or within 100 feet of it with a clear view
    B. must be awake and able to move it if necessary
    C. must know what to do in an emergency
    D. all of the above

37. If you transport Division 1.1, 1.2 or 1.3 Explosives, your carrier must:

    A. provide you with an air-conditioned truck
    B. provide you with an additional life insurance policy
    C. provide you with a copy of the FMCSR, Part 397
    D. provide you with the consignee's phone number

38. When a placarded vehicle is being refueled, the regulations state:

    A. driver must be holding a fire extinguisher ready to use
    B. someone must be at the nozzle, controlling the flow of fuel
    C. someone must be helping the driver in case a fire erupts
    D. vehicle must be 300 feet away from a building or a place where people gather

39. While driving a vehicle with hazardous materials requiring placards, you discover a tire is leaking, you should:

    A. stop as soon as you reach a safe place and repair it
    B. stop immediately and call for road service
    C. drive to the nearest phone and call CHEMTREC
    D. proceed to your destination

40. Foodstuff should not be carried in the same vehicle as:

    A. flammable gas
    B. corrosives
    C. poisons
    D. oxidizers

41. Who must certify that a shipment has been prepared according to hazardous material regulation?

    A. driver
    B. carrier
    C. consignee
    D. shipper

42. Cargo tanks have the same placarding requirements as any type vehicle transporting hazardous materials.

    True   False

43. Package labels on HAZMAT packages must be the same as on the shipping papers.

    True   False

44. Division 1.1 and 1.2 Explosives must not be transported in a combination vehicle if it includes a placarded cargo tank.

    True   False

45. You find an overheated tire during an en route inspection. If you are hauling hazardous materials, you must:

    A. wait at least two hours before continuing your trip
    B. cool the tire, then check it every two hours
    C. lower that tire's cold air pressure by at least 20 psi
    D. remove the tire and place it a safe distance from the vehicle

46. A shipment described on the Hazardous Waste Manifest may only be delivered to:

    A. another registered transporter
    B. any motor carrier with a DOT number
    C. a facility authorized to handle hazardous waste
    D. both A & C

47. The transporter of hazardous waste must keep a copy of the manifest for:

    A. 2 years
    B. 3 years
    C. 5 years
    D. indefinitely

48. Who must sign the hazardous waste manifest when delivered to a proper facility?

    A. the driver
    B. the facility dispatcher
    C. the facility operator
    D. none of the above

49. A Hazardous Waste Manifest must be treated the same as any hazardous material shipping paper:

    True   False

50. I bet you are glad you are finished with this test:

    True   False

Answer Key

1.	B	18.	D	35.	True
2.	D	19.	B	36.	D
3.	C	20.	C	37.	C
4.	A	21.	B	38.	B
5.	B	22.	B	39.	A
6.	C	23.	A	40.	C
7.	C	24.	D	41.	D
8.	B	25.	A	42.	False
9.	A	26.	A	43.	True
10.	D	27.	C	44.	True
11.	A	28.	D	45.	D
12.	A	29.	D	46.	D
13.	B	30.	B	47.	B
14.	C	31.	D	48.	C
15.	D	32.	A	49.	True
16.	A	33.	C	50.	True
17.	A	34.	D		

If you were able to answer all of the questions correctly . . . *GOOD JOB!* If you missed any, read the material again until you know it with 100% accuracy.

(Note: You will not be tested on this Table.)

Appendix B: Table of Hazard Class Definitions

HAZARD CLASS	DEFINITION	EXAMPLES
Flammable liquid Class 3	Any liquid having a flash point below 141°F.	Ethyl alcohol, gasoline, acetone, benzene, dimethyl, sulfide
Combustible liquid Class 3	Any liquid having a flash point at or above 141°F and below 200°F as determined by tests listed in	Kerosene, fuel oil
Flammable solid Division 4.1	Any solid material, other than an explosive, liable to cause fires through friction or retained heat from manufacturing or processing, or which can be ignited readily creating a serious transportation hazard because it burns vigorously and persistently.	Nitro-cellulose (film), phosphorus, charcoal
Oxidizer Division 5.1	A substance such as chlorate, permanganate, inorganic peroxide, or a nitrate that yields oxygen readily to stimulate the combustion of organic matter.	Potassium bromide, hydrogen peroxide solution, chromic acid, some bleaches
Organic peroxide Division 5.2	An organic compound containing the bivalent -0-0- structure and which may be considered a derivative of hydrogen peroxide, where one or more of the hydrogen atoms have been replaced by organic radicals.	Urea peroxide, benzoyl
Corrosive Material Class 8	Liquid or solid that causes visible destruction or irreversible alterations in human skin tissue at the site of contact. Liquids that severely corrode steel are included.	Bromine, soda lime, hydrochloric acid, sodium hydroxide solution, battery acid
Flammable gas	A compressed gas, as defined in 173.300(a), that meets certain flammability requirements.	Butane, engine starting fluid, hydrogen, liquefied petroleum gas
Non-flammable gas	A compressed gas other than a flammable gas.	Chlorine, anhydrous ammonia, oxygen

Irritating material Division 6.1	A liquid or solid substance which on contact with fire or when exposed to air, gives off dangerous or intensely irritating fumes. Poison Gas materials excluded.	Tear gas, monochloroacetone, diphenyichlorarsine
Poison Division 2.3	Extremely dangerous poison gases or liquids belong to this class. Very small amounts of these gases or vapors of these liquids, mixed with air, are dangerous to life.	Hydrocyanic acid, bromo acetone, nitric oxide, phosgene, nitrogen tetroxide, ethyidichorarsine
Poison Class 6	Substances, liquids, or solids (including pastes and semi-solids), other than Poison Gas or irritating materials, that are known to be toxic to humans. These materials cause serious sickness or death within 48 hours following skin contact, inhalation or ingestion by mouth. In the absence of adequate data on human toxicity, materials are presumed to be toxic to humans if they are toxic to laboratory animals exposed under specified conditions.	Phenol, nitroaniline, parathion, cyanide, mercury based pesticides, disinfectants
Etiologic agents Division 6.2	A viable micro-organism, or its toxin, which causes or may cause human disease.	Vibrio cholorae, clostridium botulinum, polio virus, salmonella, all serotypes
Radioactive material Class 7	A material that spontaneously emits ionizing radiation having a specific activity greater than 0.002 microcuries per gram. Further classifications are made within this category according to levels of radioactivity.	Thorium nitrate, uranium hexaflouride
Explosives Division 1.1 or Division 1.2	Explosives are chemical compounds, mixtures, or devices, the primary or common purpose of which is to function by explosion. unless such compound, mixture, or device is otherwise classified.	
	Detonate with a shock wave greater than the speed of sound and are of maximum hazard.	Dynamite, nitroglycerin
Explosives Division 1.2 or Division 1.3	Generally function by rapid combustion rather than detonation and are a flammable hazard.	Torpedo, propellant explosive

Explosives Division 1.4	Manufactured articles, such as small arms ammunition, that contain restricted quantities of class A and/or class B explosives, and certain types of fireworks. class C explosives are of minimum hazard.	Toy caps, trick matches, signal flare, some fireworks
Blasting agent Division 1.5	A material designed for blasting, but so insensitive that there is very little probability of ignition during transport.	Ammonium nitrate/fuel oil mixture
Explosive Extremely Insensitive Division 1.6	Material or substance found to be an extremely insensitive detonating substance.	
	ORM (Other Regulated Materials) is any regulated material that does not meet the definition of the other hazard classes.	
Class 9	A material which has an anesthetic, irritating, noxious, toxic, or similar property and can cause extreme annoyance or dis-comfort to passengers and crew in the event of leakage during transportation.	Trichoroethylene, carbon tetrachloride, ethylene dibromide, chloroform
Class 9	A material such as a consumer commodity, ORM-D, which, although otherwise subject to regulation, presents a limited hazard during transportation due to its form, quantity, and packaging.	Consumer commodity not otherwise specified, such as nail polish, small arms ammunition, hair spray
Class 9	A material that is not included in any other hazard class, but is subject to regulation. Materials in this class include hazardous wastes and hazardous substances named in the List of Hazardous Substances and Reportable Ouantities but not in the Hazardous Materials Table. Also marine pollutants and elevated temperature material.	phenacetin, saccharin, aldicarb, reserpine, heptachlor

Skills Test

Who is Required to Take the CDL Skills Test?

The Skills Test

The skills test is divided into three sections:

1. The Pre-Trip Inspection Test—This test is designed to see if you know how to correctly conduct an inspection of the vehicle to determine if it is safe to drive.
2. The Basic Control Skills Test—Will tell the examiner if you can safely back, park and judge the vehicle length.
3. Road Test—You will be taken on a road to test your ability to safely handle the vehicle in most on-the-road situations.

PLEASE NOTE: If you are applying for a "Class C" CDL, you will not be required to take the road test portion of the skills test.

For the Basic Control Skills Test and the Road Test, you will be required to take the test in the same type of vehicle as the type of CDL for which you are applying. In other words, if you are a municipal bus operator, you will be applying for a "Class B" CDL and will be taking the Transporting Passengers Test. If your bus is equipped with air brakes, you will also be taking the air brake test. This means that you must take your skills test in a similar type bus which is equipped with air brakes.

If you operate a tractor-trailer, you will be applying for a "Class A" CDL. You must then take your skills test in a similar type tractor-trailer.

Most of the skills test must be done by appointment. Check with your state to find what is the proper procedure. Some states are using "third parties" to administer the test. This means that the test may be held at a trucking company or bus company. Again, check with your state to find out the closest location to you.

The skills test are designed to be tough. In the states which have already started giving them, the failure rate has been high. This is because most drivers think it will be easy. *It isn't.* You must prepare for them, and you must practice. This chapter will tell you what you'll need to do, and know, but it's still up to you!

You've heard the old saying "practice makes perfect." In this case, it really is true. If you are going to pass the skills test the first time through, you must practice, practice, practice.

The Pre-Trip Inspection

Before going down to take your skills test, you must do a thorough pre-trip of the vehicle. If you get to the examiner station and discover a defect in the vehicle, the examiner will not allow the truck to be used. This will mean that you will lose your appointment and it may take several weeks to re-schedule another one.

You will need to take the following:
- tire pressure gauge
- tread depth gauge
- tire "billy"—tire "checker"
- wheel chocks
- shop rag (for cleaning lights and reflectors)
- gloves
- vehicle registrations
- proof of insurance (certain states will require this)
- any applicable permits to operate in the state
- your current driver's license

When you arrive at the examining station, the examiner will give you instructions. They will be similar to the following:

"This testing period will consist of three parts: a vehicle inspection test, a basic control skills test, and an on-the-road driving test. For the vehicle inspection test, I will ask you to do a thorough inspection of the vehicle. For the basic control skills test, you will do several backing, parking and turning exercises. For the road test, we will go out on the road for a trip that will take 30 to 45 minutes."

"At all times during this test, when you are behind the wheel, you are in charge of the vehicle. I will never knowingly ask you to do something that is unsafe or illegal."

"I will give you directions as we go along. If you have any questions, please ask—if you do not understand a direction, please ask me to clarify it."

When you are ready to begin the Pre-Trip Inspection Test, the examiner will say:

"For the vehicle inspection, please conduct a complete and thorough inspection of the vehicle. You may use the Vehicle Inspection Memory Aid from the Driver's Manual if you wish."

"As you do the inspection, <u>point to,</u> or <u>touch</u> the things you are inspecting, and explain what you are looking for."

Start by inspecting the engine compartment. Then start the engine. After you have done the start-up checks, turn off the engine and do the rest of the inspection. Do you have any questions? Go ahead and start the vehicle inspection now."

The key to doing a proper pre-trip inspection is:

- doing it the same way each time and
- practice

We suggest that you perform the pre-trip inspection following the seven-step procedure as outlined in Chapter 2, General Knowledge. Use the Vehicle Inspection Memory Aid located at the back of the manual. You are permitted to carry this with you during the pre-trip inspection test.

Practice, and do it the same way each time. By doing it the same way, you will develop a rhythm or routine. If you miss checking something you'll know it instantly. Practice until you have it down pat.

Practice until you are able to complete the entire pre-trip, checking all the items required, in 20 to 30 minutes.

When taking the pre-trip inspection test, the examiner will want you to do it in the following manner:

1. Inspect the engine compartment
2. Start engine and perform the in-vehicle checks
3. Shut down engine and perform the external inspection

This is how they want you to do it, so study and then practice it this way. Most likely, the examiner will only have you check one side of the vehicle. They figure if you do the one side correctly, then you'll know how to do the other one correctly. On a straight truck or tractor-trailer, it will be up to the examiner which side he wants checked; a bus will be inspected on the passenger door (curb) side.

If the vehicle is a COE, (cab-over-the-engine) tractor, you will not be required to jack up the cab. If you are unable to check a particular item due to the cab not being raised, you *must* say to the examiner that you are unable to check and explain what you would have looked for. By doing this, you'll get credit for having checked it.

While you are inspecting the vehicle, the examiner will be making notes or marks on his score sheet. *DON'T GET NERVOUS!* Many times he must make marks when you do something right. So don't think that since he's writing so much, that he's only writing down what you've missed—he's probably writing down those items that you've checked.

While you are doing the pre-trip you *must* call out to the examiner what you are inspecting and what you are looking for. It should sound something like this:

"I'm checking the wheel, the lugs and the nuts. I'm looking for any cracks, missing lugs or nuts, or any rust which may indicate a loose nut."

It's your job to make sure the examiner knows what you are checking. If he can't hear you, or if you don't indicate what you are checking and what you're looking for, he probably isn't going to give you credit for checking it. Too many of those, and you may have to come back a second time. Once you have checked an item, a wheel for example—when you get to the next wheel, all you need to say is that:

"I would check this wheel for the same items that I checked the other one for."

That proves to the examiner that you know what you are doing—but be sure to say it—if you don't, he may assume you just forgot to check it.

The 7-Step Pre-Trip Inspection

Step 1—Approach Vehicle

As you are walking to the vehicle you are looking for signs of obvious damage, leaks, vehicle leaning and checking the area surrounding the vehicle for any hazards or objects.

Step 2—Check Engine Compartment

Check all engine compartment components; fluid levels, wiring, belts, hoses, steering controls, front brakes, suspension, etc.

Step 3—Start Engine and Inspect Inside the Cab

Transmission in neutral (park if an automatic), brakes applied, depress clutch and start engine. Check all instruments, gauges and controls. Check all emergency equipment and vehicle registration.

Step 4—Turn Off Engine and Check Lights

Check headlights (low and high beam) and 4-way flashers on front of vehicle. Shut off headlights and 4-ways, turn on all marker and clearance lamps and right-turn signal.

Step 5—Do Walkaround Inspection

Starting at driver's door, begin checking all required items: lights, fuel tanks, wheels, mirrors, coupling devices, suspension, air line connections and air lines, brakes, doors, etc.

PLEASE NOTE: On page 290 of this manual you are told that failure to do all of the required brake checks is an automatic failure. Also know that in certain states, such as Pennsylvania, if you do any of these checks incorrectly, automatic failure will also result. For example, when pumping the brakes to check your low air pressure warning device your engine must be off.

Step 6—Check Signal Lights

Turn off all body lights, turn on brake lights and left-turn signal and check.

Step 7—Start Engine and Check Brake System

Turn off lights and perform brake system checks.

The following is a list of items which must be checked during the pre-trip inspection test, and should be checked before driving the vehicle. A description of what you must do, and what the examiner will be looking to see if you do, will follow each item.

These are not listed in the same order as you will check them during the test.

1. Air brake check—Driver should perform following air brake system checks:
   - Let air pressure build to governed cut-out pressure; should occur between 100–125 psi
   - With engine off, wheels chocked, and parking brake released, fully apply foot brake to see if air pressure drops more than 3 pounds in one minute (single vehicle) or more than 4 pounds in one minute (for combination unit). If loss exceeds this amount, there is a defect somewhere in the system.
   - Start fanning off the air pressure by rapidly applying and releasing foot brake: low air pressure warning alarm should activate before air pressure drops below 60 psi
   - Continues to fan off the air pressure: at approximately 40 pounds pressure on a tractor-trailer, the tractor protection valve should close (pop out); or on other vehicle types, the spring brake push-pull valve should pop.

2. Air buzzer sounds—If the air pressure is low, the low air pressure warning will sound immediately after the engine starts, but before the air compressor has built up pressure. You should let air pressure build to governed cut-out pressure, which should occur between 100-125 psi. The low air pressure warning should stop when the air pressure gets to 60 psi or more.

3. Air compressor—With engine off, point, touch, or press belt to test that it is tight. You should note that the belt is not frayed, no visible cracks, loose fibers, or signs of wear. If belt appears worn or loose, push it with hand, and if it deflects more than 1/2 to 3/4 of an inch, slippage is probably excessive.

4. Air leak—No audible air leaks from air brake system, or from suspension system air bags.

5. Air/electric lines—Check that air hoses are not cut, cracked, chafed or worn (steel braid should not show through); listen for audible air leaks. Air and electrical lines are not tangled, crimped or pinched, or being dragged against tractor parts. Electrical line insulation is not cut, cracked, chafed or worn (no electrical conductor showing through). None of the air or electrical lines are spliced or taped.

6. Air/electrical connectors—Check that trailer air connectors are sealed and in good condition; check that glad hands are locked in place, free of

damage, and there are no audible air leaks. Check that trailer electrical plug is firmly seated and locked in place.

7. Ammeter/voltmeter—Check that gauge shows alternator or generator is charging; or warning light is off; needle will jump and flutter, then register "charge."

8. Axle seals—No cracks or distortions in wheel/axle mounting, and no signs of leaking lubricants.

9. Cat walk secure—Cat walk is solid, securely bolted to tractor frame, and clear of loose objects.

10. Chamber (brake)—Not cracked or dented; and securely mounted.

11. Coolant level—Look at sight glass of reservoir, or remove the radiator cap and look to see the level. *NEVER REMOVE IF RADIATOR IS HOT! ADEQUATE LEVEL WILL SHOW IN SIGHT GLASS, OR BE VISIBLE IN THE RADIATOR WHEN THE CAP IS REMOVED.*

12. Clutch/gearshift—Depress clutch before turning on the starter; keep depressed until engine reaches idling speed. On an automatic transmission, the selector should be in the "park" position.

13. Doors secure (buses)—Baggage compartment doors closed securely.

14. Doors, ties secure (buses)—Doors not bent or broken; hinges secure; latches secure and fully closed. Check that there are no loose ties hanging from the side of the trailer; and/or that all cargo is securely tied down.

15. Drive shaft—Shaft not bent or cracked; shaft couplings appear to be secure.

16. Drum (brake)—No cracks or dents or holes; no loose or missing bolts. Brake linings (where visible) not worn dangerously thin.

17. Exhaust system—Outside visible parts are securely mounted; no cracks, holes, or severe dents.

18. Frame—No cracks or bends in longitudinal frame members; no loose, cracked, bent, broken or missing cross members. On truck box, or trailer frame—no signs of breaks or holes in box or trailer floor.

Note: Cracks in members are most likely to appear midway between points of attachment to vehicle assemblies; for example, half-way between tractor cab and rear tractor wheels.

19. Fuel tank—Check that tank is secure; caps are secure and have seals; no leaks or damaged tank.

20. Generator belt—With the engine off, driver points to, touches, or presses belt to test that the belt is tight. Should also note that the belt is not frayed, no visible cracks, loose fibers, or signs of wear. Should push belt with hand; if deflects more than 1/2 to 3/4 of an inch slippage is probably excessive.

21. Header board (headache rack)—If required, is securely mounted, free of damage and adequate to contain or hold cargo in the event of panic stop. Canvas or tarp, if so equipped, is securely mounted and lashed down.

22. Heater/defroster—Check that heater/defroster is working.

23. Horn(s)—Check that electric and/or air horns work.

24. Hoses (brakes)—Check for cracked, worn or frayed hoses, and for secure couplings.

25. Hub oil seal—Check wheel to see that hub oil seal is not leaking; and, if sight glass present, that oil level is adequate.

26. Kingpin/apron—Check that kingpin does not appear bent; that apron lies flat on fifth wheel skid plate; and that visible part of apron is not bent, cracked or broken.

27. Landing gear—Check that landing gear is fully raised, no missing parts, support frame not bent or damaged; crank handle is present and secured; if power operated, no air or hydraulic leaks.

28. Leaks (engine compartment)—Check for signs of fluid puddles or dripping fluids on the ground under the engine, or the underside of the engine.

29. Leaks (fuel tank area)—Check for any fuel leaks from tanks. Check that gasket is secure in cap.

30. Lighting indicators—Check that indicators illuminate when corresponding lights are turned on.

31. Lights (front)—All lights illuminate and are clean; headlights function on both high and low beams.

Note: You may mix checks of different lighting functions in with other parts of the inspection. There is no requirement to check lights in a specific order. The examiner will keep track that all lights were checked.

32. Lights, reflectors—Check that reflectors are clean; none are missing or broken; and they are of proper color (red on rear, amber elsewhere). Check that clearance lights work, are clean, not broken, and of proper color (red on rear, amber elsewhere). Check that rear running lights are clean, not

broken, and are of proper color. Rear running lights must be checked separately from signal, flasher, and brake lights.

Note: Checks of running lights and clearance lights may be done at different times in the inspection. Examiner will keep track that all lighting functions were checked.

33. Linings—On some brake drums, there are openings where the brake linings can be seen from outside the drum. For this type of drum, you should check that a visible amount of brake lining is showing. If brake linings cannot be seen because of dust covers or backing plates, you will not need to check them, but, you must mention to the examiner that the linings are covered and cannot be checked.

34. Locking pins (fifth wheel)—Look for loose or missing pins in the slide mechanism of sliding fifth wheels; if air powered—no air leaks. Check that fifth wheel is not so far forward that tractor frame will strike landing gear during turns.

35. Lug nuts—Check that all lug nuts are present; check that lugs are not loose (look for rust trails around nuts); no cracks radiating from lug bolt holes, nor distortion of the bolt holes.

36. Mirrors—Check for proper adjustment; not cracked or loose (fittings); visibility not impaired due to dirty mirrors.

37. Mounting bolts—Look for loose or missing mounting brackets, clamps, bolts, or nuts; both fifth wheel and slide mounting appear solidly attached in place.

38. Oil level—With the engine stopped, check the oil level. Level must be above the refill mark.

39. Oil pressure builds—Check that oil pressure is building to normal; the gauge shows increasing or normal oil pressure; or warning light goes off. Engine oil temperature gauge (if present) should begin a gradual rise to normal operating range.

40. Parking brake—Check that parking brake will hold vehicle by gently trying to pull forward with parking brake on.

41. Passenger emergency exits—Check that all emergency exit doors can be opened, and that they are firmly closed.

42. Passenger entry—Door correctly opens and locks closed; entry steps clear; treads not loose or worn out enough to trip passenger.

43. Passenger seating—No broken seat frames; seats firmly attached to floor.

44. Platform (fifth wheel)—No cracks or breaks in the platform structure.

45. Power steering fluid—With the engine stopped, pull out the dip stick and check fluid level. Level must be above refill mark.

46. Release arm of fifth wheel—Check that release arm is in the engaged position; and any safety latch is in place.

47. Rims—Check for damaged or bent rims; rims should not have welding repairs; no rust trails that indicate that rim is loose on wheel.

48. Safety latch—Check for damage; make sure it is working properly.

49. Safety/emergency equipment—Check for electrical fuses (if used); three red reflective triangles; and a properly charged and rated fire extinguisher.

50. Signal and brake lights—Check that both brake lights come on when brakes applied; check that each signal light flashes; and check that 4-way flashers work.

Note: Checks of brake, signal, and 4-way flasher functions must be done separately. You will likely check each function at different times in the inspection; e.g., turn on flashers at the beginning of the inspection. Examiner will keep track that all signals were checked.

51. Slack adjuster—Check for broken, loose, or missing parts; angle between push rod and adjuster arm should be a little over 90 degrees when brakes are released, and not less than 90 degrees when brakes are applied. When pulled by hand, brake rod should not move more than approximately one inch.

52. Tire spacers—Check that dual wheels are evenly separated, and that tires are not touching one another.

53. Look for broken leaves, leaves that have shifted and are in, or nearly in, contact with the tires, rim, brake drum, frame or body; missing or broken leaves in the leaf spring. For coil spring, look for broken or distorted spring.

54. Spring mount—Check for cracked or broken spring hangers; broken, missing, or loose bolts; missing or damaged bushings; broken, loose, or missing axle mounting parts.

55. Steering box secure—Look for missing nuts, bolts, cotter keys, etc.; power steering fluid leaks; damage to power steering hose.

56. Steering linkage—Connecting links, arms, rods not worn or cracked; joints and sockets not worn or loose; no loose or missing nuts or bolts.

57. Steering play—Non-power steering: you turn the steering wheel back and forth, should have less than 5-10 degrees free play (approximately 2 at the rim of a 20-inch steering wheel). Power steering: with engine running, work steering wheel from left to right and note degree of free play that occurs before front left wheel barely moves (should be less than 5-10 degrees).

58. Tires—Check tread depth (see note); tire inflation (see note); tread evenly worn; look for cuts or other damage to the tread or walls; valve caps and stem are not missing, broken or damaged; retread not separating from tire (no retreads on front wheels).

Note: Minimum tread depth is 4/32 inch on front tires, and 2/32 inch on other tires. A proper check of inflation requires use of a tire pressure gauge. A "tire billy" can be used to check that the tire is not flat. You must use a "tire billy" to check a tire to see if it is flat. If you just kick it, it will be scored as incorrect.

59. Torsion bar—Check that torsion bar assembly or torque arm is not cracked, broken or missing.

60. Water pump belt—With engine off, point to, touch, or press belt to test that it is snug. You should note that the belt is not frayed, no visible cracks, loose fibers, or signs of wear. If belt appears worn or loose, you should push belt with hand, and if it deflects more that 1/2 to 3/4 of an inch, slippage is probably excessive.

61. Windshield—Check for cracks, dirt, and illegal stickers or other obstructions to view.

62. Wipers—Check for worn rubber on blades; blades secure on wiper arm; and that wipers work.

You now know what to expect during the pre-trip inspection test. The keys to passing the first time are:

1. Practice—Practice until you can complete it in approximately 20 to 30 minutes without missing any items.
2. Be consistent—Use the 7-step method or develop your own, but do it the same way every time.
3. Study—This chapter and Chapter 2, General Knowledge—the segment on pre-trip inspections.
4. Speak up when taking the test—Tell the examiner what you are checking, and what you are looking for.
5. Be prepared—Check the truck before you go to be tested. Take with you your tire pressure gauge, tread depth gauge, "tire billy," wheel chocks, shop rag, gloves and all registrations, permits and license.

FAILURE TO DO ALL OF THE REQUIRED BRAKE CHECKS IS AN AUTOMATIC FAILURE!

CAUTION: Certain states, such as Pennsylvania, have added a simulated downgrade question. This is done after the pre-trip and before starting the road test. You are asked to simulate you are going down a long downgrade. You must say to the examiner:

1. I would test my brakes before starting down
2. I would downshift to the proper gear before starting down
3. I would not clutch or shift after I started down
4. I would constantly check my mirrors
5. I would use light steady pressure

Failure to mention any of these may result in automatic failure.

If after reading and studying about the Pre-trip Inspection, you still have questions, we have available a video that shows and explains completely how to conduct a Pre-trip Inspection.

This video, "Pre-trip Inspection—Tractor-Trailer," is the ONLY video available that shows the Pre-trip Inspection exactly as required by the state's CDL examinations.

To order the video, call 1-(800)-869-3926.

The Basic Control Skills Test

If you have ever been to a truck rodeo, you have a pretty good idea what the Basic Control Skills Test is like.

The purpose of this test is to evaluate your ability to control the vehicle and judge its position in relation to other objects. Can you safely operate the vehicle? This is what the examiner will be looking for. He will test your skill through a series of exercises which are designed to see how well you can turn, park, back, and dock your vehicle. He will also test you to see how close you can come to front and back stop lines. By doing this, he can tell how well you are able to judge the length of your vehicle.

As in the pre-trip test, you will have to practice in order to be able to pass the Basic Control Skills Test the first time through. The test isn't really that difficult, but will require you to use skills that most of you haven't used in a long time. So, you'll have to practice to get those skills back.

Basic Control of the vehicle was covered in Chapter 3 of this manual. If you haven't read it yet, *you need to read it now, before going any further in this chapter.* You must understand the basic principles of vehicle control, which are covered in Chapter 3. Once you understand the basic principles, then *practice, practice* and *practice* until you can do all of the exercises we are about to describe.

There are six different exercises which make up the Basic Control Skills Test. You won't have to do all six of them, but you'll probably have to do at least four. Since there is no way of knowing which of them you'll have to do during the test, you'll have to learn and practice all six.

The six exercises are:

1. Straight line backing—Forward stop line
2. Alley docking—Backing into a dock
3. Parallel parking—Blind side (passenger side)
4. Parallel parking—Sight side (driver's side)
5. Backward serpentine
6. Right turn

Since you won't know which ones you'll be required to execute, you must be prepared to do them all.

We can't emphasize enough that you'll have to practice. The more you practice the better you'll get. Remember how nervous you were the last time you had to take a road test? Some people get so nervous, they end up blowing the test—even drivers with 20 or 30 years of accident-free driving. We've tested hundreds of drivers over the years, and the one thing that we've noticed is that the drivers who are self-confident—who know what they have to do, are the ones who usually do very good on the road tests. So, what you have to do is practice until you get so good you could "pass this test with a blindfold on." When you have practiced to the point that you are **CONFIDENT** you can pass it, then you're ready. By being confident, you won't be nearly as nervous, and you won't make "silly" little mistakes.

You will probably take the Basic Control Skills Test after you've finished the pre-trip inspection test and before you take the road test. However, in some localities, they may not have room at their location for the Basic Control Skills Test. In that case, after you have completed the pre-trip inspection test, you will begin your road test and will stop en route at a location where your Basic Control Skills Test will be conducted.

Here are two new words with which you must become familiar:

1. **ENCROACHMENT**—Each exercise will have boundaries. These may be barrels, painted lines or traffic cones. If you touch or cross over a boundary, this is called an encroachment. Every time you have an encroachment, you lose points. Have enough encroachment, and you fail the test.

   Think of these boundaries as walls. It is possible that you can have an encroachment even if your tires don't touch the boundary. This could happen, for example, if the trailer swing crossed over a boundary. Even though the tire didn't hit, the trailer "punched through" the imaginary wall.

   If you see that you are going to hit a boundary marker, stop! Don't touch it. You must think to yourself that every boundary marker is a brand new car. Every time you hit one, it's an accident! If you see you are going to hit one, stop and pull up.

2. **PULL UP**—Is when you stop and reverse direction to get a better position. A "pull up" is much better than an encroachment. If you must pull up, be sure to pull up to a point where you can position your vehicle

exactly where you want it. Some drivers just pull up a little bit and then have to pull up again. Every pull up will cost you points! Use them if you need them, but use them correctly. Take all the space you need to position the truck correctly. Pull ups will also cost you points, but it's better to have a pull up than an encroachment.

When you're ready to begin the Basic Control Skills test, the examiner will give you the following directions:

"This test will consist of a series of basic control maneuvers."

"Try not to go over any exercise lines or hit any of the cones. These represent the boundaries of the exercise or course. Remember, it is better to do a pull up than to go over a boundary."

"The base of each cone or marker is the exercise boundary. If a wheel passes over the base of a cone, it will count as an encroachment."

"I will give you directions for each exercise as we come to it. When you finish each exercise, tap your horn to let me know."

"Under normal conditions when operating alone, before beginning to back, you would put on your parking brakes, walk to the rear of the vehicle to check to see if it is safe. For the test, I won't require you to do this."

"If you see me raise my arm like this (straight up with palms facing driver), stop the vehicle."

After receiving these instructions, you will be instructed to begin.

Straight Line Backing
Forward Stop Line

Instructions by examiner:

"Drive forward through the alley and stop with your front bumper as close as possible to the painted line at the end of the alley, without going past the line. You may stop only once. Don't pull ahead after you have stopped. Don't lean out of the window or open the door. When I get to the end of the alley, I'll wave you forward."

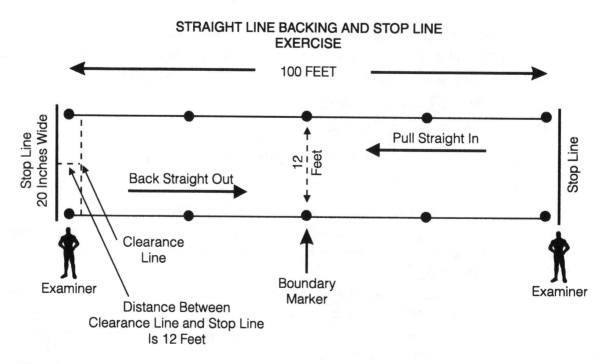

STRAIGHT LINE BACKING AND STOP LINE
EXERCISE

The purpose of this exercise is to determine how well you can judge distances to the front and rear, and how well you can control the vehicle while backing.

The course is 100 feet long by 12 feet wide. You will pull forward through the course and get as close to the stop line as possible without going over it. Once the examiner checks to see how close you came to the stop line, he will then issue these instructions:

"Continue now to pull straight ahead until the rear of your vehicle is about even with the stop line. I'll signal when you should stop. I will then wave you back, and you can proceed backing down the alley. You should try to avoid touching either side of the alley with any part of your vehicle. Stop with your front bumper about even with the stop line at the end of the alley."

You will now begin backing. Remember, if you touch any part of the boundary, or if any part of your vehicle crosses over the boundary, it will be counted as an encroachment. If it looks as if you are about to have an encroachment, STOP. Pull forward and straighten up and begin backing again. You will back until the front bumper of the vehicle is "about even" with the stop line at the end of the alley. Once you stop, the examiner will then approach you to give you your next set of instructions.

Tips:

● When pulling forward, go slow, get the vehicle straight and perfectly centered between the boundaries.

- When you stop, stop gently. The examiner will be looking for how smoothly you stop. If you stop quickly and the truck dips forward or rocks, you may lose points.
- Practice until this exercise is easy for you. Remember, stopping within 2 feet of the stop line is just as important as backing down the alley without an encroachment. Practice until you have mastered it.
- When building an alley to practice on, the alley length is 100 feet, the width between the boundaries is 12 feet. If you use cones, the 12-feet width

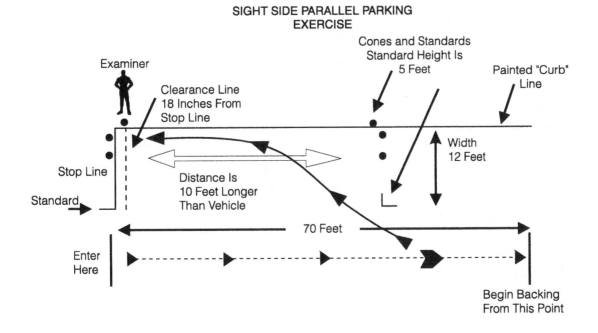

SIGHT SIDE PARALLEL PARKING EXERCISE

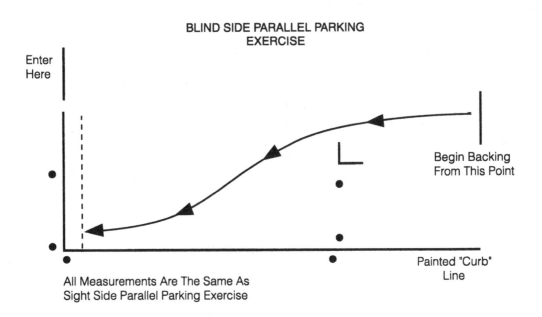

BLIND SIDE PARALLEL PARKING EXERCISE

All Measurements Are The Same As Sight Side Parallel Parking Exercise is measured from the base of the cones, not the top. The clearance line is 2 feet from the stop line. During the test, you are required to stop within 2 feet of the stop line. The clearance line is only used to see if you were within 2 feet of the stop line when you stopped. The stop line will be the wider of the two lines, it will be 20 inches wide. Practice until you can stop with your bumper between the clearance line and the stop line every time.

Instructions by examiner:

For straight trucks and buses . . .

"Drive by the parking space and then back into it. Attempt to get your vehicle as close as possible to the rear and to the curb, without crossing the lines or striking any boundaries. Try to get your vehicle completely into the space. When I wave you forward, you may proceed. Tap your horn when you have completed."

For tractor-trailers . . .

"Drive by the parking place and back the trailer into it. You are required only to get the trailer into the space. You may jackknife the tractor at any angle as long as you get the trailer into the space. Try to get your trailer as close as possible to the rear and to the curb without crossing the lines or striking any boundaries. Try to get the trailer completely in the space. When I wave you forward, you may proceed. Tap your horn when you have completed."

The purpose of this exercise is to determine how well you can control the vehicle and parallel park. Even though in everyday driving you may seldom have to parallel park (especially a tractor-trailer), the regulations require that you be able to do it if it ever becomes necessary.

Since most drivers rarely ever parallel park, a lot of practice will be needed for the sight side and the blind side (curb side) parallel parking.

The parking space will be *10 feet longer* than your vehicle. If a tractor-trailer, it will be 10 feet longer than the trailer. The width of the spot will be 12 feet. You must get within 18 inches of the rear stop line and as close to the "curb" as possible. The "curb" will not really be a curb; it will be a painted line on the pavement. The cones and standards at either end of the parking spot will be at least 5 feet high so you can see them. Check the diagram for the proper dimensions and cone placements. This will help you get familiar with how it will be laid out, so that you can create your own course for practice.

Remember, practice is the key here. Most of us have gotten "rusty" when it comes to parallel parking—so practice, practice, practice.

Alley Dock Exercise

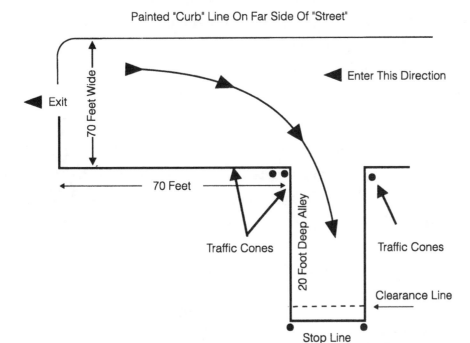

Painted "Curb" Line On Far Side Of "Street"

Instructions by the Examiner

"Drive by the entrance to the alley with the alley on your left side; then stop and back into it. Attempt to get as close to the back of the alley as possible, but don't back past it. Try not to hit or cross over any boundary lines of the alley or simulated street. I will go over and stand near the entrance to the alley. When I wave you forward, you may proceed. Tap your horn when you are in position."

When performing this exercise, you will pull into the simulated (fake) "street" and go past the entrance to the dock. As the middle of the tractor passes by the entrance, turn the steering wheel hard right and begin heading toward the course line on the far side of the street. You will then turn hard left which will point your tractor toward the exit and will line up the rear of your trailer toward the dock. You then begin backing slowly. As you back, back slowly and make minor adjustments with the steering wheel to keep the trailer positioned in the center of the alley. *Watch your trailer swing!* If the rear of the trailer passes over a cone or a boundary line, it will be counted as an encroachment. You must stop within 2 feet of the rear of the alley. The clearance line is the 2-foot marker. Once the rear of your vehicle passes the clearance line, you are within 2 feet of back of the alley. Don't back off the alley or pass over the stop line.

Tips:

- Go slow throughout this maneuver and use soft braking. The examiner will be looking to see if you can start and stop smoothly.
- Use the lowest reverse gear possible.
- As the rear of your trailer approaches the alley, have your wheels as close as possible to the two cones on the driver's side of the entrance. This will help to prevent a trailer swing encroachment on the blind side.

If you've been driving only over the road lately, and haven't done a lot of backing and docking, we suggest you practice before going down to take the test. Backing and docking is just like riding a bicycle, you never forget how to do it. You might have gotten a little rusty—but with a little practice—you'll do just fine.

The Right Turn

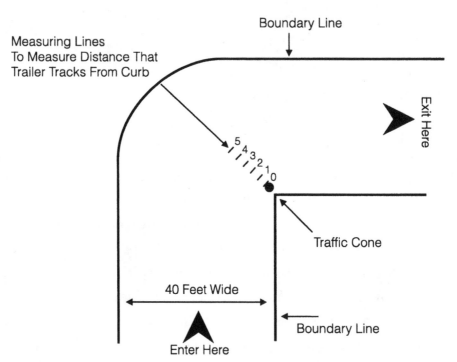

Instructions by examiner:

"Drive slowly forward and make a right turn around the cone. Try to bring your rear wheels as close to the cone as possible without hitting it. I will walk up to the cone; when I wave you forward, you may proceed."

This exercise is designed to simulate a right turn at an intersection, and to test your ability to make the turn safely.

There may be many ways to make a right turn, but only one way to do it correctly for the test.

As you enter the simulated street, stay toward the center, but still on our side, as this is supposed to represent a normal two-way street.

As you pass the cone, you will begin to turn to the right. When you begin, your turn will be determined by how much your vehicle off-tracks. A tractor pulling a trailer will off-track much more than a small straight truck. The object is to get your right rear tires as close to the cone as possible without touching it. You will lose points if you touch the cone, and you will lose points if you swing too far out. The measuring lines painted on the street will represent distances from the curb.

Before going down to take the test, determine which vehicle you will be driving during the test. Practice with that vehicle until you can stay within a few inches of the curb. If you can stay within 6 inches, you'll have a perfect score.

Tips:

- Go slow, you're not being timed.
- Don't touch or run over any of the painted boundary lines.
- After you've made the turn, continue forward until your vehicle is straight, and stop and wait for instructions.

Backward Serpentine

Boundary Line

Enter Here
Pull Forward

Exit Here
Backing

Stop
Here
And
Begin
Backing

35 Feet

Boundary Line

270 Feet

Notes:

1. Total distance is 270 feet
2. Distance between traffic cones is the *length of your vehicle*
3. Distance from traffic cones to either outside boundary line is 35 feet.
   Total distance from boundary line to boundary is 70 feet.

Instructions by examiner:

"I will adjust the distance between the cones for your vehicle. When I wave you forward, drive along the right side of the row of cones. Stop when your entire vehicle is past the third cone. Then back up in a serpentine as shown in this diagram until you back past the first cone. Try not to touch any cones or allow any part of your vehicle to pass over any cone. Also, you must keep your vehicle within the painted boundary lines."

The examiner will show you a diagram of how this exercise is to be performed. The important thing is to be sure you understand which side of the traffic cones to pass by. Study the picture above and look closely at the diagram the examiner shows you.

You will pull forward with the cones on your left side, stopping when your vehicle has passed the last cone. You will then begin to back, weaving in between the cones until you have passed the last one. When you begin backing, your vehicle must pass to the left of cone number one, to the right of the center cone and to the left of the last cone.

Remember, not only can you not touch a cone, but no part of your vehicle can pass over the cone. If it does, it will be counted as an encroachment and you will lose points. If you get into a position where you are going to hit a cone, **STOP**— pull forward and reposition the vehicle. Pull forward as far as necessary to get into the correct position. Each pull-up will cost you points, but it's much better to do this than it is to hit a cone. Also, don't cross any boundary lines. The boundary lines will be painted on the pavement. They will be 35 feet on either side of the cones. Crossing over a boundary line will also be counted as an encroachment.

We suggest you practice this maneuver quite a bit. It's tougher than you think. Build a serpentine exercise to practice on. Use the same measurement as shown in the diagram.

Tips:

- Practice—practice—practice
- Go slow—remember, you're not being timed
- Pull up if necessary, but don't hit a cone
- Don't cross over a painted boundary line

CDL Road Test

The third and final part of the skills testing is the Road Test. This test is designed to see if you can safely handle your vehicle in actual on-the-road conditions.

The test will take approximately 30-45 minutes. The examiner will take you into a variety of road conditions; such as right turns, left turns, upgrades, downgrades, railroad crossings, two-lane country roads, commercial areas and interstate highways.

In certain situations, the examiner may ask you to simulate (pretend) to do something. For example, if you take your CDL tests in Florida, you'll have some difficulty finding a hill or mountain to practice shifting or starting on an upgrade. The examiner may ask you to pull over and simulate (pretend) you're starting on an upgrade. He'll want you to tell him how you would do it smoothly and without the truck rolling backwards. Don't worry, if he asks you to simulate something, he'll give you complete instructions.

Remember one thing, *"You are the Captain of the Ship."* The examiner will never knowingly give you directions or instructions which may be unsafe or which might cause an accident. No matter what instructions he may give—you are in charge of the vehicle and responsible for its safe operation. So, should the examiner give an instruction or ask you to do something you believe to be unsafe, you have the absolute right to question his instruction and *politely* refuse to follow it. If you do decide to refuse an instruction, be sure to explain to the examiner your reason why. The examiners are not going to try to trick you, but they are only human and could make a mistake. Simply explain to them why you feel their instruction is unsafe, and you should have no problems.

Here are the instructions you can expect to receive from the examiner:

"During the road test I will give you directions as we go along. I will always give directions for turns as far in advance as possible. Along the way I may point out a location and ask you to pretend it is the top of a steep hill or maybe a railroad crossing. I will ask you to go through the motions of what you would do if it were a real hill or a railroad crossing, and at the same time tell me what you are doing and why."

"There will be no trick directions to get you to do something illegal or unsafe."

"During the test, I will be making marks on the test form. When you see this, don't get nervous; it does not necessarily mean you have done anything wrong. You should concentrate on your driving and not worry about what I'm doing."

While driving, the examiner will be looking to see if you do certain key things. Some of those key things will be:

- Starting and stopping

  Do you start smoothly and stop smoothly without jerking or bouncing the vehicle?

- Shifting

  Do you shift smoothly and without grinding gear?

  Do you use the clutch and double clutch?

- Engine control

  Do you maintain proper rpm's—no overspeeding and no lugging? If you're driving one of the new engines which shift at low rpm's, point this out to the examiner so he doesn't think you are lugging it.

- Proper following distance

  Do you maintain a safe following distance at all times?

- Turn signals

  Do you signal well in advance of a lane change or turn, and do you cancel the signal promptly after the turn?

- Proper set-up

  When making turns, do you position the vehicle properly?

- Intersections

  Do you approach the intersection cautiously and prepared to stop?

  Do you turn your head to "check out" the intersection, looking for approaching traffic and pedestrians?

  Do you stop at the stop lines?

  Do you keep transmission in neutral and foot off the clutch when stopped at traffic lights and stop signs?

  Do you stop at the stop line, and then move slowly forward?

- Transmission control

  Do you keep the truck in gear at all times, no coasting to a stop sign or light, never coasting through a turn?

- Braking

  Do you always brake smoothly—no bouncing or rebounding?

  Do you only use the brake pedal—never the hand valve?

  Do you check your mirrors when braking to see if anyone is following you too closely?

- Traffic signs and signal control

  Do you always observe the speed limits and all traffic control devices?

- Curves

  Do you slow down before entering curves? Never let the truck lean while going around a curve.

- Interstate driving

  Do you always stay in the far right lane except when you move left to allow traffic to enter?

  Do you check mirrors often?

  Do you merge smoothly?

  Do you use your turn signals when merging and changing lanes and then cancel them promptly?

  Do you look ahead 12–15 seconds?

  Do you keep the vehicle centered in your lane?

- Upgrades

  Do you maintain engine rpm's and downshift when proper?

  Can you start up on an upgrade without rolling back?

  When stopped do you always put on your 4-way flashers?

- Downgrades

  Can you maintain speed using a lower gear and slight, steady brake pressure?

  Do you check your brakes before beginning a long downgrade?

  Do you check your mirrors often for signs of overheating brakes?

- Turns

  Do you signal well in advance and turn it off after the turn is completed?

  Do you stay in the proper lane—never allowing a vehicle to squeeze between you and the curb?

  Do you keep both hands on the wheel when turning?

  Do you stay in same gear during turn—no shifting?

- Railroad crossings

  Do you turn your head from left to right, and then left and right again?

  Do you roll down your window to listen?

  If you are transporting passengers or hazardous materials, do you stop at least 15 feet from the tracks and no more than 50 feet away?

  Do you ever shift gears while crossing the tracks?

- Underpasses and bridges

    Do you check all bridge weights and height clearances? (Once you cross a bridge or pass through an underpass, the examiner may ask what the weight limit or height was—you'll need to know, so be sure to look.)

Do You Always Wear Your Seatbelt?

If you've been driving regularly, you should have no problem with passing the CDL Road Test *UNLESS* you have developed bad habits and have not studied for the test. The following bad habits can get you into big trouble quick if you do any of these on the test:

- Forget to wear your seatbelt
- Drive with one hand on the wheel
- Exceed the speed limits
- Not slow down and look when approaching an intersection or railroad crossing
- Allow vehicle to roll forward or back when stopped
- Not use turn signals or forget to turn them off
- Don't use the clutch
- Take transmission out of gear and coast up to a light or stop sign
- Run up over a curve when turning
- If the road is rough, not slow down—(if you bounce the CDL examiner all over the seat—it's probably going to cost you points)
- If you don't maintain a safe following distance

If You Have an Accident During the Test, It Is an Automatic Failure

How do you study for the road test? Simple. Read Chapter 3, the General Knowledge section in the study manual. All of the rules are covered there. You must be familiar with them to pass the test.

Don't worry if you make a mistake—the important thing is not to get nervous. Even though you might make a mistake or two, the examiner is looking to see if overall you can safely handle a commercial vehicle. A couple of minor mistakes probably will not fail you if you don't allow them to "rattle" you, and you do everything else OK.

The following are the items which the examiner has been instructed to look for while the test is being conducted. Study these items completely—and, don't worry—you're gonna do just fine.

Left Turns

Approach

Traffic check—look for any indication that the driver is observing the traffic environment ahead, to the left, right, and rear (through the mirrors)—head/body movements to left and right—eye contact with other drivers, pedestrians— uses mirrors

Signal—driver activates left turn signal

Decelerates—takes foot off accelerator—brakes gradually, evenly, smoothly—no cab bounce

Coast—does not coast—feel vehicle slows down smoothly

Lane—vehicle in left-most lane, but not over lane markings

If Stopped at Intersection

Gap—can driver see rear wheels of vehicle in front?

Stop line—not out in intersection—not over stop line on pavement or not past sidewalk, stop sign, or other marker

Full stop—driver does not coast—vehicle comes to full stop —vehicle doesn't roll

Wheels straight—wheels straight ahead while stopped

Turning

Traffic check—head/body movements to left and right—especially movement to the left (mirror)—eye contact with other drivers, pedestrians—uses mirrors

Both hands—both hands on wheel

Gears—no gear changes during turn—gear change allowed to get started away from stop

Speed—barely noticeable acceleration—no jerking, no unnecessary stops during turn—maintains smooth even speed

Wide/short—too wide—vehicle is over or touching curb—vehicle in right lane at end of turn—too short—vehicle is in lane of oncoming traffic at completion of turn—caused other traffic to back up

Complete Turn

Traffic check—head/body movements to left and right—especially movement to the right (mirror)—eye contact with other drivers, pedestrians—uses mirrors

Correct lane—vehicle finishes in the left-most lane

Signal—signal turned off after turn is completed

Accelerate, right—accelerates smoothly—signal right—driver moves into right lane when traffic is clear

Right Turns

Approach

Traffic check—look for any indication that the driver is observing the traffic environment ahead, to the left, right, and rear (through the mirrors)—head/body movements to left and right—eye contact with other drivers, pedestrians—uses mirrors

Signal—driver activates right-turn signal

Decelerates—takes foot off accelerator—brakes gradually, evenly—changes gears as necessary to keep proper rpm's

Coast—does not coast—vehicle slows down smoothly

Lane—vehicle in right-most lane, but not over markings on left side of lane unless necessary—blocks traffic from coming up right side

If Stopped at Intersection

Gap—can driver see rear wheels of vehicle in front?

Stop line—not out in intersection—not over stop line on pavement or not past sidewalk, stop sign, or other marker

Full stop—driver does not coast—vehicle comes to full stop —vehicle doesn't roll

Wheels straight—wheels straight ahead while stopped

Turning

Traffic check—head/body movements to left and right—especially movement to the right (mirror)—eye contact with other drivers, pedestrians—uses mirrors

Both hands—both hands on wheel

Gears—no gear changes during turn—gear change allowed to get started away from stop

Speed—barely noticeable acceleration, no jerking—no unnecessary stops during turn—maintains smooth, even speed

Wide/short—too short—rear wheels over or touching curb— too wide—is in lane of oncoming traffic at completion of turn—vehicle in center lane at end of turn—caused other traffic to back up—unnecessary buttonhook turn

Complete Turn

Traffic check—head/body movement to left and right—especially movement to the right (mirror)—eye contact with other drivers, pedestrians—uses mirrors

Correct lane—vehicle finishes in the right-most lane

Signal—signal turned off after turn is completed

Accelerate, right—accelerates smoothly

Railroad Crossing

Traffic check—look for any indication that the driver is checking for the presence of trains—head/body movements to left and right—roll window down to listen—may open door (bus)

Law—must stop if bus or truck with hazardous goods—not closer than 15 feet from nearest rail—may also be required to: open window, open door, and/or put parking brake on, and/or shift into neutral gear

Gears—does not change gears while on tracks

Stop—does not stop or brake on tracks—does not pass or make lane change—keeps to posted speed limit

Stop/Start on Grade

Approach

Traffic check—look for any indication that the driver is observing the traffic environment ahead, left, right and at the rear (through the mirrors)

Signal on—driver activates right-turn signal

Correct lane—vehicle in right-most or curb lane—not blocking driveways, fire hydrants, etc.

Deceleration—driver takes foot off accelerator—steady braking—driver changing gears—vehicle slows down smoothly

Not coast—driver does not coast

Stop

Parallel—vehicle parallel to curb

Not roll—vehicle does not roll forward or backward!

Signal off/4-ways on—cancels turn signal—activates 4-way flashers

Parking brake—puts parking brake on—puts gear shift in neutral—releases foot brake—foot not resting on clutch

Resume

Traffic check—head/body movements to left and right—especially movement to the left (mirror)—eye contact with other drivers, pedestrians

4-ways/signals—turns 4-way flashers off—activates left-turn signal

Parking brake—releases parking brake—puts vehicle in gear—does not turn wheel before vehicle

Not stall engine—did not stall engine when starting away

Traffic check—especially to left (mirror)

Accelerate—driver does not coast (foot on clutch)—does not let engine stall—blends smoothly with other traffic—no hard (sharp) turn into traffic—appropriate gears for speed/revs

Driving Upgrade

Proper gear—see driver change to lower gear—changes gears to maintain speed—driver does not lug engine—hands on wheel

Keep right—stays in right-most lane

4-ways if slow—uses 4-way flashers if too slow for traffic

Traffic checks—especially to left and rear (mirrors)

Driving Downgrade

Proper gear—driver changes to lower gear before grade—correct gear; only gentle-to-moderate braking needed, engine not racing—vehicle is in gear (not coasting in neutral)

Brake—driver checks brakes before starting down grade

Clutch—not ride clutch to control speed

Steady speed—driver applies light, steady brake pressure—not pump or fan the brakes—maintains even speed—increases following distance—stays in right-most lane—both hands on wheel

Traffic check—especially to left and rear (mirrors)

Intersections

Stopping

Traffic check—head/body movements to left and right—eye contact with other drivers, pedestrians—uses mirrors

Deceleration—driver takes foot off accelerator—steady braking—changing gears—feel vehicle slowing down smoothly

Coast—does not coast (foot on clutch)

Gap—can driver see rear wheels of vehicle in front

Stop line—not out in intersection—not over stop line on pavement or not past sidewalk, stop sign, or other marker

Full stop—vehicle must come to full stop—must not roll forward or backward

Driving Through

Traffic check—head/body movements to left and right—eye contact with other drivers pedestrians—uses mirrors

Yield—yields to pedestrians and other traffic already at or in intersection

Lane—does not change lanes in intersection

Gear—no gear change in intersection

Accelerate—does not stall engine—does not allow vehicle to drift back - does not cause disruption in traffic flow - does not lug or rev engine

Urban/Rural, Straight Sections

Regular traffic checks—watches for hazards at road side, or from entrances, look for indications of 12- to 15-sec. lead time (anticipates lane changes, slows for hazards or obstructions as soon as they are seen)

Selects proper lane—right lane if clear—center lane if right lane obstructed by tree branches, utility poles, etc.—center lane if using right lane requires constant lane changes—center lane if high volume of entering/exiting traffic

Keeps vehicle in lane—keeps to center of lane—does not wander

Speed—keeps up with traffic flow—times approach to hazards or obstructions to avoid continual slowing up, stopping and accelerating—maintains steady speed

Follow distance—1 sec. per 10 ft. of vehicle length when under 40 mph; add 1 sec. if over 40 mph—avoids having view blocked by large vehicles in front

Lane Changes

Traffic check—checks front and rear—especially blind spot—turns head

Signal—signals when changing lanes—cancels signal after lane change

Space—not tailgate while waiting to change lane—waits for adequate gap

Smooth change—blends smoothly with other traffic—no hard (sharp) turn—maintains speed—moves to center of lane—adequate gap front and rear after lane change

Curve

Speed: Enter through—reduces speed before curve—does not have to brake while in curve—maintains speed during curve—no Sstrong lateral accelerations

Stay in lane—keeps all vehicle wheels in lane

Traffic checks—continual traffic checks—makes extra effort to keep track of following vehicles when coming out of curve

Underpass/Bridge

Underpass—After driving under an underpass, ask driver to tell you the posted clearance (height)

Bridge—After passing over bridge, ask driver to tell you the posted weight limit

Expressway

Merge On

Traffic Check— checks both to front and rear—especially to the left (blindspot) turns head

Signal—signals at least as soon as expressway traffic can see signal

Spacing—not tailgate—avoids slowing up following traffic

No stop—merges without stopping

Merge—does not exceed ramp speed—accelerates to traffic flow in acceleration lane—no hard (sharp) turn onto expressway lane—did not lug or rev engine—moves to center of driving lane (right-most)

Cancel signal—cancels signal when merge is completed

Lane Changes

Traffic check—checks front and rear—especially blind spot

Signal— see signal indicator light flashing

Spacing—not tailgate while waiting to change lane—waits for adequate gap

Smooth change—blends smoothly with other traffic—no hard (sharp) turn— maintains speed—moves to center of lane—adequate gap front and rear after lane change

Cancel signal—cancels signal when lane change is completed

Exit Expressway

Traffic check—especially to the right (blindspot)

Signal—uses turn signal when exiting

Smooth merge to exit lane—no hard (sharp) turn onto deceleration lane—enters exit lane at start of exit lane

Decelerate in exit lane—decelerates in deceleration lane

Ramp speed—does not exceed ramp speed—no noticeable lateral acceleration on ramp curve—correct downgrade or upgrade procedure on ramp with grade

Spacing—did not tailgate on ramp

Cancel signal—cancel signal when exit maneuver is completed

General Driving Behaviors

Used clutch properly—Always used clutch to shift, double clutched non-synchromesh gears, did not over rev or lug the engine, did not coast with clutch in, did not ride clutch to control speed, did not "snap" clutch

Used gears properly—Did not grind or clash gears, generally kept in gear, did not over-rev or lug engine

Used brakes properly—Did not ride brake, braked smoothly with steady pressure, did not brake hard or pump brake

Proper steering—Kept both hands on wheel, no palming, didn't under or over-control steering

Obeyed all traffic signs—Generally obeyed signs and signals, did not exceed posted speed limits, roll through stops, or ignore traffic laws

Drove without accident—Had no physical contact with (bump into) other vehicles, objects, pedestrians, animals, etc.

Did not put vehicle over curbs or sidewalks; generally kept in correct lane; did not encroach on traffic control pavement markings, stop lines, etc.; examiner was never thrown to left right, or forward; driver was never forced to take evasive actions, *WEARS SEATBELT*

Final Examinations

General Knowledge
Combination Vehicles
Doubles and Triples
Tank Vehicles

Transporting Passengers
Air Brakes
Hazardous Materials

Instructions

During the written test, you should not use any reference material or notes. Set aside a time where you will not be interrupted while answering the questions. It is important that you take these tests seriously; don't cheat by looking up the answers on the answer sheet. Act as if this were the real test. The entire series of tests are multiple choice, just like the real CDL tests will be. If you are not sure of the answer, do the following:

1. Read the question a second time.
2. Begin reading the choices a second time, and begin to eliminate the obviously incorrect choices. By doing this you will be able to narrow it down to one or two choices.
3. Never leave an answer blank. A blank will be scored as an incorrect answer. If you just don't know, then guess! It's better than not answering it.
4. Watch out for words in the question like: "is not," "always," "never," "is not true" or "is true." These words can trip you up if you're not careful.

There is no time limit on these tests or the actual CDL tests. Take as much time as you need. When finished, check your answers with the answer sheet. If you have any incorrect answers, turn back to that chapter and find the correct answer.

It takes 80% to pass each CDL test. Read the manual until you can score at least 80% on each test at the end of the chapter and the final examination.

GOOD LUCK!

GO TO NEXT PAGE

General Knowledge Examination

This test must be taken by all applicants for a commercial driver's license.

Read each question carefully and then choose the answer that is most correct.

1. While driving you are looking ahead of your vehicle, how should you be looking?

    A. look to the right side of the roadway

    B. look back and forth and near and far

    C. stare straight ahead at all times

    D. look straight ahead and glance in your mirrors every 45 to 60 seconds

2. When you are driving at night, you should:

    A. dim your lights when you are within 300 feet of oncoming traffic

    B. watch the white line on the left side of the roadway

    C. adjust your vehicle speed so as to keep your stopping distance within your sight distance

    D. keep your high beams on at all times

3. Statistics prove that most serious skids are a result of:

    A. driving too fast for conditions

    B. improper loading of the vehicle

    C. turning too sharply

    D. winter driving conditions

4. If you drive through heavy rain or standing water your brakes may get wet, what can this cause when you apply the brakes?

    A. trailer jackknife

    B. your brakes to heat up

    C. hydroplaning

    D. hydroplaning if you were traveling faster than 30 mph when you applied the brakes

5. Which of the following is true about the use of reflective emergency triangles?

   A. The regulation requires they be placed within 5 minutes of stopping

   B. You do not need to use them if you breakdown as long as your 4-way flashers are working

   C. You do not need to use them as long as you have pulled your vehicle completely off the traveled portion of the roadway

   D. If you stop on a hill or curve, it is permissible to place them up to 500 feet in order to provide adequate warning

6. When you are driving through construction zones, you should:

   A. speed up and hurry through them so you aren't in them any longer than necessary

   B. stop before entering them, get in your low gear and proceed through

   C. watch for sharp pavement drop-offs

   D. reduce your speed only if construction workers are near the roadway

7. If you breakdown on a level, straight, four-lane, divided highway, where should you place the reflective warning triangles?

   A. one within 10 feet of the rear of the vehicle, one approximately 100 feet to the rear of the vehicle and one about 100 feet to the front of the vehicle

   B. one within 10 feet of the rear of the vehicle, one approximately 100 feet to the rear of the vehicle and another one about 200 feet to the rear of the vehicle

   C. one within 100 feet of the rear of the vehicle, one approximately 200 feet to the rear of the vehicle and one about 300 feet to the rear of the vehicle

   D. one within 50 feet of the rear of the vehicle, one about 100 feet to the rear of the vehicle and another one approximately 200 feet to the front of the vehicle

8. According to your State's Commercial Drivers Manual, why should you limit the use of the vehicle's horn?

   A. If your vehicle has air brakes, the air horn may not work while you are applying the air brakes

   B. It may startle other drivers

   C. You should keep both hands on the steering wheel at all times

   D. The Drivers Manual does not say that a driver should limit the use of the horn

9. Which of the following should you NOT do?

   A. turn on your headlights during the day if visibility is reduced due to bad weather

   B. flash your brake lights to warn vehicles behind you that you are slowing down

   C. flash your brake lights when entering a construction zone if vehicles are close behind you

   D. flash your brakes lights if someone is following you too closely

10. The proper way to load a vehicle is:

    A. keep the load balanced in the cargo area

    B. place the load at the front of the vehicle to give your drive wheels better traction

    C. place the load at the rear of the vehicle so your rear tires have better traction

    D. it makes no difference where the cargo is placed as long as you are not over the allowable gross weight

11. When driving a commercial vehicle with a height over 13 feet, you should:

    A. assume all clearances are of sufficient height

    B. height clearance is not a concern as long as you stay on a state or federal roadway

    C. if you are unsure of the clearance, stop and check before proceeding

    D. all of the above

12. Controlled braking is:

    A. applying hard brake so that the wheels lock up

    B. pressing the brakes hard enough to lock-up the wheels, then releasing and then reapplying again

    C. apply firm brake but not to the point of wheel lock-up

    D. only used if the vehicle does not have anti-lock brakes

13. You are driving on a straight and level roadway at 60 mph and suddenly a tire blows out on your vehicle. What should you do first?

    A. immediately begin light, controlled braking

    B. immediately begin stab braking

    C. grip steering wheel firmly with both hands and stay off the brakes until the vehicle has slowed down

    D. immediately begin emergency braking

14. Which of the following is true?

    A. it is permissible to use radial and bias-ply tires together on the same axle

    B. tires which are of mismatched sizes should not be used on the same vehicle

    C. 4/32 inch tread depth is the maximum allowed on drive tires

    D. 2/32 inch tread depth is permissible for steering tires

15. Why do hazardous material regulations exist?

    A. to provide for safe drivers and equipment

    B. to communicate the risk

    C. to contain the product

    D. all of the above

16. Which of the following statements about backing a commercial vehicle to the dock is NOT true?

    A. since you can't see behind you, you should back slowly until you bump the dock

    B. use a helper and communicate with hand signals

    C. you should always back toward the drivers side when possible

    D. both A and C

17. As alcohol begins to build up in the body, which of the following is affected first?

    A. muscle control

    B. coordination

    C. kidney control

    D. judgment and self-control

18. Which of the following is true concerning cold weather driving?

    A. exhaust system leaks are not of concern during cold weather

    B. if the temperature is below 32 degrees Fahrenheit, the engine cannot overheat

    C. using bleach on tires will provide increased traction

    D. you should use windshield washer fluid which contains an anti-freeze

19. Placarding, the use of hazardous material placards and labels, is an example of:

    A. containment

    B. controlling the hazardous materials risk

    C. communication

    D. all of the above

20. Controlled braking is used when:

    A. the goal is to keep the vehicle in a straight line while braking

    B. you must stop as quickly as possible

    C. is only used with hydraulic brakes

    D. only used when the vehicle is equipped with anti-lock brakes

21. What is hydroplaning?

    A. an emergency situation created when an aircraft must make an emergency landing on a highway

    B. excessive heat is built up in the radiator

    C. only occurs at high vehicle speeds

    D. when your vehicle wheels lift off the roadway on a thin film of water

22. If you are being tailgated you should:

    A. motion for the tailgater to pass you when it is safe

    B. increase your following distance

    C. turn on your 4-way flashers

    D. slam on the brakes

23. Which of the following conditions may produce a skid?

    A. driving too fast for conditions

    B. over braking

    C. over steering

    D. all of the above

24. When fighting a fire, which of the following is most correct?

    A. get downwind of the fire before using the fire extinguisher

    B. get as close to the fire as possible

    C. aim the fire extinguisher at the base of the fire

    D. aim the fire extinguisher at the top of the fire

25. When starting a commercial vehicle on level, dry pavement, it is usually not necessary to?

    A. apply parking brake

    B. use a slower acceleration

    C. press on the accelerate firmly while popping out the clutch

    D. both A and C

26. Shifting gears properly is important because:

    A. doing so helps you to maintain control of the vehicle
    B. it helps to keep the oil flowing through the crankcase
    C. it keeps the radiator cool
    D. it keeps the engine at the proper operating temperature

27. You are traveling down a long grade and you notice your brakes are not working as good as they had been, you should:

    A. continue to the bottom of the grade and then stop and check your brakes
    B. stop as quickly as you can
    C. downshift one or two gears and continue
    D. begin pumping your brake pedal

28. Water will extinguish which of the following fires?

    A. electrical
    B. diesel fuel
    C. gasoline
    D. tire

29. Convex (curved) also referred to as "bug-eye" mirrors will:

    A. make objects appear to be larger than they really are
    B. make objects appear to be smaller than they really are
    C. make objects appear closer and larger than they really are
    D. show a wider area than flat mirrors

30. Your State's Drivers Manual says you should use your horn:

    A. it may make the deer standing alongside the road move further away
    B. when a car gets in your way
    C. if it may help you to avoid a collision
    D. when you begin to change lanes

31. Which of the following is true about tire pressure?

    A. as temperature increases so does air pressure in the tires

    B. it is not necessary to check tire pressure during a trip or during a pre-trip inspection

    C. in warmer weather it is best to let out some of the air in the tires to reduce pressure

    D. all of the above

32. Which of the following happens when a tire blows at highway speed?

    A. you will experience an immediate and dramatic drop in speed to 20 mph

    B. you will feel a vibration

    C. you will hear a hissing sound

    D. the low air pressure signal device will come on

33. What is the purpose of a pre-trip inspection?

    A. to add an additional 15 minutes of time to your log book

    B. to avoid being cited by a law enforcement official

    C. to make sure the vehicle is safe to operate

    D. to see if any additional 1,000 lbs of freight can be added to maximize revenue

34. When you see a hazard in the roadway in front of you, you should:

    A. steer and countersteer around it

    B. stop quickly and get off the roadway if possible

    C. stop quickly, stay in the roadway, set out your reflective triangles and go to the rear of vehicle and flag down traffic

    D. turn on your 4-way flashers or flash your brake lights to warn others

35. At what Blood Alcohol Concentration (BAC) will you be placed out-of-service for 24 hours?

    A. at .04% or higher

    B. at .03% or higher

    C. any detectable amount

    D. at 1.0% or higher

36. Your vehicle is 40 foot long and you are traveling at 50 mph, the safe following distance is:

    A. 5 seconds

    B. 6 second

    C. 4 seconds

    D. 3 seconds

37. After you start your engine, which of the following should occur?

    A. it will take 4 to 5 minutes for oil pressure to build to normal

    B. it will take 10 to 15 minutes for the air pressure gauge to rise to normal

    C. the water temperature gauge will indicate a gradual rise to normal operating temperature

    D. the manifold exhaust indicator gauge will immediately rise to 190 degrees

38. Which of the following can you NOT check at the same time?

    A. turn signal, brake lights and 4-way flashers

    B. headlights and clearance lights

    C. taillights and clearance lights

    D. clearance lights and 4-way flashers

39. Which of the following is true about rear drive wheel braking skids?

    A. the vehicle's front wheels will slide sideways

    B. is not a cause of jackknifing

    C. the locked wheels have more traction than the wheels that are rolling

    D. if it occurs with a vehicle towing a trailer, the trailer can push the towing vehicle sideways

40. Which of the following statements is true

    A. hazards are easier to see at night than during the day

    B. many commercial vehicle accidents occur between midnight and 6 A.M.

    C. most drivers are more alert at night than during the day

    D. it is recommended that you use your high beams at all times during the period from 7 P.M. to 7 A.M.

41. Which of the following statements about causes of vehicle fires is true?

    A. an overheated radiator is the most common type of vehicle fire

    B. carrying a properly charged and rated fire extinguisher will help to prevent fires

    C. under-inflated or flat tires will NOT cause a vehicle fire

    D. poor trailer ventilation can cause cargo to catch on fire

42. "Over-The-Counter" medication used to treat the common cold:

    A. is permissible as long as the dispatcher has given the "OK" to use it

    B. can only be taken when driving during daylight hours

    C. often can make you sleepy and should not be used while driving

    D. is "OK" as long as you take just half a dose

43. Can federal inspectors inspect your truck or bus?

    A. yes, and they have the authority to place you "out-of-service"

    B. yes, but they have no authority to place you out of service

    C. yes, but only at a point of entry

    D. no

44. How many missing or broken leaves in a leaf spring will cause your vehicle to be placed "out-of-service"?

    A. one-fourth of the total number

    B. one-half of the total number

    C. one-third of the total number

    D. any

45. First offense for driving a CMV (commercial motor vehicle) under the influence of alcohol or drug will cause you to lose your CDL for at least:

    A. three years

    B. one year

    C. two years

    D. six months

46. Which of the following is a true statement?

    A. you can always trust other drivers to turn in the direction their turn signal is indicating

    B. mail or city delivery truck drivers are professionals and do not pose a hazard to you

    C. you do not have to worry about individuals driving cars with out of state license plates

    D. short-term or daily rental truck drivers are often not used to driving a large vehicle and may pose a hazard to you

47. Bridge formulas are designed to:

    A. are the same as formulas used to determine total gross vehicle weight (GVW)

    B. permit the same maximum axle weight for any axle spacing

    C. permit less maximum axle weight axles that are closer together

    D. permit less maximum axle weight for axles that are farther apart

48. When traveling down a long downgrade, you should always:

    A. apply trailer brakes to reduce speed or maintain speed

    B. use the braking effect of the engine

    C. use stab braking

    D. apply brakes when your vehicle exceeds the "safe-speed" by 5 mph

49. What three factors add up to the total stopping distance for a commercial vehicle without air brakes?

    A. perception distance, reaction distance and braking distance
    B. eye lead time, reaction distance and braking distance
    C. perception distance, reaction distance and response distance
    D. response distance and braking distance

50. Stab braking is not used on vehicles:

    A. towing trailers
    B. anti-lock brakes
    C. hauling hazardous materials
    D. never used on commercial vehicles equipped with air brakes

Answer Key

1.	B	18.	D	35.	C
2.	C	19.	C	36.	A
3.	A	20.	A	37.	C
4.	A	21.	D	38.	A
5.	D	22.	B	39.	D
6.	C	23.	D	40.	B
7.	B	24.	C	41.	D
8.	B	25.	D	42.	C
9.	D	26.	A	43.	A
10.	A	27.	B	44.	A
11.	C	28.	D	45.	B
12.	C	29.	D	46.	D
13.	C	30.	C	47.	C
14.	B	31.	A	48.	B
15.	D	32.	B	49.	A
16.	A	33.	C	50.	B
17.	D	34.	D		

A passing score is 40 correct answers. You must have at least 40 correct answers to have an 80%.

Look up any incorrect answers in the manual and study them until you know them.

If you got a score of 40 correct answers or higher, CONGRATULATIONS! You're ready to take the CDL General Knowledge Test.

Caution: Some states are going to have a test on their particular state laws. Check with your state to see if they are one of the states doing this; if so, you must obtain a coy of the state handbook from the nearest DMV and study it until you are familiar with the state laws as they pertain to commercial drivers and vehicles.

Combination Vehicles Final Examination

This test must be taken by all applicants for a "Class A" CDL.

Directions:

Same as General Knowledge Test; circle the correct answer.

You may begin now . . .

1. You are hooking a tractor to a semitrailer and have backed up but are not under it. What should you do before backing under the trailer?

   A. hook up the electrical service cable
   B. hook up the emergency and service air lines
   C. connect the ground cable
   D. nothing, back up and secure the fifth wheel to the trailer

2. After pushing in the trailer supply valve, you should not move the tractor until the whole air system is:

   A. charging
   B. at normal pressure
   C. bled down to half the maximum pressure
   D. between 50 and 60 psi

3. There are two things that a driver can do to prevent a rollover. They are (1) Keep the cargo as close to the ground as possible, and:

   A. make sure that the brakes are properly adjusted
   B. keep both hands firmly on the steering wheel
   C. reduce speed before entering turns
   D. keep the fifth wheel free play loose

4. With the engine off and the brakes released, a combination vehicle air brake system should not leak more than how many psi in one minute?

   A. 1
   B. 2
   C. 3
   D. 4

GO TO NEXT PAGE

5. The fifth wheel locking lever is not locked after the jaws close around the kingpin. This means, that:

   A. the trailer will not swing on the fifth wheel
   B. you cannot set the fifth wheel for the proper weight distribution
   C. the hand valve is released and you may drive away
   D. the coupling is not correct and should be corrected before driving the coupled unit

6. A driver crosses the air lines when hooking up to an old trailer. What will happen?

   A. the hand valve will apply the tractor brakes instead of the trailer brakes
   B. the brake pedal will work the trailer spring brakes instead of the air brakes
   C. if the trailer has no spring brakes, you could drive away but you wouldn't have trailer brakes
   D. the brake lights will not come on when the brake pedal is pressed

7. After coupling a semitrailer, you should crank up the front trailer supports (dollies) how?

   A. raised 1/2 way with the crank handle secured
   B. raised 3/4 way with the crank handle removed
   C. fully raised with the crank handle secured
   D. three turns off the top with the crank handle secured in its bracket

8. Air brake equipped trailers made before 1975:

   A. usually do not have spring brakes
   B. are easier to stop than newer trailers because they are heavier
   C. usually need a glad hand converter
   D. cannot be operated on interstate highways

9. The hand valve should be used to park a combination vehicle when?

   A. you park at loading docks
   B. parking for less than one hour
   C. when parking on a steep grade
   D. never

GO TO NEXT PAGE

10. Air lines on a combination vehicle are often colored to keep from getting them mixed up. The emergency line is _____ .

   A. red
   B. black
   C. blue
   D. orange

11. How do you supply air to the air tank on the trailer? You supply air to the trailer tank by:

   A. pushing in the trailer air supply valve
   B. pulling out the trailer air supply valve
   C. connecting the emergency line glad hand
   D. applying the trolley valve

12. In normal driving, some drivers use the trolley (hand) valve before the brake pedal in order to prevent trailer skids. Which of these statements is true?

   A. it should never be done
   B. it results in less skidding than using the brake pedal alone
   C. it lets the driver steer with both hands
   D. it is the best way to brake in a straight line

13. You are hooking up a tractor and semitrailer. You have connected both air lines. Before backing under the trailer you should:

   A. pull forward to test glad hand connections
   B. supply air to the trailer system, then pull out the air supply knob to lock the trailer brakes
   C. make sure that the trailer brakes are off
   D. blow the horn twice to alert others

14. When backing up under a trailer, you should line up:

   A. about 15 degrees off the line of the trailer
   B. the right mirror along the right edge of the trailer
   C. directly in front of the trailer
   D. the left rear inside dual wheel with the left side of the trailer

GO TO NEXT PAGE

15. If the service line disconnects while you are driving, what will happen right away?

   A. the emergency tractor brakes will come on
   B. the trailer's air tank will exhaust through the open line
   C. the emergency trailer brakes will come on
   D. nothing is likely to happen until you try the brakes

16. After hooking up, you should check the fifth wheel connection by:

   A. driving away at 20 mph and pulling down the trailer hand valve
   B. backing up with the trailer brakes released
   C. pulling the tractor ahead sharply to release the trailer brakes
   D. pulling the tractor ahead gently with the trailer brakes locked

17. When hooking a tractor to a trailer, you'll know the trailer is at the right height when the:

   A. trailer dolly wheels are fully extended
   B. kingpin is about 2-1/4 inches above the fifth wheel
   C. beginning of the kingpin is even with the top of the lower fifth wheel
   D. the coupling surface of the trailer is just below the middle of the tractor fifth wheel

18. You are driving a combination vehicle when the trailer breaks away and pulls apart the air lines. You would expect the trailer brakes to apply and:

   A. the tractor to lose all air pressure
   B. the tractor brakes to keep working properly
   C. the trailer supply valve to stay open
   D. tractor brakes to lock up

19. How much space should be between the upper and lower fifth wheel plates?

   A. about 1 inch
   B. about 1/2 inch
   C. about 1/4 inch
   D. none

GO TO NEXT PAGE

20. When not pulling a trailer, why is it a good idea to lock the glad hands together or to a dummy coupler?

A. it keeps air from escaping
B. the brake circuit becomes a secondary air tank
C. it keeps the dirt and water out of the lines
D. all of the above

Answers

1.	B	11.	A
2.	B	12.	A
3.	C	13.	B
4.	C	14.	C
5.	D	15.	D
6.	C	16.	D
7.	C	17.	D
8.	A	18.	B
9.	D	19.	D
10.	A	20.	C

A passing score is 16 correct answers. You must have at least 16 correct answers to have a score of 80%.

Look up any incorrect answers in the manual and study them until you have them memorized.

If you got a score of 16 or better, *CONGRATULATIONS!* You're ready for the CDL Combination Vehicle Test.

GO TO NEXT PAGE

Doubles and Triples Final Examination

This test must be taken by all "Class A" CDL applicants desiring to obtain a doubles and triples endorsement.

Directions:

Same as General Knowledge Test; circle the correct answer.

You may begin now . . .

1. You are driving a 100-foot-long double trailer combination at 35 mph. Pavement is dry and visibility is excellent. How much following distance in seconds should you maintain?

   A. 8
   B. 9
   C. 10
   D. 11

2. What is the best way to keep your brakes from overheating when going down a long grade?

   A. use the brake coolers
   B. drive fast enough so that the wind keeps them cool
   C. use only the trailer brakes
   D. get in proper gear, use braking effects of engine and apply brakes firmly when "safe" speed is reached

3. You are doing a walkaround inspection of a double or triple trailer rig. You should be sure the converter dolly air tank drain valves are _____ and the pintle hook is _____ .

   A. open; free
   B. closed; latched
   C. open; latched
   D. closed; free

4. There are many different types of vehicle skids. However, one rule applies to all skids; it is, in order to control the vehicle you must:

   A. accelerate
   B. countersteer
   C. restore traction to the tires
   D. use stab or controlled braking

GO TO NEXT PAGE

5. Before hooking the dolly to the rear trailer, how do you tell if the trailer height is correct?

   A. it will be slightly lower than the center of the fifth wheel
   B. the center of the kingpin will line up with the locking jaws
   C. the kingpin will be resting on the fifth wheel
   D. the fifth wheel will be touching the trailer lip

6. It is 12 noon and you are driving in a rainstorm. What does the Driver's Manual say about how much following distance you should maintain from the vehicle ahead of you?

   A. allow "the same amount of space you would at night"
   B. allow "much more space" than is needed for ideal driving conditions
   C. allow "one second to the space needed in good road conditions"
   D. allow "one car length for every 10 mph"

7. Converter dollies:

   A. often do not have spring brakes
   B. have little braking power because they are small
   C. usually need a glad hand converter
   D. all of the above

8. While driving a set of doubles, you must make a quick stop in order to avoid a crash. You should:

   A. push the brake pedal as hard as you can and hold it there
   B. use controlled or stab braking
   C. use light, steady pressure on the brake pedal
   D. use only the trailer brakes

9. Which of the following statements are true?

   A. at highway speeds, you should look at least 1/4 mile ahead of your truck
   B. good drivers shift their attention back and forth, near and far
   C. many drivers do not look far enough ahead when driving
   D. all of the above are true

GO TO NEXT PAGE

10. With the hand valve applied, you should test trailer brakes by opening the service line valve at the rear of the last trailer. When you do this, you should hear:

   A. the emergency line valve open and release air
   B. the service brakes slowly move to the fully applied position
   C. air escape from the open valve
   D. nothing, there should be no pressure in the line

11. Which of these statements is true?

   A. empty trucks require shorter stopping distances than full ones
   B. empty trucks may have poorer traction due to bouncing and wheel lockup
   C. you should always downshift while stopping an empty truck
   D. empty trucks should be stopped using only the hand valve

12. You should check trailer height before connecting a converter dolly to a second or third trailer. The trailer height is right when:

   A. the trailer will be raised slightly when the converter dolly is backed under it
   B. the center of the kingpin will line up with the locking jaws
   C. the kingpin will be resting on the fifth wheel
   D. the fifth wheel will be touching the trailer

13. When making a lane change, when should you check your mirrors?

   A. before and after signaling the change
   B. right after starting the lane change
   C. after completing the lane change
   D. all of the above

14. Which of these statements is true?

   A. the longest combination vehicles are the least likely to turn over
   B. a sudden steering movement may result in the rear trailer rolling over
   C. because of offtracking, it is easier to stop a triple bottom rig than to stop a 5-axle tractor-semitrailer
   D. rearward amplification may prevent the crack-the-whip effect from turning over all trailers

15. When is it okay to disconnect the steering axle brakes on the rig?

    A. never
    B. when the road is slippery
    C. when driving in very hilly areas
    D. when towing a trailer that has brakes

16. When pulling more than one trailer, which of the following is correct?

    A. the heaviest trailer must always be in the first position behind the tractor
    B. the lightest trailer must be in the first position behind the tractor
    C. you must make sure they are both the same weight
    D. the short trailer goes in front of the long one

17. What is the best way to make sure that you supplied air to the rear trailer?

    A. open the emergency line shut-off on the rear trailer
    B. open the hand valve with the rig parked
    C. watch for a drop of 30 psi on the air gauge
    D. apply the hand valve at 10 mph; it will stop in the same distance as one trailer at 5 mph if the brakes are working

18. What is likely to happen if you disconnect the dolly from the front trailer while it is still under the rear trailer?

    A. the trailer brakes will unlock
    B. the air lines will rupture
    C. the dolly tow bar may fly up
    D. nothing will happen unless the rig rolls forward

19. You are visually checking the coupling of a converter dolly to the rear trailer. How much space should be between the upper and lower fifth wheel?

    A. it depends on the load
    B. none
    C. 1/2 to 3/4 inch
    D. drivers are not able to visually check this coupling point

GO TO NEXT PAGE

20. Before you can supply air to the air tanks of a second trailer you need to:

    A. close the shut-off valves at the rear of both trailers

    B. open the shut-off valves at the rear of both trailers

    C. open the shutoff valves at the rear of the first trailer and close the shut-off valves at the rear of the second trailer

    D. close the shut-off valves at the rear of the first trailer and open the shut-off valves at the rear of the second trailer

Answers

1.	C	11.	B
2.	D	12.	A
3.	B	13.	D
4.	C	14.	B
5.	A	15.	A
6.	B	16.	A
7.	A	17.	A
8.	B	18.	C
9.	D	19.	B
10.	C	20.	C

A passing score is 16 correct answers. You must have at least 16 correct answers to have a score of 80%.

Look up any incorrect answers in the manual and study them until you have them memorized.

If you got a score of 16 or better, *CONGRATULATIONS!* You're ready for the CDL Doubles and Triples Test.

GO TO NEXT PAGE

Tank Vehicles Final Examination

This test must be taken by all CDL applicants desiring to obtain a tank vehicle endorsement.

Directions:

Same as General Knowledge Test; circle the correct answer.

You may begin now . . .

1. Liquid surge is caused by:

    A. movement of the fuel in the fuel tanks
    B. movement of the liquid product in the cargo tank
    C. movement of the vehicle on water-covered roads
    D. hydroplaning

2. Knowing the outage needed for the liquids is important because:

    A. you must unload some liquids at a faster rate than others
    B. tank baffles are not always legal with outage
    C. some liquids expand more than others when they get warm
    D. some of the heaviest liquids do not need any

3. What will liquid surge do to the handling of a tank vehicle?

    A. you will achieve faster trip times because it will help you to go faster
    B. surge will increase the wind resistance of the vehicle
    C. make the vehicle handle better
    D. it can move the vehicle in the same direction the liquid moves

4. When your cargo tank has bulkheads, what difference in handling can you expect?

    A. the rig will seem more heavy than it really is
    B. there will be less front-to-back surge than for a smooth bore
    C. the cargo tank will ride like it is not hooked on to the truck
    D. none, bulkheads have no effect on handling

GO TO NEXT PAGE

5. Knowing your center of gravity is important when hauling liquids.
It is best to keep the center of gravity:

   A. high
   B. wide
   C. missing
   D. low

6. Surge is generally:

   A. front to back
   B. back to front
   C. front to back and side to side
   D. bottom to top

7. How would you expect a truck with a baffled cargo tank to handle on the road?

   A. the truck will seem more heavy than it really is
   B. there will be less front-to-back surge than there is in tankers without baffles
   C. the cargo tank will feel like it is not hooked on to the truck
   D. the truck will handle the same as a tanker without baffles

8. When loading a cargo tank with liquid, you must consider which of the following?

   A. the legal weight limits in the states in which you will be driving
   B. the amount the liquid will expand during transit
   C. the weight of the liquid
   D. all of the above

9. You are driving a tank truck and the front wheels begin to skid.
Which of these is most likely to occur?

   A. you will continue in a straight line and keep moving forward no matter how much you steer
   B. liquid surge will pull the tank from the truck
   C. the truck will roll over
   D. the truck will stop in the shortest distance

10. A liquid tank with baffles can still have what kind of surge?

    A. side to side
    B. top to bottom
    C. front to back
    D. quick

GO TO NEXT PAGE

11. You are driving a loaded tank vehicle and are exiting a highway using an offramp that curves downhill. You should:

    A. use the posted speed limit for the offramp
    B. slow down to a safe speed before the turn
    C. come to a full stop at the top of the ramp
    D. wait until you are in the turn before downshifting

12. A smooth bore tank which is loaded to 50% capacity will:

    A. have less surge
    B. have the same amount of surge as one loaded to 100% of capacity
    C. make the vehicle handle better
    D. have more surge

13. A "smooth bore" tank will:

    A. have less surge than a baffled tank
    B. have less surge than a tank with bulkheads
    C. have more surge than a baffled tank
    D. all tanks have the same amount of surge

14. You need to be extremely cautious when driving smooth bore tanks. This is especially true when you are:

    A. going up or downhill
    B. starting or stopping
    C. loading and unloading
    D. hauling milk or other food products

15. Which of the following is important to remember in an emergency?

    A. stopping is always the safest action in a traffic emergency
    B. heavy vehicles can almost always turn more quickly than they can stop
    C. leaving the road is always more risky than hitting another vehicle
    D. open the door and jump out if you have time

16. When you unload the smaller tanks of a tank with bulkheads, be careful to check your:

    A. weight distribution
    B. air-to-fuel ratio
    C. water content
    D. power usage

GO TO NEXT PAGE

17. Which fires can you use water to put out?

    A. tire fires
    B. gasoline fires
    C. electrical fires
    D. all of the above

18. Which of these statements about emergency steering and tankers is true?

    A. a tanker is easier to countersteer than most vehicles
    B. when making a quick steering movement, do not apply the brakes
    C. you should wrap your thumbs around the steering wheel before starting a quick steering movement
    D. all of the above are true

19. Which of these is a good rule to follow when using a fire extinguisher?

    A. keep as close to the fire as possible
    B. stay upwind of the fire
    C. aim at the base of the fire
    D. both B and C

20. Most tankers have a high center of gravity. Which of the following is important to remember when pulling a liquid or dry bulk tanker?

    A. tankers can roll over at the speed limits posted for curves
    B. most tankers have a high center of gravity
    C. curves, exit and entrance ramps have speed limits which are safe for cars, but may be to fast for tankers
    D. all of the above

21. Which of these can cause a vehicle to skid?

    A. oversteering
    B. overbraking
    C. overacceleration
    D. all of the above

22. You are driving a tank vehicle and you must stop quickly to avoid a crash. You should:

    A. use light, steady pressure on the brake pedal
    B. push the brake pedal as hard as you can and hold it there
    C. use only the rear brakes
    D. use controlled or stab braking

GO TO NEXT PAGE

23. You should know the outage needed for the liquids you carry because:

    A. you must unload some liquids at a faster rate than others
    B. tank baffles are not always legal with outage
    C. some liquids expand more than others when they get warm
    D. delivery hose size depends on outage

24. Side-to-side surge can cause:

    A. suspension system failure
    B. overspeeding
    C. rollover
    D. tank failure

25. When should tanker drivers who have lost their brakes use truck escape ramps?

    A. never
    B. only when the tank is empty
    C. only when the tank has baffles
    D. always

GO TO NEXT PAGE

Answers

1. B	11. B	21. D
2. C	12. D	22. D
3. D	13. C	23. C
4. B	14. B	24. C
5. D	15. B	25. D
6. C	16. A	
7. B	17. A	
8. D	18. B	
9. A	19. D	
10. A	20. D	

A passing score is 20 correct answers. You must have at least 20 correct to have a score of 80%.

Look up any incorrect answers in the manual and study them until you have them memorized.

If you got a score of 20 or better, *CONGRATULATIONS!* You're ready for the CDL Tank Vehicle Test.

GO TO NEXT PAGE

Transporting Passenger Final Examination

This test must be taken by all CDL applicants desiring to obtain a Transporting Passenger endorsement.

Directions:

Same as General Knowledge Test; circle the correct answer.

You may begin now . . .

1. Buses may have recapped or regrooved tires:

    A. on any or all of the wheels
    B. only when the average speed will be less than 40 mph
    C. only on the front wheels
    D. anywhere except the front wheels

2. If a rider wants to bring a car battery or a can of gasoline or kerosene aboard your bus, you should:

    A. not allow them to do it
    B. tell them they must go to the rear of the bus
    C. instruct them to sit next to an open window
    D. have the rider pay a second fare

3. Which of the following types of emergency equipment must you have on your bus?

    A. reflectors, fire extinguisher, accident reporting kit
    B. hydraulic jack, fire extinguisher, signal flares
    C. fire extinguisher, spare electric fuses, reflectors
    D. spare electric fuses, fire extinguisher, accident reporting kit

4. You must not allow riders to stand:

    A. between the wheel wells
    B. in front of the standee line
    C. within two feet of an emergency exit
    D. within two feet of any window

GO TO NEXT PAGE

5. Your bus is disabled. The bus, with riders aboard, may be towed or pushed to a safe place only:

   A. by another bus with its 4-way flashers on
   B. by a 27,000 GVWR or larger tow truck
   C. if the distance is less than 500 yards
   D. if getting off the bus would be more risky for the riders

6. When inspecting your bus, you must make sure that:

   A. every handhold and railing is secure
   B. rider signaling devices are working
   C. emergency exit handles are secure
   D. all of the above

7. When is it best to wear your seat belt?

   A. only when you will be driving over 35 mph
   B. only if required by company policy
   C. only if your bus holds more than 27 people
   D. always

8. Which of these statements about speed management and braking is true?

   A. stopping time increases one second for each 10 mph over 20 mph
   B. you need about four times as much stopping distance at 40 mph as at 20 mph
   C. the total stopping distance of a bus is the distance it takes to stop once the brakes are put on
   D. the posted speed limit will always allow you to stop safely

9. With passengers onboard, you must never fuel your bus:

   A. with a higher grade of fuel
   B. in a closed building
   C. without a static chain
   D. with any of the windows open

10. When stopping for railroad tracks, you must stop no closer than how many feet before the nearest track?

    A. 5
    B. 10
    C. 15
    D. 20

GO TO NEXT PAGE

11. You may sometimes haul small-arms ammunition, emergency shipments of drugs or hospital supplies on a bus. The total weight of all such hazardous material must not be greater than:

    A. 100 pounds
    B. 250 pounds
    C. 500 pounds
    D. 750 pounds

12. How many folding aisle seats are permitted in a bus that is not carrying farm workers?

    A. 0
    B. 4
    C. 6
    D. 8

13. If there is no traffic light or attendant, how far from the draw of a drawbridge must you stop?

    A. 5 feet
    B. 10 yards
    C. 50 feet
    D. 100 feet

14. A bus may carry baggage or freight in the passenger area only if it is secured and meets which of the following requirements?

    A. the driver can move freely and easily
    B. any rider can use all exits
    C. riders are protected from falling or shifting packages
    D. all of the above

15. If your bus is equipped with an emergency exit door, it must:

    A. be secured when the bus is being driven
    B. always have a red door light turned on
    C. not have any signs, stickers or markings near it
    D. all of the above

GO TO NEXT PAGE

16. Which one of the folowing types of cargo must never be carried on a bus with passengers?

   A. small arms ammunition (ORM-D).
   B. tear gas
   C. emergency hospital supplies
   D. emergency drug shipments

17. When you discharge an unruly passenger, you must choose a place that is:

   A. off the regular route
   B. dark and poorly lighted
   C. as safe as possible, or the next stop
   D. the most convenient

18. When should you check your mirrors for a lane change?

   A. before and after signaling the change
   B. right after starting the lane change
   C. after completing the lane change
   D. all of the above

19. The reason you must be alert for road hazard is so:

   A. accident reports will be accurate
   B. law enforcement personnel can be called
   C. you will have time to plan your escape if the hazard becomes an emergency
   D. you can help impaired drivers

20. How many seats may be placed in the aisle if the bus is a charter and is carrying agricultural (farm) workers?

   A. 0
   B. 8
   C. 6
   D. 4

GO TO NEXT PAGE

Answers

1.	D	11.	C
2.	A	12.	A
3.	C	13.	C
4.	B	14.	D
5.	D	15.	A
6.	D	16.	B
7.	D	17.	C
8.	B	18.	D
9.	B	19.	C
10.	C	20.	B

A passing score is 16 correct answers. You must have at least 16 correct to have a score of 80%.

Look up any incorrect answers in the manual and study them until you have them memorized.

If you got a score of 16 or better, *CONGRATULATIONS!* You're ready for the CDL Transporting Passenger Test.

GO TO NEXT PAGE

Air Brake Final Examination

This test must be taken by all CDL applicants desiring to operate equipment with air brakes.

Directions:

Same as General Knowledge Test; circle the correct answer.

You may begin now . . .

1. The air loss rate for a straight truck or bus with the engine off and the brakes applied should not be more than:

   A. 1 psi in 60 seconds

   B. 1 psi in one minute

   C. 2 psi in 45 seconds

   D. 3 psi in one minute

2. Which of the following statements about brakes is true?

   A. the heavier a vehicle or the faster it is moving, the more heat the brakes have to absorb to stop it

   B. brakes have more stopping power when they get very hot

   C. brake drums cool very quickly

   D. all of the above are true

3. The purpose of engine retarders is to:

   A. provide emergency brakes

   B. help slow the vehicle while driving and reduce brake wear

   C. apply extra braking power to the non-drive axles

   D. help prevent skids and slides

4. If your vehicle has an alcohol evaporator, it is there to:

   A. get rid of alcohol that condenses in the air tanks

   B. let the driver skip the daily tank draining

   C. increase tank pressure the way superchargers boost engines

   D. reduce the risk of ice in air brake valves in cold weather

GO TO NEXT PAGE

5. The air supply pressure gauge shows the driver how much pressure:

    A. has been used in this trip
    B. is available in the air tanks
    C. is being sent to the brake chambers
    D. none of the above

6. Which brake system applies and releases the brakes when the driver uses the brake pedal?

    A. the emergency brake system
    B. the service brake system   — brake pedal
    C. the parking brake system
    D. none of the above

7. When using the parking brakes or emergency brakes, what type of pressure is being used?

    A. fluid pressure
    B. spring pressure
    C. air pressure
    D. any of the above

8. Three different systems are found on modern air brake systems: service brakes, the parking brakes, and the:

    A. emergency brakes
    B. foot brakes
    C. s-cam brakes
    D. drum brakes

9. Air loss in a single vehicle (not a combination unit) should not be more than _____ with the engine off and the brakes on.

    A. 1 psi in 30 seconds
    B. 1 psi in one minute
    C. 2 psi in 45 seconds
    D. 3 psi in one minute

GO TO NEXT PAGE

10. The vehicle must have a warning device which comes on when air pressure in the service air tanks falls below:

    A. 40 psi
    B. 50 psi
    C. 60 psi
    D. 80 psi

11. Air brake equipped vehicles must have:

    A. at least three air tanks
    B. a hydraulic braking system, in case the air system fails
    C. an air pressure gauge, to show the pressure available for braking
    D. an air application gauge, to show air used by the brake chambers for braking

12. How do you check the free play in manual slack adjusters?

    A. stop on level ground and apply the emergency brakes
    B. park on level ground, chock wheels, release the parking brakes and pull slack adjusters
    C. park on level ground and drain off air pressure before making adjustments
    D. apply the service brakes by hand at the brake chambers and watch the slack adjusters move

13. The most common type of foundation brake found on heavy commercial vehicles is:

    A. disc
    B. wedge and drum
    C. s-cam drum
    D. none of the above

14. The air compressor governor controls:

    A. the rpms of the air compressor
    B. whether the compressor is in good mechnical condition
    C. air pressure applied to the brakes
    D. when the compressor will pump air into the storage tanks

GO TO NEXT PAGE

15. The brake pedal:

    A. is the main lever in the system
    B. can be a foot rest during normal driving
    C. controls the air pressure applied to operate the brakes
    D. exerts force on the slack adjusters by rods and connectors

16. What will determine how effective the spring emergency brakes or the parking brakes work?

    A. has nothing to do with the condition of the service brakes
    B. can only be tested by highly-trained brake service people
    C. depends on the adjustment of the service brakes
    D. the braking power increases when the service brakes are hot

17. When a failure occurs in the service brake system, the system you need to stop the vehicle is the:

    A. parking brake system
    B. emergency brake system
    C. drum brake system
    D. the hand brake system

18. If your vehicle is equipped with an alcohol evaporator, every day during winter weather you should:

    A. check and fill the alcohol level
    B. change the alcohol from a new bottle
    C. oil the system with 5 weight oil
    D. drain out the alcohol which has accumulated

19. What turns on the electrical stop light switch in an air brake system?

    A. spring pressure
    B. hydraulic pressure
    C. air pressure
    D. the driver, by hand

20. Which of the following is okay to find in the air brake system?

    A. oil
    B. air
    C. water
    D. all of the above

GO TO NEXT PAGE

21. If the air system should develop a leak, what will keep the air in the tanks?

   A. the governor
   B. the tractor protection valve
   C. the emergency relay valve
   D. the one-way check valve

22. If your truck or bus has dual parking control valves, you can use pressure from a separate tank to:

   A. release the emergency brakes to move a short distance
   B. apply more brake pressure for stopping if the main tank is getting low
   C. stay parked without using up service air pressure
   D. balance the service brake system while you drive

23. In air brake equipped vehicles, you use the parking brakes when?

   A. when slowing down
   B. as little as possible
   C. whenever you park the vehicle
   D. only during pre- and post-trip inspections

24. During normal operations, the parking and emergency brakes are usually held back by:

   A. air pressure
   B. spring pressure
   C. centrifugal force
   D. bolts or clamps

25. A combination vehicle air brake system cannot leak more than _____ psi per minute with the engine off and the brakes released.

   A. 1
   B. 2
   C. 3
   D. 4

26. A straight truck or bus air brake system cannot leak more than _____ psi per minute with the engine off and the brakes released.

   A. 1
   B. 2
   C. 3
   D. 4

GO TO NEXT PAGE

27. You must make a quick emergency stop. You should brake so you:

    A. can steer hard while braking hard

    B. use the full power of the brakes and lock them

    C. can stay in a straight line and maintain steering control

    D. burn up the hand brake first

28. Why should you not fan the brakes on and off during long downgrades?

    A. air usage is less when fanning

    B. brake linings do not get hot when fanning

    C. the short time off the brakes does not allow brake cooling

    D. none of the above

29. Which of the following answers is most correct about using brakes on a long and/or steep downgrade?

    A. use the braking effects of the engine and when the vehicle speed reaches the "safe" speed, apply brakes firmly until vehicle speed is reduced to approximately 5 mph below "safe" speed

    B. use stab braking

    C. use only the trailer brakes to maintain "safe" speed

    D. apply brakes when vehicle speed reaches 5 mph over "safe" speed and then release when speed of vehicle is back at safe speed

30. To use the stab braking technique during emergency braking, you:

    A. pump the brake pedal rapidly and lightly

    B. brake hard with the pedal until the wheels lock, then get off them until the wheels begin rolling again

    C. brake hard with the pedal until the wheels lock, then get off the brakes for as long as the wheels were locked

    D. brake hard with the pedal and hand valve until you stop

GO TO NEXT PAGE

Answers

1. D	11. C	21. D
2. A	12. B	22. A
3. B	13. C	23. C
4. D	14. D	24. A
5. B	15. C	25. C
6. B	16. C	26. B
7. B	17. B	27. C
8. A	18. A	28. C
9. D	19. C	29. A
10. C	20. B	30. B

A passing score is 24 correct answers. You must have at least 24 correct to have a score of 80%.

Look up any incorrect answers in the manual and study them until you have them memorized.

If you got a score of 24 or better, *CONGRATULATIONS!* You're ready for the CDL Air Brake Test.

GO TO NEXT PAGE

Hazardous Material Final Examination

This test must be taken by all CDL applicants desiring a Hazardous Material Endorsement. The Hazardous Material Endorsement is required if you transport hazardous material in such a quantity that placards are required to be displayed on the vehicle.

Directions:

Same as General Knowledge Test; circle the correct answers.

You may begin . . .

1. There are three lists that drivers, shippers, and carriers use to find out if a material is a regulated product. Which of the following is one of them?

   A. List of Hazardous Substances and Reportable Quantities
   B. EPA Dangerous Materials Table
   C. Shippers List of Transportable Quantities
   D. Department of Transportation Hazard Chart

2. A vehicle placarded for hazardous materials is required to have placards on how many sides of the vehicle?

   A. 1
   B. 2
   C. 3
   D. 4

3. A hazard class name or ID number must not be used to describe a:

   A. non-hazardous material
   B. reportable quantity of a hazardous substance
   C. hazardous waste
   D. hazardous material

4. The intention of the hazardous materials regulations are to ensure safe drivers and equipment, to communicate the risk, and:

   A. to tax shippers correctly
   B. to contain the material
   C. to allow state enforcement
   D. none of the above

GO TO NEXT PAGE

5. If an "X" or an "RQ" is written or typed into the HM column of a shipping paper entry, the:

   A. shipment is regulated by hazardous material regulations
   B. material on that line is the biggest part of the shipment
   C. entry refers to the materials that must be top loaded
   D. entry is part of a partial shipment

6. Who do the regulations say is responsible for packaging, labeling, and preparing the hazardous material shipping papers for shipment?

   A. carrier
   B. shipper
   C. driver
   D. state auditors

7. A power unit of a placarded vehicle is required to have a fire extinguisher with a UL rating of _____ B:C or more.

   A. 5
   B. 10
   C. 15
   D. 20

8. You may not park a vehicle carrying hazardous materials within how many feet of an open fire?

   A. 100
   B. 200
   C. 300
   D. 400

9. If hazardous material is leaking from your vehicle, you must not move your vehicle:

   A. any more than 500 feet
   B. in an upwind direction
   C. off of the roadway
   D. any more than safety requires

GO TO NEXT PAGE

10. The transport index of a radioactive material tells you:

    A. the weight of the material
    B. the degree of control needed during transportation
    C. is something that only the consignee needs to worry about
    D. lets the Emergency Response Team (ERT) ignore the ID number
       on the placard

11. Only one of these shipping paper descriptions for a hazardous material
    is in the correct order. Select the correct one.

    A. hydrogen bromide, non-flammable gas, UN 1048
    B. UN 1787, corrosive material, hydriotic acid
    C. corrosive material, hydrochloric acid, UN 1789
    D. hexane, UN 1208, flammable liquid

12. A "W" in the first column of the Hazardous Materials Table indicates:

    A. a tank of water must always be in the same vehicle as this product
    B. the material is reactive to water
    C. the rules apply only if the material is waste
    D. the entry applies to water shipments that are not a RQ

13. You may not smoke around any vehicle being loaded or unloaded with:

    A. flammables
    B. oxidizers
    C. explosives
    D. any of the above

14. If a vehicle carrying explosives crashes with another object, you must
    not separate the vehicle from the other object until:

    A. at least 30 minutes have passed
    B. a firefighting crew is standing by
    C. someone has removed the explosives and placed them at least 200 feet away
    D. bomb experts have checked the explosives

15. Before loading or unloading any explosive, you must check the cargo space for:

    A. a cargo heater that could start
    B. sharp points that might damage the cargo
    C. loose floor boards or plates
    D. all of the above

GO TO NEXT PAGE

16. A liquid poison is spilling from your vehicle. If it can be done safely, how should you channel the liquid?

    A. downwind
    B. away from the leaking vehicle
    C. upwind
    D. away from streams or sewers

17. Which emergency equipment may be used to warn of a stopped vehicle which contains explosives?

    A. signal fires
    B. reflective triangles
    C. flares
    D. fuses

18. The description of a hazardous product must include the hazard class, the identification number, and its proper shipping name. Which is required to be listed first on the shipping papers?

    A. the hazard class
    B. the proper shipping name
    C. the identification number
    D. it does not matter which one appears first

19. When shippers package hazardous materials, they must certify that this was done according to the regulations. The one exception to this rule is when:

    A. the shipment is a hazardous waste
    B. the driver is given a sealed cargo compartment
    C. the shipper is a private carrier carrying their own product
    D. the trip will not cross a state line

20. When you are transporting chlorine in cargo tanks, you must have:

    A. an approved gas mask
    B. an emergency kit for controlling leaks in fittings on the dome cover plate
    C. both A and B
    D. either A or B, but not both

GO TO NEXT PAGE

21. Carriers are required to give each driver who transports Division 1.1 or Division 1.2:

    A. an extra fire bottle
    B. the consignee's phone number
    C. a copy of FMCSR, Part 397
    D. a list of rest stops the driver may use

22. When you are handling packages of explosives, you must:

    A. never use a forklift to move the freight
    B. double wrap wet boxes in plastic to prevent staining
    C. roll the packages carefully, with no sharp or jarring actions
    D. never use hooks or other metal tools

23. If the word "Forbidden" is written or typed in the hazard class column of an entry in the hazardous materials table:

    A. the carrier may not open the package or container
    B. you must never transport the product
    C. a shipment of that product must never be larger than the RQ
    D. you may transport it only with an escort vehicle

24. What is the largest allowable total transport index of all packages in a single vehicle allowed to be?

    A. 5
    B. 10
    C. 50
    D. 100

25. You are hauling 2000 pounds of a corrosive. You may park within _____ feet of the road if your work requires it and it is for a very short period of time.

    A. 5
    B. 7
    C. 12
    D. 15

GO TO NEXT PAGE

26. If you are hauling hazardous materials and you discover that one of your tires is leaking, you must:

    A. continue at reduced speed, and check that tire every 25 miles
    B. stop at the nearest safe place and fix it
    C. report it to your carrier immediately
    D. report this to the DOT

27. You should stop before crossing a railroad grade if your vehicle is carrying how many gallons of chlorine?

    A. 110 gallons
    B. 100 gallons
    C. 55 gallons
    D. any amount

28. Animal and human foodstuffs must not be loaded in the same vehicle with:

    A. explosives
    B. oxidizers
    C. poisons
    D. flammable gases

29. When fueling a placarded vehicle, someone must always be:

    A. within 10 feet of the pump with a fire extinguisher
    B. watching the fueling from a safe distance
    C. at the nozzle, controlling the fuel flow
    D. at the emergency power shut-off for the pump

30. Who do the regulations say is responsible for checking that the shipper correctly named, labeled, and marked a hazardous material shipment?

    A. shipper
    B. manufacturer
    C. carrier
    D. DOT

GO TO NEXT PAGE

31. While transporting hazardous material you stop to eat lunch at a truck stop. While you are in the truck stop, the shipping papers must be placed on the drivers seat or:

    A. in the driver's door pouch
    B. in the trailer's paper pouch
    C. on your person
    D. on the dashboard in clear view

32. During an en route inspection, you discover an overheated tire. If you are hauling hazardous materials, you must:

    A. wait at least two hours before continuing your trip
    B. cool the tire, then check it every two hours
    C. lower that tire's air pressure by at least 20 psi
    D. remove the tire and place it a safe distance from the vehicle

33. When hauling hazardous materials, you must stop your vehicle and check any dual tires at least once every:

    A. 1 hour or 40 miles
    B. 2 hours or 80 miles
    C. 2 hours or 100 miles
    D. 3 hours or 150 miles

34. During a hazardous materials emergency, you must use every available means to:

    A. keep people away
    B. prevent smoking and keep open flame away
    C. warn others of the danger
    D. do choices A, B, and C

35. If you are transporting Division 1.1 or 1.2 Explosives, you must not:

    A. transport them in a combination vehicle consisting of double trailers
    B. stop the vehicle while en route to your destination
    C. transport them in vehicle combinations if there is a placarded cargo tank in the combination
    D. both A and C

GO TO NEXT PAGE

Answers

1. A	14. C	27. D
2. D	15. D	28. C
3. A	16. D	29. C
4. B	17. B	30. C
5. A	18. B	31. A
6. B	19. C	32. D
7. B	20. C	33. C
8. C	21. C	34. D
9. D	22. D	35. C
10. B	23. B	
11. A	24. C	
12. D	25. A	
13. D	26. B	

A passing score is 28 correct answers. You must have at least 28 correct to have a score of 80%.

Look up any incorrect answers in the manual and study them until you have them memorized.

If you got a score of 28 or better, *CONGRATULATIONS!* You're ready for the CDL Hazardous Material Test.

GO TO NEXT PAGE

True and False CDL Tests

Several states have changed the CDL tests from multiple choice to true and false.

As a service to our customers who live in those states we are including true and false tests in this manual.

If you live in a state giving true and false tests, you should practice by taking the tests which begin after this page.

If you don't know which type of tests your state is giving, call your local Department of Motor Vehicles (DMV) office.

If you live in a state giving multiple choice tests, you don't need to take the following tests, but of course it wouldn't hurt. Remember practice makes perfect.

General Knowledge

This test must be taken by all applicants for a commercial driver's license.

Directions:

Study each question carefully and then draw a circle around the letter which is most correct:

1. Hydroplaning can occur at speeds as low as 30 mph.   T   F

2. Braking in a curve helps prevent skidding.   T   F

3. When going down a long steep hill, you should use a light, steady pressure on the brake pedal.   T   F

4. When making a pre-trip inspection on the engine compartments, you should check for worn electrical wiring insulation.   T   F

5. When traction is poor, you should accelerate quickly.   T   F

6. If the drive wheels start to spin, you should take your foot off the accelerator.   T   F

7. You should hold the steering wheel with both hands, one near the top and the other near the bottom.   T   F

GO TO NEXT PAGE

8. You should keep about one second for each 25 feet of vehicle length in front of you when traveling at speeds over 40 mph.   T   F

9. When driving a large vehicle, you should always stay as close to the right of the lane as possible.   T   F

10. Steering wheel play of more than 10 degrees is dangerous.   T   F

11. Brake pads should have plenty of brake fluid on them.   T   F

12. Retarders increase brake wear.   T   F

13. You should inspect your tires every two (2) hours or 100 miles in very hot weather.   T   F

14. Air pressure in tires increases when the temperature rises.   T   F

15. When you are about half-way down a long and/or steep downgrade you should shift to a lower gear.   T   F

16. The driver is responsible for recognizing overloads, whether or not he loaded the cargo himself.   T   F

17. Liquid surge tends to push the vehicle in the opposite direction the wave of liquid is moving.   T   F

18. When traveling at 55 mph in good conditions, it will take about six seconds to stop your vehicle.   T   F

19. When driving on a wet road, you should reduce your speed about 1/3.   T   F

20. Perception distance + reaction distance + braking distance = total stopping distance.   T   F

21. It is safest to back your vehicle towards the driver's side whenever possible.   T   F

22. When backing, you should not use a helper because you might hit him.   T   F

23. When double clutching, you should release the accelerator several seconds before pushing in the clutch.   T   F

GO TO NEXT PAGE

24. The posted speed limit on off-ramps may not be safe for larger or heavily loaded vehicles.   T   F

25. The symbol for a "Slow Moving Vehicle" is a red triangle with an orange center.   T   F

26. You should never countersteer after making a quick turn to miss an object.   T   F

27. Stab braking is one method to stop quickly and keep your vehicle in a straight line.   T   F

28. Understeering is one of the steps to correct a drive-wheel braking skid.   T   F

29. Most front-wheel skids are caused by driving too fast for conditions.   T   F

30. An A:B:C fire extinguisher should be used to put out a fire burning a cargo of wood.   T   F

31. Coffee and fresh air can help a drinker sober up.   T   F

32. Alcohol affects reaction time.   T   F

33. Placards are charts showing chemical equations for hazardous materials.   T   F

34. When making a pre-trip inspection in winter weather, you should pay extra attention to the wipers and washers.   T   F

35. When driving on slippery roads, you should pass slower vehicles as soon as possible.   T   F

36. If your brakes become wet, the best way to dry them out is to speed up and let the air dry them.   T   F

37. Conditions can make the posted height at an overpass incorrect.   T   F

38. When making a right turn in a large vehicle, you should turn wide to the left as you start the turn.   T   F

GO TO NEXT PAGE

39. You should signal when the vehicle ahead of you is turning to let drivers behind you know the vehicle is turning.   T   F

40. When stopped on a two-lane highway, you should place one reflective triangle 100 feet to the front of the vehicle, one 10 feet to the rear, and one 100 feet to the rear.   T   F

41. When traveling at highway speed, you should look about 1/4 mile ahead of your vehicle.   T   F

42. You should have at least 4/32 of an inch tread depth on front tires.   T   F

43. Mismatched lock rings are not a sign of problems with the wheel or rim.   T   F

44. If your hydraulic brakes fail, you can downshift to slow the vehicle.   T   F

45. If you notice a sign of tire failure, you should steer onto the shoulder before slowing down.   T   F

46. When driving a heavy vehicle, you need a smaller gap to enter traffic than cars.   T   F

47. The only safe cure if you become sleepy while driving is to get off the road and get some sleep.   T   F

48. When driving at night, you should be able to stop within 100 feet.   T   F

49. You should never load a cargo tank totally full because liquids expand as they warm.   T   F

50. You should use light, steady braking pressure when traveling down a long and/or steep downgrade.   T   F

GO TO NEXT PAGE

Answers

1. True	14. True	27. True	40. True
2. False	15. False	28. False	41. True
3. True	16. True	29. True	42. True
4. True	17. False	30. True	43. False
5. False	18. True	31. False	44. True
6. True	19. True	32. True	45. False
7. False	20. True	33. False	46. False
8. False	21. True	34. True	47. True
9. False	22. False	35. False	48. False
10. True	23. False	36. False	49. True
11. False	24. True	37. True	50. False
12. False	25. True	38. False	
13. True	26. False	39. False	

GO TO NEXT PAGE

Combination Vehicles

This test must be taken by all applicants for a " Class A" CDL.

Directions:

Same as General Knowledge Test

Circle the correct answer

You may begin now . . .

1. Fully-loaded rigs are 10 times more likely to roll over in a crash than empty rigs.   (T)   F

2. Cargo should be kept as close to the ground as possible.   (T)   F

3. Rearward amplification causes the crack-the-whip effect.   (T)   F

4. Lightly loaded trailers are less likely to jackknife than heavily loaded ones.   T   (F)

5. It takes a bobtail longer to stop than a tractor-semitrailer loaded to maximum gross weight.   (T)   F

6. You should use the trailer hand brake to straighten out if you go into a trailer skid.   T   (F)

7. You should swing wide to the left before starting a right turn.   T   (F)

8. You should never use the trailer hand valve for parking.   (T)   F

9. The rear wheels of the trailer will offtrack the most.   (T)   F

10. The tractor protection valve keeps air in the tractor if the trailer breaks away.   (T)   F

11. Emergency air lines are often coded with the color blue.   T   (F)

12. The tractor protection valve closes automatically when the air pressure rises too high.   T   (F)

13. Dummy, or dead-end, couplers prevent water and dirt from getting into the coupler and air lines.   (T)   F

GO TO NEXT PAGE

14. If the fifth wheel plate is not kept lubricated, it could
cause steering problems.   (T)   F

15. Never back your tractor under a trailer at an angle.   (T)   F

16. The trailer should remain perfectly level when the tractor
is backed under it.   T   (F)

17. The tractor emergency air line should be connected to the
trailer emergency glad hand.   (T)   F

18. Crossed air lines are only dangerous if you do
not have a tractor emergency brake.   T   (F)

19. Fifth wheel jaws should close around the shank of the
kingpin when properly coupled.   (T)   F

20. When testing the brake system for a combination vehicle,
you should not hear air escaping when you open the
emergency line shut-off valve.   T   (F)

Answers

1.	True	11.	False
2.	True	12.	False
3.	True	13.	True
4.	False	14.	True
5.	True	15.	True
6.	False	16.	False
7.	False	17.	True
8.	True	18.	False
9.	True	19.	True
10.	True	20.	False

GO TO NEXT PAGE

Double and Triple Trailers

True and False Final Examination

This test must be taken by all "Class A" CDL applicants desiring to obtain a doubles and triples endorsement.

Directions:

Same as General Knowledge Test; circle the correct answer.

You may begin now . . .

1. Always couple the heaviest trailer to the rear of the combination when pulling two trailers.   T   F

2. The converter dolly should be positioned in front of the second trailer and in line with the kingpin.   T   F

3. There should be no space between the upper and lower fifth wheel when properly coupled.   T   F

4. Never unlock the pintle hook with the dolly still under the rear trailer.   T   F

5. The trailer should be slightly lower than the center of the fifth wheel.   T   F

6. You should release dolly brakes before disconnecting the dolly air and electric lines when uncoupling the rear trailer.   T   F

7. To set the trailer emergency brakes if the second trailer does not have spring brakes, you should drive the tractor close to the trailer air tank and disconnect the emergency line.   T   F

8. When inspecting double trailers, the shut-off valves at the rear of the last trailer should be open.   T   F

9. When pulling double trailers, you should brake a little more firmly while going through a curve.   T   F

GO TO NEXT PAGE

10. You should check for air at the rear of the second trailer
    by opening the emergency line shut-off.   T   F

11. Double trailers jackknife more easily when loaded.   T   F

12. If the dolly has air brakes, you release them by opening
    the air tank petcock.   T   F

13. You should use the trailer brakes to stop a skid.   T   F

14 You should pull the tractor forward gently while the
    trailer brakes are still locked to check that the trailer
    is locked onto the tractor.   T   F

15. When the full weight of a trailer is resting on the tractor,
    you should hit the landing gear only after turning
    more than 45 degrees.   T   F

16. It is a good idea to chock the wheels before coupling a
    second trailer to your rig.   T   F

17. To hook the dolly to the front trailer, you should lock
    the pintle hook and secure the converter gear
    support in a raised position.   T   F

18. When performing a vehicle inspection in a two-trailer rig,
    the shut-off valves at the rear of the front trailers should be open.   T   F

19. When coupling a second semitrailer, the dolly should
    always be at least two feet away from the nose of
    the trailer.   T   F

20. You should release the pintle hook on the first semitrailer
    before pulling clear of the converter dolly.   T   F

GO TO NEXT PAGE

Answers

1. False

2. True

3. True

4. True

5. True

6. False

7. True

8. False

9. False

10. True

11. False

12. True

13. False

14. True

15. False

16. True

17. True

18. True

19. False

20. True

GO TO NEXT PAGE

Tank Vehicles

True and False Final Examination

This test must be taken by all CDL applicants desiring to obtain a Tank Vehicle Endorsement.

Directions:

Same as General Knowledge Test; circle the correct answer.

You may begin now . . .

1. Tank vehicles have a low center of gravity.   T   F

2. Tankers can turn over at the speed limits posted for curves.   T   F

3. Liquid surge tends to push the truck in the direction the wave of liquid is moving.   T   F

4. Baffled tanks have bulkheads with holes in them.   T   F

5. Liquid surge is less dangerous in poor driving conditions.   T   F

6. Baffled tanks control side-to-side surge.   T   F

7. Sanitation regulations forbid the use of baffled tanks to transport food products.   T   F

8. You should always leave room for expanding liquids when loading a cargo tank.   T   F

9. Because of bulkheads, weight distribution is not as big a factor for tanker drivers.   T   F

10. Tank vehicles tend to be top heavy.   T   F

11. Dense liquids, such as some acids, are likely to exceed legal weight limits if the tank is fully loaded.   T   F

12. Forward and back surge is especially high in unbaffled tankers.   T   F

13. The driver is only responsible for an overloaded vehicle if he loaded it himself.   T   F

GO TO NEXT PAGE

14. Too much weight on the driving axles is likely to cause poor traction.   T   F

15. Dry bulk tank loads tend to have a high unstable center of gravity.   T   F

16. A bridge formula permits less maximum axle weight for axles that are closer together.   T   F

17. When hauling liquids in bulk, it is less important to know the outage requirements.   T   F

18. Starting and stopping in a smooth bore tanker requires extreme caution.   T   F

19. Baffles divide a tank into several smaller tanks.   T   F

20. Too much weight on the steering axle can cause hard steering.   T   F

Answers

1.	False	11.	True
2.	True	12.	True
3.	True	13.	False
4.	True	14.	False
5.	False	15.	True
6.	False	16.	True
7.	True	17.	False
8.	True	18.	True
9.	False	19.	False
10.	True	20.	True

GO TO NEXT PAGE

Passenger Vehicles

True and False Final Examination

This test must be taken by all CDL applicants desiring to obtain a Transporting Passenger endorsement.

Directions:

Same as General Knowledge Test; circle the correct answer.

You may begin now . . .

1. Front wheels on a bus must not have recapped or regrooved tires.   T   F

2. Buses can never carry "Class A" poison.   T   F

3. Riders should be allowed to only leave one piece of
    baggage in the aisle.   T   F

4. A rider should be allowed to transport a car battery only
    if it is securely packed and clearly labeled.   T   F

5. When driving a bus, you should scan the interior of the
    bus as well as the road ahead.   T   F

6. You must stop a bus between 5 and 15 feet before
    railroad crossings.   T   F

7. The posted speed for curves is always the safest speed
    for a bus.   T   F

8. Intersections are some of the most common places for bus crashes.   T   F

9. You should stop at least 50 feet before a drawbridge
    without a signal control or attendant.   T   F

10. Never refuel your bus with riders on board in a closed building.   T   F

11. A brake-door interlock is to be used in place of the parking brake.   T   F

12. Disruptive riders should always be discharged immediately.   T   F

GO TO NEXT PAGE

13. If you are getting sleepy near the end of your route, it is a good idea to start a conversation with a passenger to help keep you alert.　　　　　　　　　T　　F

14. Do not allow a rider to stand forward of the rear of the driver's seat unless there is no room anywhere else.　　　　　　　　　T　　F

15. Every bus should be equipped with a fire extinguisher and emergency reflectors.　　　　　　　　　T　　F

16. Hazardous materials labels are diamond shaped.　　　　　　　　　T　　F

17. There is only one exception to the rule that all seats must be securely fastened to the bus.　　　　　　　　　T　　F

18. When driving at the safest speed, your bus should lean slightly to the outside on a banked curve.　　　　　　　　　T　　F

19. You should not change gears while crossing railroad tracks.　　　　　　　　　T　　F

20. Emergency windows may be opened only half-way while driving.　　　　　　　　　T　　F

GO TO NEXT PAGE

Answers

1.	True	11.	False
2.	True	12.	False
3.	False	13.	False
4.	False	14.	False
5.	True	15.	True
6.	False	16.	True
7.	False	17.	true
8.	True	18.	False
9.	True	19.	True
10.	True	20.	False

GO TO NEXT PAGE

Air Brakes

True and False Final Examination

This test must be taken by all CDL applicants desiring to operate equipment with air brakes.

Directions:

Same as General Knowledge Test; circle the correct answer.

You may begin now . . .

1. Slack adjusters on s-cam brakes need adjustment if they move more than two inches where the push rod attaches.   T   F

2. With the engine at operating rpm, the air pressure should build from 85 to 100 psi in about 45 seconds in a dual air system.   T   F

3. Air pressure loss in a combination vehicle should not be more than 1 psi per minute while pressure is on the brake pedal.   T   F

4. At 55 mph on dry pavement, the air brake's lag distance adds about 32 feet to total stopping distance.   T   F

5. Air brakes cool very quickly.   T   F

6. Trying to slow down from too high a speed too many times may cause too much heat to build up in your air brakes.   T   F

7. If the low air pressure warning comes on, you should stop and safely park your vehicle as soon as possible.   T   F

8. You should drain your air tanks at the end of each working day to remove moisture and oil.   T   F

9. When the spring brakes come on, lightly loaded vehicles will build air pressure quickly.   T   F

10. The most common type of foundation brakes is s-cam drum.   T   F

11. The supply pressure gauge tells you how long before the s-cam turns.   T   F

GO TO NEXT PAGE

12. Drum bakes are the only type of brakes in which brake fade occurs. T F

13. The emergency brake on a heavy vehicle is usually held in place by spring pressure because air pressure can leak away. T F

14. Some vehicles have a separate air tank which can be used to release the spring brakes. T F

15. A dual air brake system has two systems—primary and secondary. T F

16. When air pressure drops too much, the spring brakes come on. T F

17. You should not use the parking brakes when the brakes are very hot. T F

18. The total stopping distance for an average driver at 55 mph under good traction and brake conditions is about 100 feet. T F

19. Modern air brake systems use three braking systems combined—service, parking, and emergency. T F

20. The air compressor regulator controls when air compressor will pump air into the air storage tanks. T F

21. The alcohol evaporator condenses the air in the brake system. T F

22. The first tank the air compressor pumps air to is installed with a safety relief valve to protect the tank and the rest of the system from too much air pressure. T F

23. If your vehicle pulls to one side while testing the service brakes, there may be a problem with the service brakes. T F

24. The braking effects of the engine when going down a long and/or steep downgrade should be supplemented by the use of the brakes. T F

GO TO NEXT PAGE

25. When the wheels lock up, you should maintain steady pressure on the brakes and hold the steering wheel firmly to keep the vehicle in a straight line.   T   F

Answers

1. True   14. True

2. True   15. True

3. False   16. True

4. True   17. True

5. False   18. False

6. True   19. True

7. True   20. True

8. True   21. False

9. False   22. True

10. True   23. True

11. False   24. True

12. False   25. False

13. True

GO TO NEXT PAGE

Hazardous Materials

True and False Final Examination

This test must be taken by all CDL applicants desiring a Hazardous Material Endorsement. The Hazardous Material Endorsement is required if you transport hazardous material in such a quantity that placards are required to be displayed on the vehicle.

Directions:

Same as General Knowledge Test; circle the correct answers.

You may begin . . .

1. Column 3 of the Hazardous Materials Table shows the date of shipping.   T   F

2. Forbidden materials can never be transported.   T   F

3. If the words "Inhalation Hazard" are on the shipping paper, you must use poison placards in addition to any others needed by the product.   T   F

4. You should keep your shipping papers describing hazardous materials in a pouch under the passenger seat.   T   F

5. A placarded vehicle must have placards on the front, rear, and both sides.   T   F

6. Each item description on a shipping paper shows the material's hazard class.   T   F

7. Regulated products appear on the Hazardous Materials Table and the Regulated Products Table.   T   F

8. The basic description of a hazardous product must always include the name of the hazardous material.   T   F

9. The most important package marking is the name of the hazardous material.   T   F

GO TO NEXT PAGE

10. When transporting hazardous waste, you must sign and carry a Uniform Hazardous Waste Manifest.   T   F

11. Always use placards to transport any amount of material listed in Table 2.   T   F

12. The power unit of placarded vehicles must have a fire extinguisher with a UL rating of 10 B:C or more.   T   F

13. You must stop 50 to 100 feet before the nearest rail of a railroad crossing when driving a placarded vehicle.   T   F

14. A driver transporting chlorine in cargo tanks must have an approved gas mask in the vehicle.   T   F

15. When loading explosives, you must disable the cargo heaters.   T   F

16. You should not load nitric acid in stacks more than two feet high.   T   F

17. The transport index tells which hazardous materials in the load being transported require placards.   T   F

18. "Class 6" poisons must be transported in containers with inter-connectors.   T   F

19. An accident involving hazardous materials must be reported to the proper government agency by the shipper.   T   F

20. The driver is responsible for keeping hazardous materials shipping papers in the proper place.   T   F

21. A shipment of hazardous materials is described by Hazardous Materials Transportation papers.   T   F

22. The labels on hazardous materials packages are diamond shaped.   T   F

23. The driver should immediately clean up any leaking hazardous material he discovers.   T   F

GO TO NEXT PAGE

24. Before pulling apart two vehicles carrying explosives
that have been in a collision, you should move the explosives
just enough to stabilize the load.   T   F

25. You can leave a placarded vehicle unattended if you are
not within 100 feet of a public road.   T   F

26. You must have a written route plan when transporting
Division 1.1 explosives.   T   F

27. You should stop and check your tires every two hours
or 100 miles, whichever comes first.   T   F

28. Before transporting flammable cryogenic liquids, a driver
must have had special training within the last two
years.   T   F

29. Containment rules tell drivers how to load, transport,
and unload bulk tanks of hazardous materials.   T   F

30. The intent of hazardous materials regulations is to en-
sure safe drivers, contain the material, and hide the risk.   T   F

GO TO NEXT PAGE

Answers

1.	False	16.	True
2.	True	17.	False
3.	True	18.	False
4.	False	19.	False
5.	True	20.	True
6.	True	21.	False
7.	False	22.	True
8.	True	23.	False
9.	True	24.	False
10.	True	25.	False
11.	False	26.	True
12.	True	27.	True
13.	False	28.	True
14.	True	29.	True
15.	True	30.	False

GO TO NEXT PAGE

- 500 feet - use your low beams

- Pull off the Road in a safe legal place to use the equipment

- Provide enough traction to steer and push vehicle through snow

- begin turning your vehicle when you are halfway though the intersection.

- poor traction
  To the right side of the road.
- show a wider area than flat mirrors show.

- only

- You need both hands on the wheel to turn safely.

- loss of sterring control

- On a vehicle with a trailer, the trailer can push the towing vehicle sideways

- start at the inside lane and swing right as you turn

- the vehicle's speed and how quickly you want to stop.

PRETRIP INSPECTION CHECKLIST

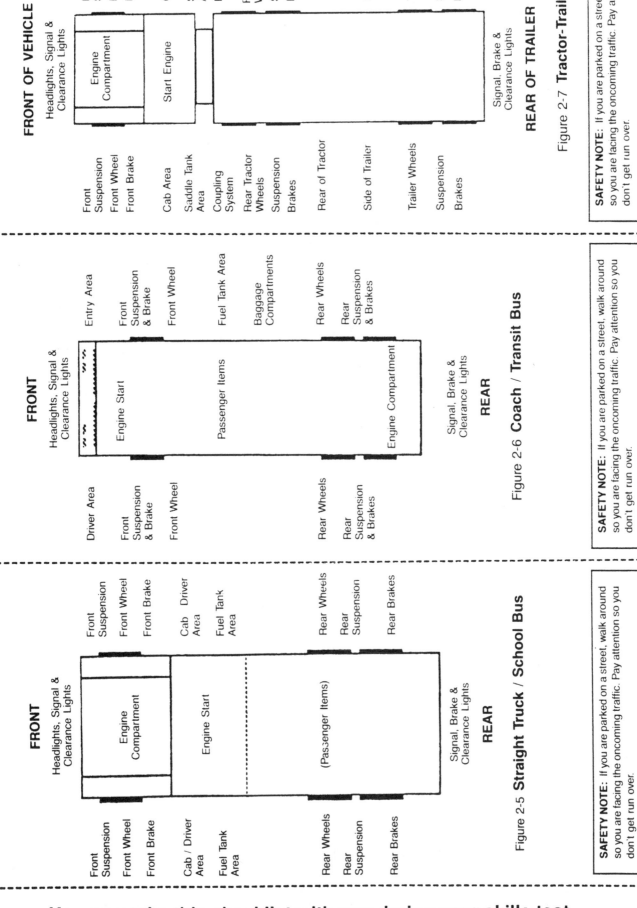

FRONT OF VEHICLE

Headlights, Signal & Clearance Lights

Engine Compartment

Start Engine

Top labels:
- Front Suspension
- Front Wheel
- Front Brake
- Cab Area
- Saddle Tank Area
- Front of Trailer
- Rear Tractor Wheels
- Suspension
- Brakes
- Side of Trailer
- Trailer Wheels
- Suspension
- Brakes

Signal, Brake & Clearance Lights

Bottom labels:
- Front Suspension
- Front Wheel
- Front Brake
- Cab Area
- Saddle Tank Area
- Coupling System
- Rear Tractor Wheels
- Suspension
- Brakes
- Rear of Tractor
- Side of Trailer
- Trailer Wheels
- Suspension
- Brakes

REAR OF TRAILER

Figure 2-7 **Tractor-Trailer**

SAFETY NOTE: If you are parked on a street, walk around so you are facing the oncoming traffic. Pay attention so you don't get run over.

Always put vehicle key in your pocket — or someone might move the vehicle while you are checking underneath it.

FRONT

Headlights, Signal & Clearance Lights

Engine Start

Passenger Items

Engine Compartment

Top labels:
- Entry Area
- Front Suspension & Brake
- Front Wheel
- Fuel Tank Area
- Baggage Compartments
- Rear Wheels
- Rear Suspension & Brakes

Signal, Brake & Clearance Lights

Bottom labels:
- Driver Area
- Front Suspension & Brake
- Front Wheel
- Rear Wheels
- Rear Suspension & Brakes

REAR

Figure 2-6 **Coach / Transit Bus**

SAFETY NOTE: If you are parked on a street, walk around so you are facing the oncoming traffic. Pay attention so you don't get run over.

Always put vehicle key in your pocket — or someone might move the vehicle while you are checking underneath it.

FRONT

Headlights, Signal & Clearance Lights

Engine Compartment

Engine Start

(Passenger Items)

Top labels:
- Front Suspension
- Front Wheel
- Front Brake
- Cab Driver Area
- Fuel Tank Area
- Rear Wheels
- Rear Suspension
- Rear Brakes

Signal, Brake & Clearance Lights

Bottom labels:
- Front Suspension
- Front Wheel
- Front Brake
- Cab / Driver Area
- Fuel Tank Area
- Rear Wheels
- Rear Suspension
- Rear Brakes

REAR

Figure 2-5 **Straight Truck / School Bus**

SAFETY NOTE: If you are parked on a street, walk around so you are facing the oncoming traffic. Pay attention so you don't get run over.

Always put vehicle key in your pocket — or someone might move the vehicle while you are checking underneath it.

You may take this checklist with you during your skills test.

The following pages contain a Hazardous Materials Marking, Labeling, and Placarding Guide from the U.S. DOT.

U.S. Department of
Transportation
**Research and
Special Programs
Administration**

DOT CHART 10
Hazardous Materials Marking,
Labeling & Placarding Guide

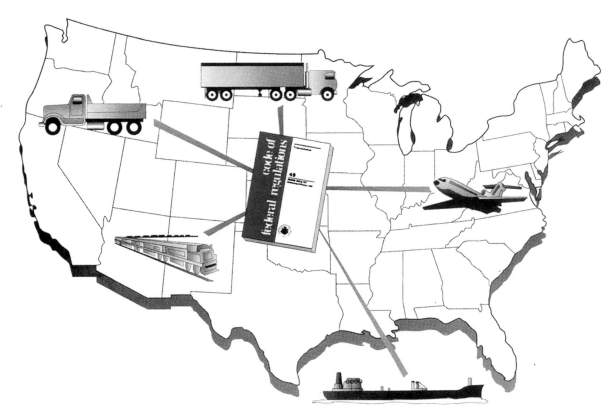

Refer to 49 CFR, Part 172:

Marking - Subpart D

Labeling - Subpart E

Placarding - Subpart F

Emergency Response - Subpart G

NOTE: **This document is for general guidance only and must not be
used to determine compliance with 49 CFR, Parts 100-199.**

Hazardous Materials Warning Labels

CLASS 1 Explosive 1.1 1.2 1.3	CLASS 1 Explosive 1.4	CLASS 1 Explosive 1.5	CLASS 1 Explosive 1.6	CLASS 2 Division 2.1	CLASS 2 Division 2.2	CLASS 2 Division 2.2
EXPLOSIVE ** 1 *Include appropriate division number and compatibility group letter.	1.4 EXPLOSIVE * 1 *Include appropriate compatibility group letter.	1.5 BLASTING AGENT * 1 *Include appropriate compatibility group letter.	1.6 EXPLOSIVE * 1 *Include appropriate compatibility group letter.	FLAMMABLE GAS 2 Flammable gas	NON-FLAMMABLE GAS 2 Non-flammable gas	OXYGEN 2 Oxygen

CLASS 2 Division 2.3	CLASS 3	CLASS 4 Division 4.1	CLASS 4 Division 4.2	CLASS 4 Division 4.3	CLASS 5 Division 5.1	CLASS 5 Division 5.2
POISON GAS 2 Poison gas	FLAMMABLE LIQUID 3 Flammable liquid	FLAMMABLE SOLID 4 Flammable solid	COMBUSTIBLE 4 Spontaneously Combustible	DANGEROUS WHEN WET 4 Dangerous when wet	OXIDIZER 5.1 Oxidizer	ORGANIC PEROXIDE 5.2 Organic peroxide

CLASS 6 Division 6.1	CLASS 6 Division 6.1	CLASS 6 Division 6.2		CLASS 7 I	CLASS 7 II	CLASS 7 III
POISON 6 Poison-Packing Group I and II	HARMFUL STOW AWAY FROM FOODSTUFFS 6 Poison-Packing III	INFECTIOUS SUBSTANCE 6 Infectious substance	ETIOLOGIC AGENTS BIOMEDICAL MATERIAL IN CASE OF DAMAGE OR LEAKAGE NOTIFY DIRECTOR CDC ATLANTA GEORGIA 404 633 5313 42 CFR 72.3 Etiological agent label may apply.	RADIOACTIVE I 7	RADIOACTIVE II 7	RADIOACTIVE III 7

CLASS 8	CLASS 9	SUBSIDIARY RISK LABELS			FOR AIRCRAFT	
CORROSIVE 8 Corrosive	9	** Explosive Flammable gas Flammable liquid Flammable solid Corrosive Oxidizer Poison Spontaneously Combustible Dangerous when wet The class number may not be displayed on a subsidiary label (see Section 172.402).	EMPTY Empty		Cargo Aircraft Only DANGER	MAGNETIZED MATERIAL KEEP AWAY FROM AIRCRAFT COMPASS DETECTOR UNIT

TRANSITION-2001	TRANSITION-2001	TRANSITION-2001	TRANSITION-2001	TRANSITION-2001	TRANSITION-2001	TRANSITION-2001
EXPLOSIVE A 1	EXPLOSIVE B 1	EXPLOSIVE C 1	BLASTING AGENT 1	CHLORINE 2	FLAMMABLE SOLID 4	IRRITANT 6

HAZARDOUS MATERIALS PACKAGE MARKINGS

INNER PACKAGES COMPLY WITH PRESCRIBED SPECIFICATIONS
§173.25(a)(4)

§172.312(a)

MARINE POLLUTANT
§172.322

HOT
§172.325

DANGER
The lading of this car has been
FUMIGATED or
TREATED
with
_____
(Name of poisonous liquid, solid,
or gas)
BEFORE UNLOADING, open both doors
and DO NOT ENTER until car is free
of gas. REMOVE ALL POISONOUS
MATERIAL before release of empty
car.
§173.9

INHALATION HAZARD
§172.313(a)

CONSUMER COMMODITY
ORM-D
§172.316(a)

CONSUMER COMMODITY
ORM-D-AIR
§172.316(a)(1)

Keep a copy of the DOT Emergency Response Guidebook handy!

Hazardous Materials Warning Placards

CLASS 1

EXPLOSIVES
*Enter Division Number 1.1, 1.2, or 1.3 and compatibility group letter, when required. Placard any quantity.

CLASS 1

EXPLOSIVES 1.4
*Enter compatibility group letter, when required. Placard 454 kg (1,001 lbs) or more.

CLASS 1

EXPLOSIVES 1.5
*Enter compatibility group letter, when required. Placard 454 kg (1,001 lbs) or more.

CLASS 1

EXPLOSIVES 1.6
*Enter compatibility group letter, when required. Placard 454 kg (1,001 lbs) or more.

CLASS 2

OXYGEN
Placard 454 kg (1,001 lbs) or more, gross weight of either compressed gas or refrigerated liquid.

CLASS 2

FLAMMABLE GAS
Placard 454 kg (1,001 lbs) or more.

CLASS 2

NON-FLAMMABLE GAS
Placard 454 kg (1,001 lbs) or more gross weight.

CLASS 2

POISON GAS
Placard any quantity of Division 2.3 material.

CLASS 3

FLAMMABLE
Placard 454 kg (1,001 lbs) or more.

CLASS 3

GASOLINE
May be used in the place of FLAMMABLE on a placard displayed on a cargo tank or a portable tank being used to transport gasoline by highway.

CLASS 3

COMBUSTIBLE
Placard a combustible liquid when transported in bulk. See §172.504(f)(2)for use of FLAMMABLE placard in place of COMBUSTIBLE placard.

CLASS 3

FUEL OIL
May be used in place of COMBUSTIBLE on a placard displayed on a cargo tank or portable tank being used to transport by highway fuel oil not classed as a flammable liquid.

CLASS 4

FLAMMABLE SOLID
Placard 454 kg (1,001 lbs) or more.

CLASS 4

SPONTANEOUSLY COMBUSTIBLE
Placard 454 kg (1,001 lbs) or more.

CLASS 4

DANGEROUS WHEN WET
Placard any quantity of Division 4.3 material.

CLASS 5

OXIDIZER
Placard 454 kg (1,001 lbs) or more.

CLASS 5

ORGANIC PEROXIDE
Placard 454 kg (1,001 lbs) or more.

CLASS 6

HARMFUL
STOW AWAY FROM FOODSTUFFS

KEEP AWAY FROM FOOD
Placard 454 kg (1,001 lbs) or more.

CLASS 6

POISON
POISON
Placard any quantity of 6.1, PGI, inhalation hazard only. Placard 454 kg (1,001 lbs) or more of PGI or II, other than PGI inhalation hazard.

CLASS 7

RADIOACTIVE
RADIOACTIVE
Placard any quantity of packages bearing the RADIOACTIVE III label. Certain low specific activity radioactive materials in "exclusive use" will not bear the label, but RADIOACTIVE placard is required.

CLASS 8

CORROSIVE
Placard 454 kg (1,001 lbs) or more.

CLASS 9

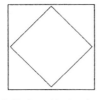

MISCELLANEOUS
Not required for domestic transportation. Placard 454 kg (1,001 lbs) or more gross weight of a material which presents a hazard during transport, but is not included in any other hazard class.

DANGEROUS
Placard 454 kg (1,001 lbs) gross weight of two or more categories of hazardous materials listed in Table 2. A freight container, unit load device, motor vehicle, or rail car which contain non-bulk packagings with two or more categories of hazardous materials that require placards specified in Table 2 may be placarded with a DANGEROUS placard instead of the separate placarding specified for each of the materials in Table 2. However, when 2,268 kg (5,000 lbs) or more of one category of material is loaded at one facility, the placard specified in Table 2 must be applied.

SUBSIDIARY RISK PLACARD

CORROSIVE

Class numbers do not appear on subsidiary risk placard.

RAIL
Placard empty tank cars for residue of material last contained.

Required background for placards on rail shipments of certain explosives and poisons. Also required for highway route-controlled quantities of radioactive materials (see §§172.507 and 172.510).

UN or NA Identification Numbers

MUST BE DISPLAYED ON TANK CARS, CARGO TANKS, PORTABLE TANKS AND OTHER BULK PACKAGINGS

PLACARDS OR ORANGE PANELS →

 and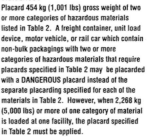

Appropriate Placard must be used.

Response begins with identification!

General Guidelines on Use of Warning Labels and Placards

LABELS

See 49 CFR, Part 172, Subpart E for complete labeling regulations.

- Until October 1, 1993, all of the labels appearing on the Hazardous Materials Warning Labels chart may be used to satisfy the labeling requirements contained in Subpart E.
- On and after October 1, 1993, those labels in boxes marked "TRANSITION-2001" on the chart will not be authorized for use under Subpart E. (NOTE: these labels may be used IF they were affixed to a package offered for transportation and transported prior to October 1, 2001, and the package was filled with hazardous materials prior to October 1, 1991.)
- For classes 1,2,3,4,5,6 and 8, text indicating a hazard (e.g., "CORROSIVE") IS NOT required on a label. The label must otherwise conform to Subpart E [Section 172.405].
- Any person who offers a hazardous material for transportation MUST label the package, if required [Section 172.400(a)].
- The Hazardous Materials Table [Section 172.101] identifies the proper label(s) for the hazardous material listed.
- When required, labels must be printed on or affixed to the surface of the package near the proper shipping name [Section 172.406(a)].
- When two or more labels are required, they must be displayed next to each other [Section 172.406(c)].
- Labels may be affixed to packages when not required by regulations, provided each label represents a hazard of the material contained in the package [Section 172.401].

PLACARDS

See 49 CFR, Part 172, Subpart F for complete placarding regulations.

- All of the placards appearing on the Hazardous Materials Warning Placards chart may be used to satisfy the placarding requirements contained in Subpart F.
- Each person who offers for transportation or transports any hazardous material subject to the Hazardous Materials Regulations shall comply with all applicable requirements of Subpart F.
- Placards may be displayed for a hazardous material even when not required, if the placarding otherwise conforms to the requirements of Subpart F.
- For other than Class 7 or the OXYGEN placard, text indicating a hazard (e.g., "CORROSIVE") is not required on a placard [Section 172.519(b)].
- Any transport vehicle, freight container, or rail car containing any quantity of material listed in Table 1 (Section 172.504) must be placarded.
- When the gross weight of all hazardous materials covered in Table 2 is less than 454 kg (1,001 lbs), no placard is required on a transport vehicle or freight container [Section 172.504].

Effective October 1, 1994, and extending through October 1, 2001, these placards may be used for HIGHWAY TRANSPORTATION ONLY.

Illustration numbers in each square refer to Tables 1 and 2 below.

Poisonous Materials

§172.554

INHALATION HAZARD

§172.313

Materials which meet the inhalation toxicity criteria have additional "communication standards" prescribed by the HMR. First, the words "Poison-Inhalation Hazard" must be entered on the shipping paper, as required by Section 172.203(m)(3). Second, packagings must be marked "Inhalation Hazard" in accordance with Section 172.313(a). Lastly, transport vehicles, freight containers, portable tanks and unit load devices that contain a poisonous material subject to the "Poison-Inhalation Hazard" shipping description, must be placarded with a POISON or POISON GAS placard, as appropriate. This shall be in addition to any other placard required for that material in Section 172.504.

Table 1 (Placard any quantity)

Hazard class or division	Placard name
1.1	EXPLOSIVES 1.1
1.2	EXPLOSIVES 1.2
1.3	EXPLOSIVES 1.3
2.3	POISON GAS
4.3	DANGEROUS WHEN WET
6.1 (PGI, PIH only)	POISON
7 (Radioactive Yellow III)	RADIOACTIVE

Table 2 (Placard 1,001 pounds or more)

Hazard class or division	Placard name
1.4	EXPLOSIVES 1.4
1.5	EXPLOSIVES 1.5
1.6	EXPLOSIVES 1.6
2.1	FLAMMABLE GAS
2.2	NON-FLAMMABLE GAS
3	FLAMMABLE
Combustible Liquid	COMBUSTIBLE
4.1	FLAMMABLE SOLID
4.2	SPONTANEOUSLY COMBUSTIBLE
5.1	OXIDIZER
5.2	ORGANIC PEROXIDE
6.1 (PGI or II, other than PGI PIH)	POISON
6.1 (PGIII)	KEEP AWAY FROM FOOD
6.2	NONE
8	CORROSIVE
9	CLASS 9
ORM-D	NONE

For complete details, refer to one or more of the following:
- Code of Federal Regulations, Title 49, Transportation. Parts 100-199. [All modes]
- International Civil Aviation Organization (ICAO) Technical Instructions for Safe Transport of Dangerous Goods by Air [Air]
- International Maritime Organization (IMO) Dangerous Goods Code [Water]
- "Transportation of Dangerous Goods Regulations" of Transport Canada. [All Modes]

**U.S. Department of Transportation
Research and Special Programs Administration**

Copies of this Chart can be obtained by writing OHMIT/DHM-51, Washington, D.C. 20590

CHART 10
REV. FEBRUARY 1994